The Founding Fathers Reconsidered

R. B. BERNSTEIN

The Founding Fathers Reconsidered

OXFORD
UNIVERSITY PRESS

OXFORD
UNIVERSITY PRESS

Oxford University Press, Inc., publishes works that further
Oxford University's objective of excellence
in research, scholarship, and education.

Oxford   New York

Auckland   Cape Town   Dar es Salaam   Hong Kong   Karachi
Kuala Lumpur   Madrid   Melbourne   Mexico City   Nairobi
New Delhi   Shanghai   Taipei   Toronto

With offices in
Argentina   Austria   Brazil   Chile   Czech Republic   France   Greece
Guatemala   Hungary   Italy   Japan   Poland   Portugal   Singapore
South Korea   Switzerland   Thailand   Turkey   Ukraine   Vietnam

First published by Oxford University Press, Inc., 2009
198 Madison Avenue, New York, NY 10016
www.oup.com

First issued as an Oxford University Press paperback, 2011

Oxford is a registered trademark of Oxford University Press

Library of Congress Cataloging-in-Publication Data
Bernstein, Richard B., 1956–
The Founding Fathers reconsidered / R. B. Bernstein.
p.   cm.   Includes bibliographical references and index.
Summary: "This concise study reintroduces us to the history that shaped the
founding fathers, the history that they made, and what history has made of them.
It gives the reader a context within which to explore the world of the founding
fathers and their complex and still-controversial achievements and legacies."
—Provided by publisher.
ISBN 978-0-19-533832-4 (hardcover); 978-0-19-983257-6 (paperback)
1. Founding Fathers of the United States.
2. Founding Fathers of the United States—Historiography.
3. United States—Politics and government—1775–1783.
4. United States—Politics and government—1783–1809.   I. Title.
E302.5.B47 2009   973.3092'2—dc22   2008045313

Frontispiece and title page: In John Trumbull's 12- by 18-foot painting, now hanging in the U.S. Capitol,
John Adams, Roger Sherman, Robert R. Livingston, Thomas Jefferson, and Benjamin Franklin
present their draft of the Declaration of Independence to the Second Continental Congress.
Library of Congress LC-USZ62-115965.

9 8 7 6 5 4 3 2 1
Printed in the United States of America
on acid-free paper

Contents

Preface

THE FOUNDING FATHERS WERE CREATORS OF the United States and of American national identity, symbols of constitutional democracy, and icons of disinterested statesmanship. They risked all in the service of their great dream of a free, peaceful, and happy nation immune from the corruptions of the Old World and destined to spread across a new, rich continent. They wrote the words and the music to the great American story that posterity has lived by from their time to ours. As we revere them, celebrate their lives, and extol their achievements, we despair of measuring up to them. That is one popular view.

Another view is the photographic negative of the first: The founding fathers were selfish, intolerant, bigoted representatives of a corrupt establishment. They reluctantly gave the great body of the people opportunities to realize their dreams of independence and self-fulfillment, only to smother those dreams by creating a new, powerful general government that suppressed the people and choked their creative energies. Only a peaceful democratic revolution of which Thomas Jefferson was the figurehead and the wordsmith undid the founding fathers' plans. Even then, Jefferson and those whom he led scorned the claims of oppressed groups such as enslaved African Americans, Native American peoples, and women. Instead of burning incense before their pedestals, we should knock them down, taking them to task for their sins against democracy.

A third view is much more instrumental. Whether demigods or demons, the founding fathers, creators of the Constitution and the American constitutional system, are the sole determiners of what the Constitution means and how we should apply it to solve pressing constitutional problems. We must pore over the evidence they left behind: the records of their debates both formal and informal, the drafts they prepared and revised and reshaped, the letters they exchanged, the memoranda they wrote for themselves and for the future, and even the diaries that they intended for no eyes other than their own. Only by reference to their words and deeds can we interpret the Constitution responsibly. Otherwise, we would have no restraint on constitutional interpretation, leaving those dreaded and dangerous creatures, free-wheeling judges, free to write into the Constitution whatever ideas or meanings they persuade themselves and us that they can find there.

Readers might object that these three approaches to the founding fathers are caricatures—and they would be both right and wrong. Though exaggerated for dramatic effect, the paragraphs above capture the essence of three prevailing approaches to the founding fathers and their record of achievements and failures.

None of these three approaches to the founding fathers is true. All oversimplify the story of the founding fathers and what that remarkable, fractious group of statesmen, politicians, journalists, farmers, and soldiers did and tried to do. For more than forty years, historians and other scholars have worked to give us a fresh, complex, and nuanced perspective on the founding fathers and their world. Sadly, general readers have little knowledge of this fascinating scholarship, in part because too many scholars write only for one another in gnarled, murky prose and in part because the three caricatures set forth above have achieved such popularity with the reading public that they eclipse any other way of looking at the subject.

In this short book, I propose to brush aside those caricatures of the founding fathers and to offer general readers a distilled introduction to the subject, synthesizing the remarkable work that so many of my colleagues have produced. Chapter 1 explores the words, images, and meanings that we so often associate with the founding fathers and clears the ground for the substantive inquiry the rest of this book presents. Chapter 2 sketches three contexts— geographical, political, and intellectual—that shaped the founding fathers. Chapter 3 explores the array of great challenges that the founding fathers faced, meeting most but not all of them and leaving others for future generations to solve. Taken together, those challenges met and those challenges shirked define the founding fathers' creation of the United States and its constitutional and political systems. Chapter 4 traces the ways that posterity has sought to understand the founding fathers and has come to terms with their labors and ambiguous legacies. The Epilogue uses the words of five great African American orators to explore the concept of perfecting the Union as a way to answer enduring questions about our thorny and conflicted relationship with the founding fathers and their legacies.

I propose to take the founding fathers down from their pedestals without knocking them down. At the same time, I set their achievements and their failures within the context of their own time and place, while making clear that those achievements were not great beyond the bounds of mortal men and that those failures were not blameworthy beyond human beings' normal capacity to err. If we rework our relationship with the founding fathers so that we meet them eye to eye instead of gazing reverently upward or sneering contemptuously downward, perhaps we can form a more pragmatic sense of who they were, what they did and failed to do, and why we care.

Chronology

1776–1777	First wave of state constitution-making
1777	New York frames and adopts state constitution
	Battle of Saratoga
	Congress proposes Articles of Confederation to states
1778	Franklin negotiates alliance with France
1779–1780	Massachusetts frames and adopts state constitution
1781	Maryland's ratification puts Articles of Confederation into effect
	Battle of Yorktown
1782	Adams negotiates treaty with Netherlands and loans to United States
1782–1783	Negotiations between Franklin, Adams, and Jay and British diplomats
1783	Treaty of Paris ends American War of Independence
	Washington quells Newburgh Conspiracy
	British evacuate occupied American states
	Washington resigns as commander-in-chief
1784	Congress adopts Ordinance of 1784
1785	Congress adopts Land Ordinance of 1785
	Mount Vernon Conference between Maryland and Virginia
1786	Annapolis Convention.
1787	Federal Convention frames Constitution of the United States
	Congress adopts Northwest Ordinance of 1787
1787–1788	Ratification controversy; Constitution adopted by 11 of 13 states
1788	Confederation Congress declares Constitution adopted, arranges transition
1789	Washington unanimously elected first President of United States

The Founding Fathers Reconsidered

CHAPTER 1

Words, Images, Meanings

N O MATTER HOW MANY HISTORIANS SEEK TO drive a stake through its heart, the phrase "founding fathers" remains a core component of the way Americans talk about politics and government, one with remarkable rhetorical power. Given this fact, we might assume that "founding fathers" has had as long and honorable a history as "All men are created equal." And yet, for an expression so central to Americans' understanding of their past, and so fruitful a source of legal, political, and historiographic controversy, "founding fathers" has a surprisingly short life. It did not enter the political lexicon until the early twentieth century, and its inventor is no one you might expect.

On June 7, 1916, Senator Warren G. Harding of Ohio delivered the keynote address at that year's Republican National Convention in Chicago. Standing before his enthusiastic audience, Harding seemed the embodiment of a statesman—tall and commanding, his silver hair contrasting dramatically with his dark eyebrows and olive skin. A former newspaper publisher who had won election to the Senate after a failed 1910 campaign for governor of Ohio, Harding was known—and often mocked—for his "bloviation," Ohio political slang for empty, windy oratory. Now he told the cheering crowd of delegates, "We ought to be as genuinely American today as when the founding fathers flung their immortal defiance in the face of old world oppressions and dedicated a new republic to liberty and justice."[1]

This 1916 speech is the first recorded appearance of the phrase "founding fathers"—but Harding had come close four years before, when, at the 1912 Republican National Convention, also in Chicago, he nominated President William Howard Taft for a second term. Facing a divided and contentious audience (nearly half of whom later bolted from the convention to propel Theodore Roosevelt into a third-party candidacy), Harding was determined to hold the stage for his candidate. Launching his customary long-winded detour through American history, he proclaimed, "Human rights and their defense are as old as civilization; but, more important to us, the founding American fathers wrote the covenant of a people's rule into the bond of national life, beyond all erasure or abridgment."[2] In 1916, he dropped the intervening "American" and coined a phrase—though at the time nobody noticed.

Over the next five years, Harding periodically revived the phrase "founding fathers." On February 22, 1918, as the featured speaker at a Washington's Birthday commemoration hosted by the Sons and Daughters of the American Revolution, he declared: "It is good to meet and drink at the fountain of wisdom inherited from the founding fathers of the Republic." Then, in 1920, after the weary party leaders at the deadlocked Republican convention in Chicago fixed on the Ohio senator as their presidential nominee, Harding twice invoked the "founding fathers" in his acceptance speech. Finally, in his 1921 inaugural address, President Harding intoned: "Standing in this presence, mindful of the solemnity of this occasion, feeling the emotions which no one may know until he senses the great weight of responsibility for himself, I must utter my belief in the divine inspiration of the founding fathers. Surely there must have been God's intent in the making of this new-world Republic."

Harding's creation, with its attendant aura of sanctity, was abroad in the land—passing into general use so swiftly and easily that its origins were soon forgotten. Not until the 1960s, when a television writer posed the question to the Library of Congress's Congressional Research Service, did Harding receive belated credit for creating "founding fathers." Given Harding's weak historical reputation, "founding fathers" may be his most enduring political and intellectual legacy.[3]

The phrase that Harding coined seemed tailor-made to fit a corresponding image (derived from the history paintings of eighteenth-century Europe) that American artists have adapted and revisited with enduring popularity for more than two centuries. From John Trumbull and Amos Doolittle in the early Republic, to Junius Brutus Stearns in the mid-nineteenth century, to Howard Chandler Christy, Henry Hy Hintermeister, and Barry Faulkner in the early twentieth century, to Louis Glantzman during the Constitution's bicentennial, painters and engravers all depicted the nation's founding moments in standard form: a group of carefully dressed, somber politicians, standing or sitting together in a legislative chamber, their attention focused on a document.

Some of these pictures have achieved the status of patriotic icons, in part because of their placement in the temples of the nation's civic religion. For example, John Trumbull's "The Declaration of Independence" and Howard Chandler Christy's "The Signing of the Constitution" hang in the U.S. Capitol, attracting the reverent gaze of thousands of tourists. So, too, Barry Faulkner's murals "The Declaration of Independence" and "The Constitution of the United States" loom above visitors to the National Archives, the building that houses the original parchments of the Declaration and the Constitution. Some of these paintings are genuine works of art, whereas others are lifeless assemblages of familiar faces in a standard matrix. The overall effect is always the same—a staid group of white men, frozen in time.

This conjunction of words and images raises the question of what Harding's emblematic phrase means. Most scholars identify as founding fathers the politicians, soldiers, jurists, and legislators who held leadership positions during the American Revolution, the Confederation period, and the early Republic.[4] This category has two subsets, each keyed to one of two founding images. First are the Signers, the delegates to the Second Continental Congress who in July 1776 in Philadelphia's State House (now called Independence Hall) declared American independence and revised and adopted Thomas Jefferson's draft of the Declaration of Independence. Second are the Framers, the delegates to the Federal Convention who met in the same building from May through September of 1787 and framed the Constitution of the United States.

At a minimum, the roster would include the seven key leaders named by the historian Richard B. Morris in his 1973 book *Seven Who Shaped Our Destiny*: Benjamin Franklin, George Washington, John Adams, Thomas Jefferson, John Jay, James Madison, and Alexander Hamilton. (John Jay, however, was neither a Signer nor a Framer; Adams and Jefferson were Signers but not Framers; and Madison and Hamilton were Framers but not Signers.)[5] These seven men played such central roles throughout the long era of the American Founding that we may plausibly deem them the core of the group known as the founding fathers; for that reason, readers will encounter them regularly in the pages that follow.

Despite these conventional boundaries, "founding fathers" is a protean phrase with varying meanings depending on who has used it and when. Most often, it includes participants on both sides of the 1787–1788 controversy over ratifying the Constitution. Some have expanded the phrase to embrace not only the usual cadre of elite white males but also Americans of the middling and common sorts who served in the militia or the Continental Army or Navy during the American Revolution, who voted for delegates to the state conventions that were to ratify the Constitution, and who helped to bring the new government into existence.[6]

WORDS, IMAGES, MEANINGS ⸗ 7

Some historians substitute the phrase "revolutionary generation"—though this group actually spanned three or even four generations, from Benjamin Franklin to Albert Gallatin.

Some political writers highlighting the role of women in American history confer the honorific term "founding mothers" on women such as Abigail Adams, Mercy Otis Warren, and Deborah Sampson.[7] Other biographers affix the term to historical figures falling outside its chronological boundaries—from John Winthrop, the first governor of the Massachusetts Bay Colony, to the late Senator Samuel J. Ervin, Jr. (D-NC), who won fame as chairman of the Senate's Watergate Committee in 1973–1974, to Brian Lamb, founder of C-SPAN.[8] Finally, biographers studying major historical figures falling within the category of founding fathers stress the point by labeling their subject as a "forgotten founder," a "forgotten founding father," or, in the case of Aaron Burr, a "fallen founder."[9] Significantly, however, the phrase usually has excluded those who were not white, whether African American or Native American—though a controversial 1987 monograph labels Native Americans as "forgotten founders" and a 2008 biography of the African American clergyman Richard Allen dubs him a "founding father."[10]

Whatever the group's extended membership, the core meaning of "founding fathers" remains constant. It designates those who, by word or deed, helped to found the United States as a nation and a political experiment. Thus, beyond the "seven who shaped our destiny" named by Richard B. Morris, the term includes those who sat in the Congress that declared American independence; it even includes a delegate such as John Dickinson of Pennsylvania, who opposed independence and refused to sign the Declaration but fought for the American cause in the Revolutionary War, and a polemicist such as Thomas Paine, who only briefly held political office but was an extraordinarily effective educator and mobilizer of public opinion. It also encompasses others who fought on the American side in the war, or played important roles (as framers, ratifiers, opponents, or effectuators) in the origins of the Constitution of the United States and the system of government it outlines.

In studying the founding fathers, we study a political elite, though a more porous and open elite than those holding sway in Europe.[11] In addition, that elite increasingly had to interact with the people during the Revolution and in the eras of the Confederation and the early Republic. Though they may have sought to direct the course of events, at least as often they had to respond to changes coming from below and to shifts of opinion among the people, who increasingly were inclined to express their own views, follow their own lead, and challenge the primacy of their ostensible governors. One of the most rewarding and disturbing subthemes of current scholarship is the profusion of carefully researched studies again casting doubt on the disinterestedness of the founding fathers, highlighting clashes of ideals and interests between different levels of American society, causing at least some among the "ordinary people" to wonder whether the American victory in the Revolution was a hollow triumph. For these reasons, reconsidering the founding fathers within their historical context illuminates the evolution of American politics and democracy, complementing the work of those who concentrate their attention on the great body of the people or on those other groups previously excluded from historical study.[12]

Yet another point to keep in mind when reconsidering the founding fathers is that they sought to order the world, not primarily by force but with words, by framing and adopting a series of documents of political foundation: constitutions, declarations or bills of rights, treaties, and laws. John Adams rightly called his time "the age of revolutions and constitutions."[13] The possibilities and limitations of ordering the world with words is a theme running through their writings—giving them hope and causing them frustration, often at the same time. In this light, reexamining the founding fathers helps us to recover a broader sense of the possibilities and purposes of political thought and action.

Finally, reconsidering the founding fathers makes it necessary to explore the complex story of their historical reputations, both as members of that fabled group and as individuals, as well as their legacies in the two centuries since the Revolution. As the political scientist Seymour Martin Lipset argued, the United States is "the first new nation"—the first nation to be created at a specific time and place, in a specific act of political invention, having at its core not shared ethnicity or language or religion but rather shared commitment to a set of defining principles as a national "political creed" or "civil religion."[14] Inevitably, this defining quality of American national identity and American nationalism focuses attention on the founding fathers and their handiwork.[15] Among other things, American history is an ongoing story of how successive generations have wrestled with the clashing imperatives of preserving the founding fathers' legacies and reforming or transforming them in the face of changing values, problems, and circumstances. We argue over ideas such as liberty, equality, national identity, separation of church and state, the purposes of constitutional government, and the proper workings of that government in terms invented or shaped by the founding fathers. Just as often, we either invoke them as oracles guiding modern constitutional government or reject them as irrelevant to very different modern issues. To put it another way, we continue the process that they began of struggling to order the world with words, sometimes quarreling over how best to interpret the words they used and sometimes seeking to revise or add to the words and texts they left us.

The founding fathers still draw the attention not only of scholars but of Americans in all walks of life; their words are still accessible to us, and the challenge of understanding what they meant or should have meant is irresistible and urgent. Major constitutional crises, spawning disputes over whether and how "original intent" can resolve them, intersect with public uncertainty about the lessons that the "usable past" can or should teach.[16] On the one hand, we celebrate the founding fathers for erecting a standard of wise statesmanship for posterity to emulate and leaving a precious legacy for posterity to preserve. On the other hand, we argue bitterly over whether and why the founding fathers failed to confront the central moral and constitutional issue of their era: chattel slavery and its attendant implications for issues of race and equality.

The recent sense of crisis that has enveloped the American people has brought with it a resurgent reverence for the founding fathers. To be sure, this is nothing new in American history. In 1941, with the United States poised on the brink of World War II, the novelist and critic John Dos Passos wrote in his book analyzing the American political creed, *The Ground We Stand On:* "In times of change and danger, when there is a quicksand of fear under men's reasoning, a sense of continuity with generations gone before can stretch like a lifeline across the scary present and get us past the idiot delusion of the exceptional."[17] Dos Passos's words apply equally well, six decades later, to the American state of mind in the wake of *Bush v. Gore* (2000) and the terrorist attacks on New York City and Washington, D.C., on September 11, 2001.[18] In this troubled era, many question the ability of the constitutional system to respond to grave national problems. At the same time, looking back to history for reassurance, many Americans found in John Adams a Churchillian figure of reassuring toughness, in Alexander Hamilton a forthright, realistic champion of national interests, and in Thomas Jefferson an eloquent spokesman for values and principles under attack in a hostile world. Notwithstanding sharp differences between scholarly and popular understandings of the Revolution and the Constitution, once again the appeal of a mythologized cadre of founding fathers has become nearly overwhelming.

The influence of the founding fathers extends beyond the borders of the United States. Beginning in the mid-1980s and continuing in the twenty-first century, people around the world have tried to replace corrupt, oppressive governments with constitutional democracies, and in the process have sought guidance from the American founding. This is only the latest chapter of a story reaching back to the era of the founding fathers— beginning with the efforts of liberal French politicians and *philosophes* such as the Marquis de Lafayette and the Marquis de Condorcet to frame the French Declaration of the Rights of Man by reference to American exemplars (with a discreet assist from the American minister to France, Thomas Jefferson). The trend continued—in the early nineteenth century, when new republics broke free of Spain's disintegrating Latin American empire; in the decades following the Second World War, when European nations dismantled their colonial empires and emerging nations in Asia and Africa experimented with the blessings of constitutional self-government; and in the decades since 1989, when former members of the Warsaw Pact and other former tyrannies rejected dictatorship in favor of constitutional democracy.

Even though most nations have adopted a form of government—parliamentary democracy—significantly different from the presidential system outlined in the U.S. Constitution, they still have adopted the idea of a democratic government with a written constitution and declaration of rights at its core. The example of "political building" they follow is American, even if the constitutional and political architecture they build is their own.[19] The experiment launched by the founding fathers retains significance for a wider world. We now must turn to the ways that the wider world shaped the founding fathers, more than two centuries ago.

CHAPTER 2

Contexts

The History That Made the Founding Fathers

WE RISK THINKING OF THE FOUNDING FATHERS as existing apart from history, in some austere and timeless realm of godlike statesmanship far beyond the powers of ordinary human beings. Such an idealized vision could not be further from the truth. The founding fathers never thought or acted in magnificent, disinterested isolation. Rather, they sought to act in tandem with the people whom they sought to lead—though sometimes they found themselves in conflict with a people increasingly ready to think for themselves.[1] Just as important, they and their contemporaries lived within and were shaped by three interlocking contexts—first, as people living on the periphery of the Atlantic world; second, as citizens first of British North America and then of an independent but fragile United States of America still wrestling with their heritage of English constitutional liberty; and, finally, as participants in the intellectual world dominated by the trans-Atlantic phenomenon known as the Enlightenment.

One historical episode dramatizes the value of reconsidering the founding fathers in context. On February 12 and 13, 1766, Benjamin Franklin stood in the well of the British House of Commons in London and answered a series of questions put to him by members of Parliament about the effects of the Stamp Act of 1765 on the British colonies on the North American mainland. He was the star witness of a series of hearings called by the government, newly formed by the Marquis of Rockingham, to meet the growing public demand in Great Britain for the repeal of the Stamp Act. Rockingham's ministry had taken office after the fall of the ministry led by George Grenville, the principal author and advocate of the Stamp Act, and hoped to use these hearings to bolster its standing and tarnish the standing of its predecessor. Franklin was to be the star witness—and he lived up to the role in which Rockingham's government cast him.

The man who quietly identified himself as "Franklin, of Philadelphia" was not the genial homespun philosopher of historical legend. Rather, Franklin, who had turned sixty nearly a month before, was a polished, suave, diplomatic figure who had made himself the most admired American in the world. Born on the fringes of the British Empire, in the town of Boston, the tenth son of a candlemaker, he had worked hard to remake himself, and now he had established himself at the empire's core as valued and estimable. Dressed with quiet elegance, he was indistinguishable in appearance and bearing from those questioning him. He had lived in London for seven years, showing no desire to return to Philadelphia. He was a colonial agent, or lobbyist, for Georgia, Massachusetts, and New Jersey, as well as for the Pennsylvania Assembly; he was also rising through the tangled structure of the British colonial administration, having won in 1753 the post of joint deputy postmaster-general for North America. Renowned throughout the western world as the man who explained electricity and who devised a series of memorable experiments for its scientific study, he was a leading figure of the trans-Atlantic Enlightenment.[2]

Thus, when he stood before Parliament, Franklin embodied the three contexts within which he and the other founding fathers emerged to shape—and to be shaped by—the development of

American history. Having penetrated from the fringes of the British Empire to its epicenter, he symbolized the effort to transcend the difference between periphery and center that overshadowed relations between the American colonies and the mother country. He also embodied the American colonists' understanding of themselves as free-born English subjects when that vision, not shared by the Crown's officials or by most members of Parliament, had begun to provoke crisis within the empire. And he drew much of his authority from his stature as an avatar of the Enlightenment—as the master of electricity, a newly elected member of the Royal Society in London, the recipient of an honorary doctorate from Scotland's University of St. Andrews, and a founder of Philadelphia's American Philosophical Society. In all these ways, he symbolized the pursuit of useful knowledge that was the Enlightenment's hallmark.

In four hours of testimony spread over two days, Franklin did his best to explain America to Britain. Sparring with Grenville, who did his best to defend his policies by casting doubt on American motives for disliking the Stamp Act, Franklin painted a picture of his fellow colonists as among George III's most ardent and loyal subjects. Asked what the American view of Britain was before the Stamp Act, he replied:

> The best in the world. They submitted willingly to the government of the Crown, and paid, in all their courts, obedience to acts of Parliament. Numerous as the people are in the several old provinces, they cost you nothing in forts, citadels, garrisons, or armies, to keep them in subjection. They were governed by this country at the expense only of a little pen, ink, and paper. They were led by a thread.

Answering a follow-up question about American views of their relationship to the mother country since the Stamp Act, Franklin said that those views were "very much altered," and that American respect for Parliament had been "greatly lessened" from the time when Americans had seen Parliament as "the great bulwark and security of their liberties and privileges." In one last exchange,

Franklin painted a memorable word-picture of the colonists' determination to resist what they saw as unjust taxation:

> Q: What used to be the pride of the Americans?
> A: To indulge in the fashions and manufactures of Great Britain.
> Q: What is now their pride?
> A: To wear their old clothes over again till they can make new ones.

Many observers, including the Marquis of Rockingham himself, credited Franklin's testimony with persuading Parliament to repeal the Stamp Act (though Parliament coupled that repeal with a new piece of legislation, the Declaratory Act, that asserted Parliament's right to legislate for the colonies "in all cases whatsoever").[3]

As Franklin testified before Parliament, other Americans were making their way in the world, all valuing their connection with the British Empire. George Washington, a veteran of the French and Indian War, was a wealthy Virginia planter anxiously awaiting the arrival of his thirty-fourth birthday (few men in his family had survived beyond their fortieth year), remembering his exploits as a colonial militia officer during the war and recalling with resentment the disdain with which British regular officers had treated him.[4] John Adams was twenty-nine years old, a rising member of the Massachusetts bar, married less than two years and brooding over how he might advance his career and make a name for himself.[5] Thomas Jefferson, not yet twenty-three years old, was in his last year of study for the Virginia bar, a shy, quiet, gangling young man, the protégé of one of the two finest lawyers in the colony, and a friend of the royal governor.[6] John Jay, just turned twenty-one years old and known for his sense of his own dignity and for his level-headedness, was studying for the bar in New York City, having graduated from King's College.[7] James Madison, two months short of his fifteenth birthday, was excelling in his studies at his father's plantation in Virginia and looking forward someday to attending college—if his frail health would stand the strain.[8] And Alexander Hamilton, just turned eleven years old, was a clerk in a shipping firm in Christiansted, on Ste. Croix, in the West

Indies, dreaming of ways that he might achieve fame and glory.[9] Franklin was arguing for all of them, as well as for all other residents of British North America.

As he had been all his adult life and as he would continue to be for nine years more, Franklin was an enthusiastic advocate for the British Empire and a canny, shrewd strategist bent on securing an ever-more-central and honorable place in that empire for Britain's North American colonies in general and for himself in particular. He would have deemed the idea of independence incomprehensible at best and a horrific nightmare at worst. Little did he or anyone in the House of Commons expect that the controversy they were seeking to navigate was the first of a series of crises that ultimately would tear the Empire apart, make the thirteen North American colonies a new nation determined to challenge the conventional wisdom of history, and transform Franklin himself from an ardent British imperialist to an American founding father.[10]

LIVING ON THE PERIPHERY OF THE WESTERN WORLD

The America of 1787 had changed little from the America of 1766—save for its legal and constitutional transformation from a collection of colonies to a confederation of independent states. Thus, in the spring of 1787, as the aged Benjamin Franklin prepared to attend the first session of the Federal Convention, the independent United States for which he had labored as a delegate and diplomat occupied the same place on the fringe of Atlantic civilization that it had when he had attempted to explain the colonies and the mother country to one another in his testimony before Parliament.

In 1787, the United States of America had been an independent nation for just over a decade and a nation at peace for less than five years. Yet, as successor to the colonial system known as British North America, the United States also embodied one hundred seventy years of continuous British presence and Anglo-American political experience in the New World. Europeans may have found America rustic and provincial—but the Americans had mastered the art of politics, had evolved a thriving and complex society, and were working to forge a national social, economic, and cultural identity.

By far the most astonishing aspect of the United States was its size. From north to south the new nation spanned about twelve hundred miles, and from the Atlantic coast to the Mississippi River about six hundred miles. Most of the thirteen American states were at least as large as a medium-sized European nation, and England could have fit almost exactly within the state of New York. The United States seemed blessed almost beyond imagining with natural resources and room for growth. Even if the American population doubled every twenty years, as Benjamin Franklin had predicted in 1751, there still seemed room enough in the new republic for "the thousandth and thousandth generation," as Thomas Jefferson confidently asserted in 1801.[11]

Although the United States was the largest nation in the western world except for Russia, its population was comparatively sparse. Fewer than four million inhabitants occupied the populated strip extending about two hundred miles inland from the Atlantic coast. Beyond this frontier lay the territory ceded by Great Britain after the Revolution; this area was largely the domain of Native American nations, with a scattering of American and British forts. The British maintained a military presence in this territory despite the stipulation in the Treaty of Paris of 1783 that they were to evacuate the region; they argued that they were entitled to keep their forts until the Americans met their treaty obligations to repay debts owed to British creditors.

No less important as a force shaping the new nation than its size was its remoteness from Europe. Though the Atlantic Ocean was the principal highway of commerce in goods and ideas linking the New World to the Old World, it also was a tremendous barrier, fraught with peril for those who dared to cross it. It could take as long as two months for a ship to sail between Europe and America, and although those who crossed the Atlantic in the eighteenth century had amassed geographic knowledge and made technological advances beyond those of their counterparts of the sixteenth century, the challenge of leaving the Old World for the New World remained daunting.[12] Beyond the separation imposed by geography loomed another, less tangible but no less difficult separation—the difference between the center and the periphery. For those who lived in the capital city of one of the great imperial powers, whether London or Paris or Madrid or Vienna, Americans seemed quaint and backward. During his time as an American agent in London, even so cosmopolitan a figure as Benjamin Franklin chafed with resentment at the condescension shown to him by those whom he had formerly seen as fellow Britons.

The facts of geography played a significant part in creating a diverse nation composed of people from different states and regions who were unsure that they could come together to create a united nation. In every intercolonial and interstate gathering from the Albany Congress of 1754 through the Federal Convention of 1787, delegates from different colonies or states observed one another narrowly, penning detailed descriptions of the cultural, religious, and political differences among them and wondering what weight to give such differences in pursuing their shared goals—and whether union was even possible. New England divines, merchants, and lawyers found it difficult to establish common ground with Southern planters, and vice versa. And those from both New England and the South had difficulty understanding the fast-talking, tolerant, commercial entrepreneurs of the middle states such as New York, New Jersey, and Pennsylvania. These cleavages and divergences separating states and regions were among the most daunting obstacles to a firm American union.

The United States was a nation of farmers, although a few writers such as the Pennsylvanian Tench Coxe predicted a glorious future for the United States as a manufacturing and commercial nation.[13] Even the tenth of the population who practiced the professions—lawyers, doctors, and the clergy—never fully abandoned agriculture as a source of income or provisions. Agriculture was central not only to the American economy but also to most Americans' political and social thinking. Of the seven of ten Americans who earned their livelihood by working on small farms, three were laborers on farms owned by others, whereas four owned the land they tilled. Most of these farms consisted of about 96 to 160 acres, but only a few acres were in active cultivation; the rest was used for pasture, grazing livestock, or growing timber, or was left fallow. Even so, these farms required the full commitment of a farmer and his wife, their children, and hired hands—or, in the South, the labor of a few slaves.

The lives of these Americans were closely tied to the rhythms of the agricultural economy, with its cycles of plantings and harvests. Farmers and their families rarely saw anyone outside their own household on a daily basis. Sometimes they did travel, usually to the nearest town to buy provisions that they could not grow or produce themselves, to sell their cash crops, and to find out the latest news. If they were members of a church, they might also make the effort to attend religious services; although by the late eighteenth century church membership and attendance were on the decline, this demographic pattern did not mean a corresponding drop in intensity of religious commitment.[14] Their existence was hard, with few amenities or opportunities for entertainment, but their standard of living was high—in many ways the highest in the western world.

Most Americans at first did not take an active part in the new republic's political life, contenting themselves with voting if they met the requirements established by state constitutions and laws. All the states maintained some form of property test for voting and still higher property qualifications for holding elective office. These requirements grew out of two assumptions about politics dominating eighteenth-century thought. First, one ought to have a stake in society and be able to prove it before one could have a voice in directing that society's affairs. Second, only truly independent voters, whose independence could be proved by satisfying the property test, should take part in public life. Just how many Americans in this period met the property tests for voting is a matter of vigorous dispute, though it now seems that those tests were easier to satisfy than was previously believed.[15]

Of the fraction of the population who could play a role in the political process, however, few aspired to hold office. The society that had evolved since the first English settlements at Jamestown in 1607 was governed by unspoken assumptions and principles bound up in the shorthand term *deference*. There were two categories of Americans: gentlemen, who did not need to worry about earning a living and thus were well-suited to hold office and shape policy, and everyone else, usually lumped together as "the common sort." For the most part, the common sort usually did not challenge the assumption that the elite were entitled to dominate the political system, but the doctrines let loose by the American Revolution buffeted and weakened the deferential society of colonial America, and as a result the distinction between gentlemen and the common sort began to erode significantly.

That distinction, however, was not a rigidly defined class barrier of the type found in Europe. It was possible for the tenth son of a Boston tallow-chandler, a runaway apprentice, to relocate to Philadelphia virtually penniless and eventually to become wealthy, respected, and powerful. This was the achievement of Benjamin Franklin, whom his admiring compatriots saw as a symbol of the possibilities of America. Similarly, a brilliant illegitimate child born on a small Caribbean island could find backing to finance his education at King's College (now Columbia University) and ultimately to become a distinguished attorney and a leading advocate of a stronger national government. Such was the climb of Alexander Hamilton, who nonetheless strove to obscure the circumstances of his early life. The idea of the self-made man came early to American thought, though it still was the exception rather than the rule.

American society was divided not only by occupation but also by religion. The American people exhibited what seemed to bewildered European observers (and even to some Americans) a staggering diversity of religious beliefs and practices—though, to later generations, a spectrum composed mostly of differing forms of Protestant Christianity may seem not much of a spectrum. Accompanying this diversity was a corresponding diversity of forms of church–state relations. In some states, a few large sects or denominations constituting a religious majority secured fiscal support by taxation, imposing religious tests often disqualifying members of dissenting sects from holding office. In other states, no sect received any preferred status, though there was an unspoken assumption that nonbelievers had to defer to believers. And in two states, Virginia and Rhode Island, absolute religious liberty existed. This range of experimentation with church–state relations evolved without a set plan, yet soon dominated Americans' thinking on proper relations between church and state.[16]

Other divisions pervaded American society—though these divisions operated for the most part outside the boundaries of what the historian Henry Adams called the "political population."[17] Perhaps the largest group excluded from direct participation in voting and governing was women.[18] For the most part, laws—whether statutes or the rules of the common law imported from the mother country—barred both single and married women from voting. The doctrine of coverture was an integral part of the institution of marriage in all the states. Under its sway, the married couple constituted one unit for all purposes, political and economic, and only the husband could represent the married couple in the public realm. Even a wife who had launched and was running a business on her own could not sue or be sued without her husband acting as co-plaintiff or co-defendant. Only in New Jersey, from 1776 until 1806, when the state changed its statute regulating the franchise, could single women cast ballots.

To be sure, during and after the Revolution, women took part indirectly—by organizing and taking part in boycotts of British goods, by preparing supplies for American soldiers, and by providing vital intelligence. Mercy Otis Warren wrote polemical pamphlets, including an influential 1788 essay opposing ratification of the Constitution; she also became one of the Revolution's first historians, publishing her *History of the Rise, Progress, and Termination of the American Revolution* in 1805. Though we do not know of other women who took part in the pamphlet wars of the Revolution and the early Republic, it is likely that Warren was not unique. Politicians' wives often were their principal advisors and sources of political information from their home districts or communities. And women were expected to teach their children the values of republican virtue so that their sons would grow up to be good republican citizens and their daughters would continue the tradition of "republican mothers." Some women, such as Abigail Adams, protested privately that the Revolution ought to "remember the ladies," but they found that their calls went unheeded.[19]

The most visible of these lines of division was race, which in turn was entangled with the institution of slavery. In 1787, every state but Massachusetts retained the institution of chattel slavery, and although some northern states such as New York had significant populations of free people of color, ideas about race, slavery, and the link between the two still rested on the unexamined assumption that whites were somehow inherently superior to blacks. Although individual slaveowners freed their slaves,[20] and although some religious groups such as the Quakers denounced slavery as violating the laws of God and man, there was no general movement for emancipation or abolition in the United States. Groups such as the New York Manumission Society, which numbered John Jay and Alexander Hamilton among its founders, and the Pennsylvania Anti-Slavery Society, founded by Benjamin Franklin and like-minded friends, focused on encouraging individual action among slaveowners rather than urging any concerted political or governmental action against slavery as an institution.

At the Revolution's start, the African American poet and slave Phillis Wheatley penned verses in honor of George Washington, and received his thanks and possibly even a visit from him—but she also had to face an inquiry organized by the leading figures of Boston to determine whether her poetry was genuine or an artful fraud of which she was a mere figurehead.[21] In one of the most important American books published before 1800, *Notes on the State of Virginia*, Thomas Jefferson, then American minister to France, put forth one of the first "scientific" cases for the racial inferiority of those of African descent—an argument that stirred little controversy in the United States or in Europe.[22] Even though free African Americans in a few states satisfied property qualifications and thus could vote, they were the exception rather than the rule; for most Americans a black skin meant slavery and racial inferiority as well. Most supporters of the Revolution sought to avoid issues of race and slavery, though George Washington privately recognized the uncomfortable analogy between the Americans' objections to what they deemed the British attempt to reduce them to a state of slavery and "the blacks we rule over with such arbitrary sway."[23] Only opponents of the American Revolution, such as the Tory literary critic, lexicographer, and wit Dr. Samuel Johnson, asked (in his 1775 pamphlet *Taxation No Tyranny*) the biting question: "How is it that we hear the loudest yelps for liberty among the drivers of negroes?"[24]

Both within the states and on the new nation's borders, Native American nations raised other troubling questions about the racial makeup of the United States. Whoever won the American Revolution, historians agree that Native American nations were the biggest losers. Those who had allied themselves with the British found themselves deprived of land, exiled from their ancestral

homes, and targeted for reprisal by vengeful Americans. Even treaties negotiated between the United States and individual Native
American nations were violated repeatedly by white Americans,
with state governments spurning any attempt to invoke the treaty
as a bar to these actions; in fact, one key reason for the calling of
the Federal Convention was to create a general government that
would have the power to restrain states from violating such treaties.[25] The question was further confused by the status at law of
what most white Americans called Indian tribes. In most cases, they
were separate nations and peoples, and they insisted on being
treated as such, rather than as American citizens.[26]

Perhaps those who felt most passionately about being excluded
from public life but are least visible to modern eyes were those
white men who were too poor to have a legitimate voice in politics. Some, though solvent, could not meet the various property
qualifications imposed on voting and holding political office; others wrestled with the problem of debt. Both these groups com-
prised what contemporaries called the "middling" or "common"
sort, as opposed to the "better sort" who expected and mostly
received the deference that they felt was their due. The former
group tended during the colonial period to leave politics to the
elite who dominated office-holding, showing up to vote at election time but otherwise tending to their own needs and concerns.
The latter group, which included members of the better sort who
were struggling with their fiscal obligations, sometimes demanded
that governments respond to their plight by easing laws regulating
debtor–creditor relations. The Revolution launched what the historian Richard B. Morris called "a cautiously transforming egali-
tarianism" that slowly began to open up American public life to
those previously excluded or uninterested.[27]

It was on this crowded and complicated stage that the story
of the founding fathers unfolded. Beginning in 1706 with the
birth of Benjamin Franklin in Boston and continuing onward
through the next six decades, those who became leading figures

of the American Revolution and the early Republic were born into a remarkable variety of families, occupations, religious allegiances, and geographic settings. Some, such as George Mason, George Washington, and Thomas Jefferson of Virginia, Charles Cotesworth Pinckney and Charles Pinckney of South Carolina, and Philip Schuyler of New York, came from the landed gentry and the leading religious denomination, as sons of leading families destined to take their places in the ruling elite. Jefferson varied from the pattern by choosing to pursue the law as a profession, as did his close contemporary John Jay of New York. Others, born among the middling sorts of New England, such as Roger Sherman of Connecticut, John Adams of Massachusetts, and Benjamin Rush of Pennsylvania, seized on the law or medicine as a professional path to distinction.

Still others were born in one part of America but chose to seek their fame and fortune in other colonies. Benjamin Franklin, for example, forsook Boston for Philadelphia, and Abraham Baldwin left Connecticut for Georgia. Joining this mix were immigrants from other parts of the British Empire. James Wilson, for example, left Scotland to settle in Philadelphia, where he became a leading figure in the colonial bar. Among his clients was Irish-born Robert Morris, whose rise was even swifter and more spectacular than Wilson's rise had been; amassing a fortune based on trade and land speculation, Morris became one of the wealthiest men in America. And eventually Wilson and Morris acquired as one of their strongest political and intellectual allies the brilliant, Caribbean-born—and illegitimate—Alexander Hamilton of New York.

Despite their successes and the promise that so many of them foresaw in the future of the new nation, the founding fathers and their contemporaries in America were always conscious that they were living on the edge of the Atlantic civilization. They knew all too keenly that Europe was the center of that civilization's economics, culture, politics, diplomacy, and war, and they fretted that Europeans either would not give them the respect that they felt their nation was due or, worse yet, seek to exploit America for European advantage. This conflicted relationship with the Old World was a key factor shaping Americans' efforts to build a free, wealthy, and happy nation with a wise and sound form of government. Though they knew themselves to be children of Europe, the founding fathers, like most Americans, sought to establish their independence from what Thomas Jefferson called "the parent stem."

FREE-BORN ENGLISH SUBJECTS

If Franklin sought to make one point to Parliament in 1766, it was that a great bond united Americans and Britons even in the face of the differences threatening to divide them—their shared loyalty and deep pride in being free-born English subjects. Franklin also sought to explain how that loyalty and pride entwined with Americans' deep insecurity about how they were seen within that empire—insecurities fueled during the French and Indian War by their often frustrating contacts with British soldiers and administrators.[28] Franklin was undertaking a difficult, perhaps impossible project: to bolster Americans' loyalty to Great Britain while trying to remind Britain what it was about being British that meant so much to those living in British North America.

The idea of "the free-born Englishman," endowed with a rich heritage of liberty rooted in centuries of experience, was a core component of British national identity. England's bloody history of civil wars and regicide, culminating in the Glorious Revolution of 1688, resulted in a stable constitutional and political order that extolled English liberty and seemed to Europeans to approach the kind of perfection usually associated with natural law.[29] Somehow, it appeared, England had emerged from the crucible of revolution cleansed and purified, exhibiting to the world the spectacle of an orderly polity and society, at once stable and energetic, rational and enterprising, and reaping the rewards of empire. All of this the

English attributed to their "ancient constitution," a form of government not codified in a single authoritative document framed and adopted at an identifiable time and place but having paradoxically evolved and developed over centuries while at the same time retaining its core principles of liberty untainted and undisturbed.[30]

Admiration for the unwritten English constitution and its protection of liberty pervaded European perceptions of Great Britain and found its way into some of the most popular and influential literature of the era—literature that American readers such as John Adams studied as eagerly as their European counterparts.[31] Even opera goers attending Wolfgang Amadeus Mozart's *The Abduction from the Seraglio* were treated to the spectacle of Blonde, Kostanze's English maid, who in Act Two, protesting efforts to kidnap her for the harem of the Pasha Selim, declares, "I'm an Englishwoman, and I defy anyone who would attempt to enslave me."[32]

American colonists gloried in their English constitutional heritage, but in the years between 1765 and 1776 that heritage came under siege from an unexpected quarter—the mother country itself. The dispute over British colonial policy that sent the British Empire spiraling into civil war was wrenching and unexpected, and Americans searched frantically for an explanation of what had gone wrong. The controversies of that crucial period posed one agonizing question: How did the English constitution apply to Britain's exercise of authority over her American colonies?

The controversy began when, in the years following the last of the great colonial wars fought between Britain and France in the eighteenth century, Britain sought to require Americans to assume a share of the financial burden generated by those wars of empire. The assumption undergirding this policy shift was simple: because those wars had been fought largely to protect Britain's American colonies from French ambition, Americans ought to assist Britain in paying for those wars. The means the British chose to achieve this goal was the power to tax. In 1765, Parliament enacted a series of measures imposing taxes on the colonists. The most notorious was the Stamp Act, which imposed a tax on printed goods, from legal documents to playing cards, symbolized by an affixed stamp.[33] British authorities expected no controversy—nor did Americans residing in London, including Benjamin Franklin, an ardent advocate of Britain's imperial future. At first, Franklin even sought to name some of his relatives as stamp distributors in America—posts that ordinarily would have been well paid and imbued with high status.

To Britain's surprise—and to Franklin's as well—Americans objected to the Stamp Act and resisted paying the tax. Those who opposed the measure argued that it violated a key principle of the unwritten British constitution—the idea of "no taxation without representation." Under this principle, only taxes levied by legislatures elected directly by those being taxed were legitimate and constitutional. The British rejected this argument, insisting that all members of Parliament had the duty to represent and keep in mind the interests of all those residing within the British Empire. Americans thus were *virtually* represented in Parliament, having no need for actual representation. (The British authorities did not want to address a byproduct of the Americans' arguments—that Parliament was radically unrepresentative, with only a few hundred thousand electors having the power to choose members of the House of Commons while cities such as Manchester and Birmingham, which arose after the establishment of the system of boroughs and counties represented in Parliament, had no direct representation either.)[34]

This dispute over British colonial policy forced both sides to a more basic and ominous level of argument. The colonists insisted that as free men and women who had settled the North American continent by choice, their ancestors carried their birthright of English constitutional liberty with them and transmitted it by inheritance to their descendants. By contrast, British authorities and pamphleteers insisted that Britain had conquered the land forming the American colonies; thus, they concluded, the American colonists had only those rights that the mother country chose to recognize and protect.

This framework of argument formed the rhetorical arena for the next decade of dispute between the colonists and the mother country. Even after Parliament recognized the political realities touched off by the Stamp Act and repealed it in 1766, it linked this repeal to a new statute, the Declaratory Act, which asserted that Parliament had the right to bind the colonies "in all cases whatsoever." Americans who put aside celebrating their victory over the Stamp Act long enough to read the Declaratory Act realized that the argument was not over. In succeeding stages of the dispute, they maintained, at first politely but with increasing vehemence and alarm, that Parliament was violating a core principle of the English constitution as Americans understood it—its restraint on arbitrary (unchecked) power. In theory, the House of Lords or the Crown could check the excesses of the House of Commons. In reality, no English monarch since Queen Anne, who had died in 1714, had vetoed any act of Parliament, and the House of Lords nearly always deferred to any measure passed by the House of Commons. Thus, the American measures enacted by Parliament were exercises of unchecked and thus arbitrary power.

In vain, spokesmen for Parliament and the mother country rejected the colonists' understanding of the English constitution— insisting that Parliament was not arbitrary but merely supreme within the English constitutional system, having earned that central role by defending English constitutional liberty against the pretensions and tyrannical designs of the Stuart monarchs Charles I and James II. Because Parliament had shown that it could be trusted to defend English constitutional liberty against tyrannical Stuart kings, Americans should trust Parliament to exercise its authority over them.

Increasingly the two sides in this elaborate constitutional argument were arguing past each other, for each side rooted its arguments in one of two conflicting visions of the English constitution.

The American version, growing out of the seventeenth-century battles pitting Charles I and later James II against Parliament, taught that the English constitution was a restraint on arbitrary power from whatever source or institution, including Parliament itself. By contrast, the British embraced the eighteenth-century version of the English constitution as enshrining the supremacy of Parliament, the institution that had preserved constitutional liberty and thus should receive pride of place in the constitutional system.[35]

Thus, each new set of tax measures and each experiment with organized resistance to those measures raised the stakes in the dispute between Britain and America. Following the Stamp Act, Parliament enacted the Townshend Acts of the late 1760s, supplanting them in turn in 1773 with the Tea Act. This last statute grew out of a crisis faced by the semiprivate East India Company. Parliament and the king's ministers reasoned that there was a way to solve a whole series of otherwise unrelated problems with one stroke. A relatively modest three-pence tax on tea would generate proceeds to bolster the sagging East India Company and to raise revenue; in addition, it would put an end to all other sources of dispute between America and Britain—or so Parliament and the king's ministers thought. The American response was the spectacular political theater of the Boston Tea Party in December 1773, in which "Sons of Liberty," costumed as Native American warriors, boarded a fleet of three British tea ships at anchor in Boston Harbor, broke open their holds, dumped the tea (which they regarded as illegal contraband) into the harbor, repaired the locks on the holds (thus proving their respect for private property), and went home.[36]

Parliament and the ministry responded with anger to this dramatic act of disobedience. Either missing or choosing to ignore the point that the Americans were trying to make, Britain enacted a series of statutes to punish the people of Massachusetts. One rescinded the royal charter of Massachusetts and placed the colony and its capital, Boston, under martial law; a second closed the port of Boston to commerce; and a third fined the people of Boston for the value of the lost tea. Quickly dubbed the "Intolerable Acts" by their opponents, these measures goaded Americans into calling a Continental Congress to meet in Philadelphia to debate a coordinated American response to Britain's assault on American rights.

All the while, the British government suspected that Americans really wanted to sever ties with the empire and become independent. The colonists, even the fiercest critics of British policy, rejected this charge as slanderous and unfair. The colonists were deeply proud of their connection to the freest empire on earth, symbolized by their king, George III. This pride and loyalty fueled the bitterness of the Americans' resentment of British colonial policy and spurred their constitutional arguments against it. For them, the mother country was betraying the most cherished possession of English subjects wherever they resided: constitutional liberty.

Only after the terrible events of April 19, 1775, when British forces fired on Massachusetts militiamen, first at Lexington and next at Concord, and then suffered a humiliating defeat at the hands of that same militia, did some American politicians begin to believe that the argument had deteriorated beyond the point of resolution within the empire. Even then, radical delegates such as John Adams could not prevent the Second Continental Congress from launching one final conciliatory appeal, the "Olive Branch Petition" addressed directly to King George III. To the moderates' dismay, George III refused even to receive this petition, and issued a proclamation declaring the colonies out of his allegiance and protection and authorizing a wide array of means and measures to quell the rebellion. Once news of his refusal and his proclamation reached America in the last weeks of 1775, independence became a serious option for Americans.

American politicians still valued the constitutional legacy that Americans had inherited from the former mother country and designed new constitutional systems to preserve principles and doctrines that were part of that legacy.[37] The challenge of preserving what was best in the British constitutional tradition, combined with the trauma of having to leave the empire that was supposed to safeguard that tradition, helped to shape the Americans' responses to the constitutional and political problems they faced as an independent nation and people.

Even after they had won independence, Americans could not agree about how to think of Great Britain. In 1785, when he was presented to his former monarch as the first American minister to Great Britain, John Adams took pains to assure George III that Americans and Britons could restore "an entire esteem, confidence, and affection, or, in better words, the old good nature and the old good humor between people who, though separated by an ocean, and under different governments, have the same language, a similar religion, and kindred blood."[38] Some Americans agreed with him, for reasons both principled and pragmatic. Others, such as Thomas Jefferson, were too embittered to share Adams's hopes. They still cherished ideals of ancient English liberty, but they had concluded that the mother country was too far gone in corruption to be seen with anything but suspicion and hostility. This conflict of perceptions also helped to shape the Americans' efforts to establish their independence and govern themselves.

THE GREAT CONFLUENCE

In February 1766, Franklin had reason to expect that the members of Parliament assembled to hear his testimony would accord his words great weight. For nine years he had been working to represent American interests in the capital of the British Empire, rising to high rank in the Empire's administrative structure. But it was as "Dr. Franklin" that he was best known throughout Europe. In 1759, the University of St. Andrews in Scotland had even conferred an honorary doctorate on him for his work explaining that electricity was a natural phenomenon that could be analyzed and

explained by the scientific method.[39] For Franklin and his contemporaries, electricity symbolized man's continuing efforts to
understand and control the natural world, in the spirit of Lord
Francis Bacon, author of the adage "Knowledge is power." With
his customary shrewdness, Franklin saw beyond the specific consequences of his work for the advancement of scientific knowledge; he used his international reputation as an American scientist
to promote recognition that America was the stage of continuing
work to expand human knowledge of the natural world, and thus
by implication a bulwark of learning in the New World.[40]

At the same time that Franklin was testifying before Parliament,
Bostonians three thousand miles away were reading and debating a
pamphlet, *A Dissertation on the Canon and Feudal Law*, published the
previous fall. That pamphlet, the first major political work by a
thirty-year-old attorney from Braintree named John Adams, was not
a staid, abstract work of historical or legal scholarship. Rather, it was
a vigorous, slashing polemic that began by painting for its readers a
vivid picture of the domination of medieval England by a corrupt
aristocracy and a tyrannical Catholic church that used canon law
and feudalism as their instruments of oppression. Adams then deftly
built an analogy between those benighted times and the first stirrings of British colonial policy as represented by the Stamp Act. In
the climax of his essay, Adams issued a call to arms to his countrymen, not to an actual war, but to a war of words and arguments:

> Let us dare to read, think, speak, and write. Let every order and degree
> among the people rouse their attention and animate their resolution. Let
> them all become attentive to the grounds and principles of government,
> ecclesiastical and civil. Let us study the law of nature; search into the spirit
> of the British constitution; read the histories of ancient ages; contemplate
> the great examples of Greece and Rome; set before us the conduct of
> our own British ancestors, who have defended for us the inherent rights
> of mankind against foreign and domestic tyrants and usurpers, against
> arbitrary kings and cruel priests, in short, against the gates of earth and
> hell. Let us read and recollect and impress upon our souls the views and
> ends of our own more immediate forefathers, in exchanging their native
> country for a dreary, inhospitable wilderness.[41]

In this passage, Adams not only mapped the relevant bodies of ideas and experience that he and his fellow colonists sought to use in their campaign against Britain; he embodied that spirit of wide-ranging reading and synthesis so characteristic of the Enlightenment in general and the American Enlightenment in particular. Throughout the era of the Revolution, the Confederation, and the early Republic, Americans continued to heed Adams's mandate, "Let us dare to read, think, speak, and write." And in heeding that mandate they emulated and extended his practice of drawing on a diverse, rich medley of history and philosophy in the service of political, constitutional, and legal reform.

In their attempts to interpret the American Enlightenment, modern historians often seek to assert the primacy of one or another body of thought or experience—whether the lessons of classical civilization in general and the Greek democracies and the Roman Republic in particular,[42] the constitutionalism of the Anglo-American world,[43] the political experience and documents of political foundation of the American colonies,[44] the ideas of civic republicanism,[45] or the philosophical doctrines taught by great thinkers such as Charles de Montesquieu, David Hume, or John Locke.[46] It is all but impossible to make a convincing case for any single candidate, and perhaps the most sensible position to take on the question is that a wide variety of constellations of ideas and assumptions reigned in a wide variety of Americans, with the only thing they had in common being the habit of gathering and synthesizing diverse bodies of thought associated with the Enlightenment.[47]

Americans' awareness that they were participants in a trans-Atlantic intellectual world both empowered and frustrated them. They knew that they lived on the periphery of the Atlantic civilization, and they chafed at the condescension with which Britons and other Europeans regarded them—a condescension that contributed to the worsening and increasingly conflicted relationship they had with the British empire—but at the same time they believed and insisted that they were full participants in the intellectual world of the Atlantic civilization, a world dominated by the cluster of ideas and habits of thought often summed up in the word "Enlightenment."[48] Many of them were conversant with, and obsessed by, the extraordinary explosion of intellectual creativity that spanned the century between Isaac Newton and Adam Smith.[49]

On both sides of the Atlantic, Newton was the greatest hero of the age.[50] The man who discovered and articulated natural laws that governed everything from the movements of the heavens to a falling rock, and who articulated a model of scientific inquiry that profoundly shaped the rise of modern science, Newton fired the imaginations of his contemporaries and successors. For his epitaph, Alexander Pope composed a couplet that captured Newton's gigantic reputation and influence: "Nature and nature's laws lay hid in night: / God said, Let Newton be! and all was light."[51] The quest for natural laws exemplified by Newton's work—and the work of later scientists, such as Franklin himself, building on Newton's achievements—inspired daring hopes. If Sir William Herschel could apply Newton's laws to the motions of the six known planets, deduce the existence of a seventh, previously unknown planet, and find it exactly where he said it would appear; if Reverend Joseph Priestley could add oxygen to the ranks of the chemical elements and Antoine Lavoisier could explain its role in combustion; if Benjamin Franklin could transform electricity from a parlor trick into a respectable, comprehensible scientific phenomenon—in short, if the age could identify natural laws binding God Himself and His creation, perhaps other Enlightenment thinkers could identify, elucidate, and apply equally valid and binding natural laws regulating society, politics, and government. This great goal, and the enduring fame that would come with it, inspired many Americans to blend practical politics with searching inquiries into the history of politics, government, and society. Among the ranks of American philosophical politicians we find the leading thinkers of the American enlightenment, including John Adams, Thomas Jefferson, James Madison, James Wilson, and Alexander Hamilton.

The eighteenth century was perhaps the last era of western history in which one person in quest of such natural laws could hope to command and distill the accumulated wisdom and experience of the ages, and scores of philosophers and savants throughout the western world accepted the challenge, preparing vast treatises on every subject under the sun. For those who lacked the fixed purpose to master this body of knowledge firsthand, other savants published great multivolume compilations—such as the French Comte de Buffon's *Natural History* comprising nearly forty volumes plus at least a dozen volumes of elegant engraved plates; Charles Rollin's encyclopedic and popular *Ancient History*; and, towering above the rest, the vast, collaborative *Encyclopédie Méthodique* planned and edited by Denis Diderot.[52] The French even coined a new word to describe theorists engaged in the service of reform: *philosophe*.[53]

This intellectual world, and its interaction with the realities of the Americans' place in Atlantic civilization and the British Empire, gave the American colonists the intellectual tools and weapons to meet the constitutional, political, diplomatic, and military challenges that they faced when the ties binding them to the British Empire began to dissolve. Once they ceased to be colonists and became independent Americans (in their own eyes and the eyes of the world), they continued to apply the lessons of the Enlightenment to the political and constitutional problems confronting them—if anything, devoting greater energy and urgency to that task.

Different founding fathers felt and responded to the Enlightenment in different ways. Some, such as Thomas Paine and to a lesser extent Benjamin Franklin, Thomas Jefferson, and Benjamin Rush, saw it as a welcome chance for the radical act of uprooting oppressive old ways of all kinds. Rush, for example, urged that American education be reformed by dropping what he deemed to be the useless rubbish of teaching Latin and Greek. Others, such as John Adams and Alexander Hamilton, saw the Enlightenment as an opportunity for a gigantic project of sorting human wisdom—identifying and conserving what was worth conserving in the best of the past while setting aside what had to be revised or replaced.[54]

Although the Enlightenment spanned international borders and even the Atlantic Ocean, we can trace subtly different flavors of the movement as it took form in different nations, shaped by the context of social, political, and cultural forces operating within each nation.[55] The American version of the Enlightenment focused on institutions of government, movements for constitutional and legal reform, and works on constitutionalism, government, and politics. American literature in the era of the Revolution, the Confederation, and the launching of the Constitution took the form of works of political thought and argument such as Thomas Paine's *Common Sense,* John Adams's *Thoughts on Government* and *A Defence of the Constitutions of Government of the United States,* J. Hector St. John de Crèvecoeur's *Letters from an American Farmer,* and Thomas Jefferson's *Notes on the State of Virginia.* The rich literature spawned on both sides of the ratification controversy in 1787–1788 deserves special mention. Though posterity tends to focus on Alexander Hamilton's, James Madison's, and John Jay's essays collected as *The Federalist,* the latest authoritative modern edition of commentaries on the Constitution published in 1787–1788 fills six stout volumes and has ranged beyond *The Federalist* to recover for modern readers neglected classics such as John Jay's *Address to the People of the State of New-York,* the anonymous *Letters from the Federal Farmer to the Republican,* and the pseudonymous *Letters of Brutus.*[56] Pride in these achievements led Americans to think of their nation as "the empire of reason."[57]

Thus, all three contexts—the intellectual context of the Enlightenment; the political context within which former provincials were seeking at once to preserve their Anglo-American constitutional heritage while improving it beyond the parent model; and the social, economic, and cultural context formed by the Americans who resided on the periphery of the Atlantic world—helped to shape the founding fathers, their sense of their role in American and world history, and their political and constitutional achievements.

CHAPTER 3

Achievements and Challenges

The History the Founding Fathers Made

ON NOVEMBER 30, 1787, WRITING AS "PUBLIUS," James Madison published *The Federalist No. 14* in *The New-York Packet*. In this installment of the series of essays that he, Alexander Hamilton, and John Jay were writing to defend and explain the Constitution, Madison sought to justify the theory of the "extended republic" at the Constitution's core. He closed with a memorable challenge to the Constitution's critics:

> But why is the experiment of an extended republic to be rejected merely because it may comprise what is new? Is it not the glory of the people of America, that whilst they have paid a decent regard to the opinions of former times and other nations, they have not suffered a blind veneration for antiquity, for custom, or for names, to overrule the suggestions of their own good sense, the knowledge of their own situation, and the lessons of their own experience? To this manly spirit, posterity will be indebted for the possession, and the world for the example of the numerous innovations displayed on the American theatre, in favor of private rights and public happiness.[1]

Not only did Madison present an eloquent verbal picture of the founding fathers' complex relationship with the past—he also defined for us a valuable perspective from which we should reconsider our relationship with them.

The founding fathers engaged in a creative argument between past and present about the future. From 1765, when American colonists first realized that their interests were diverging from those of Great Britain, to 1836, when (several weeks before his death) the aged Madison penned his last "Advice to My Country," the founding fathers played pivotal roles in creating an American nation and in devising and putting into effect its new constitutional system. They had no guarantees that their efforts would succeed; success was not foreordained. And though the calm, static group paintings by artists such as John Trumbull might suggest otherwise, the founding fathers often disagreed, even fought bitterly, about every step they—and the people they proposed to lead—took to achieve independence, nationhood, and constitutional government. Exacerbating these divisions was a belief that gripped them all—that their labors not only would determine their own fates and the fates of future generations of Americans, but also would answer the age-old question of whether human beings, in the words of Alexander Hamilton, were "capable or not, of establishing good government by reflection and choice, or whether they were forever destined to depend, for their political constitutions, on accident and force." A wrong choice, they knew, might well become "the general misfortune of mankind."[2]

Two themes undergird the founding fathers' struggles. The first is their sense of firstness. From the time when independence became both feasible and necessary, they faced the task of defining what independence would mean, and that task entailed defining what kind of government they would have as an independent people, what kind of politics they would practice under that government, and what kinds of laws they would make. The second is their sense of connectedness to the past and to posterity—to generations gone before and generations yet to come. They linked in their minds their acute sense of being situated in historical time with their equally strong belief that theirs was a pivotal era in human history. Their sense of firstness did not divorce them from the past nor from the future but rather intensified their connections with past and future.[3]

INDEPENDENCE

Though the founding fathers led the first successful colonial revolution—the first not only to claim independence but also to make good on that claim—many of them were reluctant revolutionaries, reacting with sorrow and anger against a mother country that in their view had lost its soul and rejected them in the process, forcing them into a dangerous enterprise that might plunge them and America into disaster.

Especially after the revolutionaries' goal had shifted from resistance to revolution,[4] the Revolution's leaders and foot soldiers all knew that the odds were stacked against them—though some put a brave face on the matter. In *Common Sense*, for example, Thomas Paine, defying conventional wisdom, offered a powerful argument that independence was desirable, well-deserved, and within reach; Paine's case for independence was one strong reason for the popularity of *Common Sense*. Paine and other pamphleteers repeatedly invoked the rallying cry of independence to bolster Americans' commitment to the war, and many called the war that raged from 1775 to 1783 the War of Independence.

Throughout that long, difficult war, those commanding American forces, particularly George Washington, paid close attention to the ideological and political goals the war was supposed to achieve, and took pains to fix those goals in the minds of the forces under their command. The war was a learning experience for Washington and for those he led. Both the commander-in-chief and ordinary soldiers in the line had to overcome parochial and regional loyalties, customs, and habits, and to think of themselves as Americans taking part in a common cause. The shared capacity of Washington, his officers, and his men to absorb and act on these lessons was crucial to the ultimate victory by the Continental Army and its allies.[5]

For Washington, the Revolution brought unprecedented burdens. Not only was he the Continental Army's commander-in-chief—he soon found himself becoming the symbol of the American cause, embodying the Revolution in a way that no other founding father could match. The responsibility he felt proved almost unendurable, yet he struggled to carry it while rejecting the delusion of indispensability that had afflicted earlier revolutionary leaders such as Oliver Cromwell.[6]

In particular, throughout the war, Washington defended the principle that civil authority is and should be superior to military power. In 1783, he thwarted a plan by officers under his command (resenting that they had not been paid for months) to challenge the Confederation Congress's authority. In Washington's view, this Newburgh Conspiracy posed a dire threat to the American cause—even though some nationalist politicians (such as the Confederation's Superintendent of Finance Robert Morris and Washington's former aide-de-camp Alexander Hamilton) thought it might be a useful prod to win additional powers for Congress. Rejecting this scheme, Washington quelled the conspiracy by the sheer force of his personality. At the close of 1783, once British forces evacuated New York City, Washington tendered his resignation to the Confederation Congress. In so doing, he emulated the Roman Republic's revered hero Lucius Quinctius Cincinnatus, who left his plow to lead Rome's armies in time of danger, but, once the crisis was ended, resigned his command and returned to his farm.

Washington's resignation became a cornerstone of his historical and political reputation; his countrymen often cited his willingness to yield power as a reason why they could trust him with power. Reluctantly agreeing to attend the Federal Convention in 1787, and then privately backing ratification of the proposed

Constitution, Washington found that his countrymen were determined to make him their first president; James Madison and Alexander Hamilton argued that his duty to the Union and the Constitution required him to accept the post, and he was elected unanimously. Washington found the presidency a burden at least as painful as his tenure as commander-in-chief had been. In 1792, it took the efforts of Secretary of State Thomas Jefferson and Secretary of the Treasury Alexander Hamilton, who agreed on almost nothing else, to persuade him to accept a second term. In September 1796, nearly thirteen years after his first great renunciation of power, Washington rejected the idea of a third term and announced that he would retire from the presidency on March 4, 1797, the day his second term would end. He thus defined a standard of conduct that shaped the presidency for generations to come; not until 1940 did any president breach the two-term tradition that Washington created. Washington's politics of renunciation also helped to define the nature of American independence; he confirmed the American commitment to constitutional government in general and the principles of rotation in office and civilian supremacy over the military power in particular.[7]

As Washington and his contemporaries understood, independence meant more than either military victory or legal separation from Britain. Inextricably bound up with the question of independence was the question of what kind of independent entity the United States would be. What kind of government would it have? What kind of laws would it adopt? What pursuits would its citizens follow? These questions focused the attention of the founding fathers on devising forms of government for the newly independent states, the form of government uniting those states, and the principles upon which the United States of America would chart the American people's independent course.

Though rumors circulated that leaders of the Continental Congress and then the Federal Convention were seeking a royal candidate to become the first American king, nothing ever came of such reports. Indeed, a deliberate leak from the Convention to a Pennsylvania newspaper on August 22, 1787, declared: "[T]ho' we cannot tell you, affirmatively, what we are doing, we can tell you, negatively, what we are not doing—we never once thought of a king."[8] Nonetheless, the idea of an American monarchy raised troubling questions well into the early nineteenth century. Chief among them was whether the American Revolution would turn out to be truly a revolution or merely the swapping of one king for another. If Americans were fighting only for the right to have a king of their own, how revolutionary was the Revolution? Even as the issue of an American monarchy hovered on the edge of public debate, other issues, at least as pressing and far more real, linked all discussions of constitution-making to the central issue: would the form of government under discussion, whether state or national, help to maintain or threaten to undermine American independence?

The pivotal act of defining what independence meant was the Second Continental Congress's adoption of the Declaration of Independence. That document emerged from the set of resolutions offered on June 7, 1776, by Richard Henry Lee of Virginia; immediately becoming the focus of Congress's agenda, these resolutions distilled the formula for independence.[9] The central resolution declared "that these united colonies are, and of right ought to be, free and independent States, that they are absolved from all allegiance to the British Crown, and that all political connection between them and the State of Great Britain is, and ought to be, totally dissolved." Congress debated two other accompanying resolutions—one authorizing Congress to send diplomatic representatives to European nations to secure alliances and win recognition of American independence and the other authorizing the framing of "articles of confederation and perpetual union" to bind the thirteen states together into an American Union.

Congress named three committees—one to draft articles of confederation, a second to plan diplomatic initiatives to seek allies and financial support, and a third to frame a declaration of independence. The third committee's handiwork, which Congress approved two days after adopting Lee's central resolution, fused in American memory with the decision to declare independence, in the process becoming the enduring statement of the Revolution's goals and Americans' shared principles and purposes.[10]

The draft Declaration—the presentation of which is the subject of John Trumbull's iconic painting—was the work of Thomas Jefferson, with editorial assistance from John Adams and Benjamin Franklin. Congress subjected Jefferson's draft to skilled, rigorous editing that, despite Jefferson's later complaints, improved the document's cogency and force. Jefferson gave the Declaration a three-part structure. The first part stated principles justifying the Americans' decision to declare independence and offered those principles as a basis for a new, independent America. The middle part focused its wrath on King George III, accusing him of destroying the last clear chance to avoid civil war and of violating his kingly responsibilities to his American subjects. This itemized indictment was by far the Declaration's most controversial part in 1776.[11] The concluding part, incorporating Lee's resolution, declared independence as the American response to the facts proved in the indictment.

The Declaration was Janus-faced; like the ancient Roman god of past and future, it looked backward and forward at the same time—backward to tie off the eleven-year argument with Britain by putting the Americans' last word in that argument on record,[12] and forward to define the principles for which the Americans declared independence and by which they hoped to govern themselves should they win independence. It was addressed to the American people, to the rest of the world, and to later generations—seeking to shape the meaning of American independence for all these audiences.[13]

Independence was the lodestar of the diplomats sent by the Continental Congress to European capitals.[14] Benjamin Franklin,

John Adams, and John Jay used an array of approaches to the sensitive question of the Americans' place in great-power politics, but they shared the same goal—to enlist European support for American independence without compromising that independence by tying the United States too closely to its allies. The diplomats battled among themselves and sometimes appealed over one another's heads to a distracted, frustrated Continental Congress. Adams charged that Franklin was too lazy, dilatory, subservient, and bedazzled by France to safeguard American independence and vital American interests. Franklin complained in turn that Adams was not just undiplomatic but too bullheaded, quarrelsome, parochial, peevish, and suspicious to be a good diplomat—indeed, that he was endangering the cause of independence by offending the new nation's greatest ally.[15]

Though their disputes threatened at times to overwhelm their constructive efforts, both Franklin and Adams helped to advance American interests in Europe and to aid the war effort. Franklin had to his credit the creation of the 1778 alliance with France following the American victory in the Battle of Saratoga in 1777; Adams could cite his negotiation of a treaty with the Netherlands and—at least as important—his arranging a series of loans from Dutch bankers to Congress to help finance the American cause.

Joining Adams and Franklin in Paris in 1781 after two frustrating years seeking an American alliance with Spain, John Jay tipped the scales. Cooler than Adams but more suspicious of the French and their attempts to control Congress than Franklin, Jay helped to set in motion the crucial negotiations with Great Britain and to define their tone.[16] The diplomats dealt directly with Britain, leaving to Franklin the delicate task of explaining why the Americans had made a separate peace without consulting their great and powerful ally. The Treaty of Paris of 1783 gave shape to the vision of independence that Americans had crafted throughout the war. The British not only conceded American independence but also ceded all territories between the Allegheny

Mountains and the Mississippi River, doubling the new nation's size. This cession made certain that the American future would include the goal of western expansion and development.

Despite American and French military success at the battle of Yorktown in 1781, and the diplomatic success of Franklin, Adams, and Jay in Paris in 1782–1783, independence remained only a legal and diplomatic fact. The new nation continued to suffer from vulnerabilities of all sorts—economic, social, cultural, and political— that threatened regularly to undermine American independence. For decades after 1783, Americans faced the ever-present threat that their own government's inability to secure vital American interests would endanger the independence that they had won in the Revolution. In the 1780s, supporters and opponents of strengthening the government of the United States divided over how best to preserve the fruits of the Revolution; this division became acute in the struggle over ratifying the Constitution in 1787–1788. Supporters of the Constitution (known as Federalists) insisted that it had to be adopted because a government too weak to protect American interests would fail, destroying the achievements of the Revolution. By contrast, their adversaries (saddled against their will with the name Anti-Federalists) argued that in 1776 Americans had revolted against a strong general government, adding that such a government would drain the states' legitimate powers, destroy individual liberty, and create a tyranny as dangerous as that against which Americans had fought during the Revolution.[17]

Independence continued to be a touchstone for national politics and public policy even after the adoption of the Constitution. In this period, Americans continued to use the concepts of independence and the Revolution interchangeably, regarding a threat to one as a threat to the other. The new partisan alliances dominating national politics, Federalists and Republicans, each claimed to be the Revolution's true guardians and denounced their foes as endangering American independence. For example, in 1793, Federalists and Republicans divided over whether the United

States should maintain its neutrality in the wars convulsing Europe or take sides with Revolutionary France against the league of conservative monarchies led by Great Britain. Republicans cited the critical role that the French–American alliance had played in the winning of independence. Federalists answered that Louis XVI's execution in 1792 abrogated the 1778 treaty of alliance, and that the United States had to maintain neutrality to preserve its independence and not become a vassal of France.[18]

Arguments invoking independence persisted into the early nineteenth century, reaching a high point of political danger during the War of 1812. Republicans viewed that struggle as a second American Revolution against Britain, whereas Federalists denounced the conflict as a mad enterprise endangering American independence. So bitter did the controversy become that some conservative Federalists, including the draftsman of the Constitution, Senator Gouverneur Morris of New York, and New England Federalists such as Harrison Gray Otis and Timothy Pickering of Massachusetts, flirted with the idea of taking their states out of the Union and forming a separate confederation or petitioning to return to the British Empire. Only the news of the Treaty of Ghent of 1815, soon followed by the news of General Andrew Jackson's epic victory in the Battle of New Orleans, derailed these enterprises of disunion and repudiation of the Revolution's central achievement.[19]

In the period from the 1760s to the 1820s, independence evolved from aspiration and goal (in the 1770s and early 1780s), to independence as an achievement requiring defense and preservation (from the late 1780s to the early nineteenth century), to independence as an assumed fact (following the end of the War of 1812). That evolution becomes clear in Thomas Jefferson's last public letter, written ten days before his death, in which he declined with regret an invitation from the mayor of Washington, D.C., Roger C. Weightman, to take part in the city's celebration of the fiftieth anniversary of the Declaration. Calling the Declaration "an instrument pregnant with our own, and the fate of the world," and noting that in 1776 the delegates to Congress faced "the bold and doubtful election we were to make, for our country, between submission, or the sword," Jefferson expressed his happiness that new generations continued "to approve the choice we made." He then set the Declaration in the context of world history:

> May it be to the world what I believe it will be, (to some parts sooner, to others later, but finally to all), the Signal of arousing men to burst the chains, under which monkish ignorance and superstition had persuaded them to bind themselves, and to assume the blessings & security of self government. That form which we have substituted restores the free right to the unbounded exercise of reason and freedom of opinion. All eyes are opened, or opening to the rights of man. The general spread of the light of science has already laid open to every view the palpable truth, that the mass of mankind has not been born, with saddles on their backs, nor a favored few booted and spurred, ready to ride them legitimately, by the grace of god. These are grounds of hope for others. For ourselves, let the annual return of this day for ever refresh our recollections of these rights, and an undiminished devotion to them.[20]

CONSTITUTION-MAKING

The central means to give enduring meaning to American independence was the framing and adoption of state and national constitutions. The founding fathers sought not only to reestablish lawful government, which had collapsed in 1775–1776 with the breakdown of British imperial rule; they also sought to safeguard American independence, to give it institutional form, and to define what it would mean for the American people. A revolution succeeds only if it both tears down an unjust existing order and replaces it with a new, more just order. Franklin used the memorable phrase "political building" in his last speech to the Federal Convention to evoke this constructive component of revolution.[21] The era of political building, which Jefferson memorably called "an age of experiments in government," resulted in an array of new written constitutions, both for the individual states and for the United

States, that formed the founding fathers' most enduring achievement.[22] This achievement had two linked parts: first, the actual forms of the constitutions the Americans wrote and adopted, and, second, the means by which they framed and ratified them.

Constitution-making was on the American agenda even before the Second Continental Congress's declaration of American independence. Beginning in the summer of 1775, royal officials in the colonies fled their posts, leaving behind a void of legitimate government. To fill this void, the people in each colony accepted the leadership of provincial congresses and conventions, although most Americans saw these arrangements as temporary expedients only. Casting about for a more permanent and valid way to restore lawful government, Americans recalled their long experience of governments built around charters granted by the mother country. These charters had become focal points of controversy, with colonial legislatures using them as standards by which they evaluated and often opposed actions of royal governors and Crown officials.[23] In a new, untried political world, Americans realized, framing and adopting a written constitution as a successor to a lapsed colonial charter would help to restore a sense of governmental legitimacy. For this reason, American politicians sought ways to devise new written constitutions and guidance as to the form that those constitutions should take.

Many veterans of the First and Second Continental Congresses knew that one of their colleagues, John Adams of Massachusetts, was renowned for his learning in constitutional government and law and for his skill as an advocate in the dispute with Britain. Deluged in the months from late 1775 to early 1776 with appeals for advice, Adams wrote letter after letter, revising and expanding a sketch that he had first sent to Richard Henry Lee of Virginia. Finally, in April 1776, he wearied of recopying the letter and reworked it as a pamphlet, *Thoughts on Government*, which he published in Philadelphia and which friends republished in Boston and elsewhere. *Thoughts on Government* soon became the most influential work that Adams ever published, shaping American thinking on the writing of constitutions and the devising of constitutional government throughout the thirteen states.

Explaining in a letter to his friend James Warren that his "Design [in writing *Thoughts on Government*] is to mark out a Path, and putt Men upon thinking," Adams embraced the chance to distill for his countrymen his years of studying and pondering constitutional government.[24] In addition to answering his colleagues' pleas for guidance, Adams wanted to counter what he saw as a well-meant but dangerous prescription for new state governments, a plan that Thomas Paine had set forth in the last section of his pamphlet *Common Sense*. Adams valued Paine's plain-spoken eloquence and his formidable arguments for American independence—but Paine horrified Adams by rejecting the need for checks and balances and separation of powers, in particular the need for separate and clearly defined institutions of government.

To Paine, the idea of a two-house legislature coupled with a powerful executive was an unnecessary and dangerous throwback to outmoded ways of thinking. Precisely because this model echoed the British model of King, Lords, and Commons, Paine found it offensive. If, as Paine insisted, the people were to be sovereign, to have ultimate political power, they did not need to protect themselves from themselves. In Paine's view, intricate systems of separation of powers and checks and balances were nothing but schemes of mystification intended to put government beyond the understanding of the great body of the people, reserving it for the educated and wealthy, who could manipulate such complexities to keep themselves in power at the people's expense.[25]

Offended and disgusted by Paine's ideas, Adams insisted that the amassed wisdom of history taught that the people could be just as oppressive as a king or an aristocracy, and that only a checked, balanced, and separated form of government such as the one that he was proposing in *Thoughts on Government* could guard against such dangers. Thus, Adams's pamphlet envisioned a constitution providing for a two-house legislature large enough to form an exact portrait in miniature of the society at large, with a powerful governor holding the balance between them. (Neither Paine nor Adams devoted much attention to what form a government for the entire United States should take, reflecting the general American uncertainty in 1776 about that issue.)

In the late 1770s and early 1780s, Americans adopted an array of state constitutions—with the two models offered by Paine and Adams forming the poles of a spectrum of experiments in government.[26] In Connecticut and Rhode Island, the legislatures revised their colonial charters by deleting all references to England and the king; these revised charters served as constitutions for those states into the nineteenth century. In the other eleven states, new constitutions supplanted colonial charters, while incorporating institutional arrangements and language found in those earlier documents.

These experiments in government formed two great waves of Revolutionary constitution-making at the state level. In the first wave, constitution-makers devoted little attention to the process of creating a new form of government. A revolutionary congress or provincial convention (usually a lame-duck session of a colonial legislature) would vote itself the power to frame a new constitution, draft such a document based largely on the old colonial charter with some liberalizing provisions, and either declare the new constitution to be in effect or call for elections while announcing that the new legislators and executive officials would be bound by the new constitution.

One notable innovation that emerged from this first wave was the written declaration or bill of rights. Virginia's 1776 constitution began with a declaration of rights penned by the planter George Mason, with assistance on the religious-liberty provisions from the twenty-five-year-old James Madison, then making his start in Virginia politics. Mason intended his declaration, codifying right things or principles rather than judicially enforceable individual rights, as a source of guidance for voters in evaluating the conduct of their elected officials. The declaration soon found a host of imitators in other states, and many of the new state constitution-makers followed Virginia's lead in prefacing their constitutions with a written declaration of rights.[27]

Most of these first state constitutions, while preserving English constitutional principles in an American setting,[28] reacted against the American experience of the previous decade. Remembering that colonial governors and judges had sided with Parliament and the Crown, many state constitution-makers either did away with such institutions (Pennsylvania and Georgia had no governor—only a relatively weak president of the state's Supreme Executive Council) or put them firmly under the thumb of large, popularly elected state legislatures. In an ironic twist, these constitution-makers echoed the thinking of British constitutionalism after the Glorious Revolution of 1688–1689. Just as Britain had given pride of place to Parliament, these constitution-makers gave pride of place to legislatures, ruthlessly cutting back on the power and independence of executive and judicial officials.

A reaction set in against this first version of Revolutionary constitutionalism—a development that John Adams insisted was due to the influence of his pamphlet *Thoughts on Government*. In New York in 1777, and in Massachusetts in 1779–1780, this reaction took shape as a new model of constitutional government. Constitution-makers in New York—a small group of politicians led by John Jay—worked in the midst of a civil war convulsing the state. The New York constitution adopted in 1777 created a governor to be elected directly by the people for a three-year term and armed with powers—shared with a Council of Revision and a Council of Appointment—to veto legislation and appoint executive-branch officials. Though this constitution did not have a separate declaration of rights, its framers scattered rights-declaring provisions through the document, including the first guaranteeing due process of law (article XIII).[29]

Massachusetts built on and extended New York's achievements. Its constitution of 1780 was the product of three turbulent years of political and constitutional dispute. In 1778, the state legislature announced, just before state elections, that those elections would empower the legislature to draft a constitution. The legislature then prepared a draft constitution and submitted it to the state's town meetings for the voters' approval—the first time that a constitution was submitted to the electorate for its approval. To the legislature's surprise and dismay, the electorate rejected the 1778 constitution by a margin approaching four to one. Reports of deliberations (known as "results") sent by the town meetings to the state legislature expressed anger at the constitution's unfair apportionment of the legislature benefiting the eastern counties at the expense of the western counties; at its lack of a declaration or bill of rights; and at its failure to establish a clear principle of separation of powers. Chastened, the legislature voted to call elections for a new, popularly elected convention, which would have the sole task of drafting a new constitution that again would go to the town meetings for approval.

The invention by Massachusetts of the constitutional convention was a major advance in the theory and practice of constitutional government. The convention met in Cambridge, where its nearly two hundred delegates chose a three-member drafting committee—James Bowdoin, Samuel Adams, and John Adams; that committee assigned the task of drafting to John Adams, who was on leave between diplomatic assignments. Adams threw himself into the task and produced perhaps the most eloquent of the state constitutions. It is difficult to document what the convention did with Adams's draft, for all we have is the final version that the delegates sent to the town meetings. Over the next several months, the towns debated the proposed constitution clause by clause and again prepared detailed "results" indicating which parts they approved, which they rejected, and why. In the fall of 1780, the convention sifted these "results" and, with a bit of juggling, declared every provision of the constitution adopted by the needed two-thirds majority. On October 25, 1780, the new constitution went into effect.[30] In 1784, New Hampshire was the first state to revise its constitution based on the Massachusetts pattern, and the 1780 Massachusetts constitution, along with the 1777 New York constitution, served as models for the drafters of the United States Constitution in 1787.

A key point of these American experiments in state constitution-making is that these projects, taken together, formed the most important and far-reaching efforts to define what kind of independence the American people would have. Drawing both on the teachings of the French jurist Montesquieu's *The Spirit of the Laws* and on their own decades of political experience, Americans across the political and social spectrum recognized a direct relationship between the kind of government a society had and the shape that society was to take, the values it would foster, and the purposes it would seek to achieve.[31]

When in 1787 the delegates to the Federal Convention assembled in Philadelphia, they had in the various state constitutions a series of precedents and prototypes to guide their efforts. And yet they faced a daunting, unprecedented challenge: Could they devise a republican form of government, the only form that Americans found acceptable after the trauma of monarchic betrayal in 1776, for a nation as large as the United States?

At first, the delegates had to decide whether they would act as a constitutional convention or not. About half the states had chosen delegates to the convention on the understanding that the delegates would propose only amendments to the Articles of Confederation, rather than replacing the Articles with a new constitution. Only after the delegates decided that revising the Articles would not solve the problems facing the United States did the meeting become a true constitutional convention. Even then, they knew that they could only propose a constitution, not put it into effect. The exercise of the power to constitute a government for the United States ultimately would rest with the people of the several states.

The document that the Federal Convention met to revise or replace, the Articles of Confederation, was the product of more than a year of congressional debate and a process of ratification that had dragged on for more than three years. Fearful of the dangers posed by a strong central government, yet recognizing that some form of union was needed if Americans were to win their independence, Congress had created "a firm league of friendship" (Article III) that fell short of being a consolidated Union or a true government for the United States. Even the rickety Articles, which Congress proposed to the states on November 15, 1777, seemed too threatening, and not until March 1, 1781 did the holdout state, Maryland, provide the decisive thirteenth vote of ratification.[32]

To be sure, the Confederation Congress authorized by the Articles had many successes to its credit. It had fielded an army that won the war (with French aid) and a team of diplomats that secured vital alliances and funding for the new government and negotiated a successful peace treaty. Further, in working out a new system for administering the western lands won from Britain under the 1783 peace treaty, the Confederation Congress had devised a solution to the age-old problem of colonialism, providing that these western lands would be organized into territories that ultimately would join the Union as states equal in status to the original thirteen.[33]

Nonetheless, the problems facing the Confederation raised the question whether Americans could preserve the great principles animating the American Revolution and its greatest achievements—independence, liberty, and Union.[34] Never forgetting this question, the delegates to the Federal Convention struggled to find the best way of answering it. They recognized that the United States needed a stronger government than the one limned in the Articles, but balked at the idea of consolidating the states under one national government, because nobody believed that a single unified nation as large as the United States could preserve its liberty. Even the word "nation" terrified all but Alexander Hamilton, the most vehement advocate of national power at the Convention, and the delegates spoke instead of the "general" government.[35] How could they create a general government that could vindicate American interests against hostile activities of European powers? How could they create a general government that would have power to act directly on individual citizens without endangering their liberties or the just powers of the states?

In wrestling with these challenges, the constitution-makers of 1787 never forgot a central lesson about constitutional design—that a constitution grants power as well as limiting it. The complicated and challenging task facing the Convention was to empower a new government for the United States while limiting those powers at the same time.

The efforts to create these documents of political foundation, whether the state constitutions, or the Articles of Confederation, or the Constitution of the United States, often divided Americans, including the founding fathers. John Adams, for example, railed against Thomas Paine and Benjamin Franklin for rejecting the principles of separation of powers and checks and balances that he thought were essential; he denounced their preferred model, the Pennsylvania constitution of 1776, for having a one-house legislature that had no separate executive or judicial institutions to check its sway. Similarly, the issue of church–state relations placed Patrick Henry and his allies, who favored government support of Protestant Christian churches, against James Madison, George Mason, and their allies, who insisted on strict separation of church and state. In contrast, Madison, who always retained skepticism about the power of a written declaration of rights to protect liberty in the face of a determined majority, found himself divided from his old friend Thomas Jefferson, who insisted on the value and necessity of a bill of rights. And many key figures in the leadership of the Revolution could not agree with one another on how much power to give to the general government of the United States. These disagreements and divisions fostered a series of profound debates about the nature of liberty and power, the proper design of a constitution, and the appropriate means for framing and adopting a constitution that have been profoundly influential through the rest of American history, and eventually around the world.

In the millennia preceding the American Revolution, most constitutions had been the handiwork of a single great lawgiver, the most famous being Solon of Athens, Lycurgus of Sparta, and Publius Valerius Publicola of the Roman Republic. However, the American experiments in government were products of collective deliberation. That truth is one of the continuing sources of fascination exerted by the debates in the Federal Convention. In its four months of confidential discussions, shielded from public view and public criticism by a rule of secrecy the delegates adopted at the start of the Convention, the framers of the Constitution wrestled with nearly the full range of questions about designing a constitution for the United States. The delegates struggled against what they understood as the conventional wisdom of Atlantic civilization that so large and extensive a nation as the United States could not possibly have a republican form of government, which was suited only for a small territory whose inhabitants knew one another and had a narrow range of interests. They also struggled with the linked question of the conflicting roles that experience and theory were to play in constitution-making: should they seek merely to apply the lessons of history as they could deduce them, or should they engage in a creative and challenging argument with the past? Should they frame the best constitution that human wisdom could contrive, or should they limit themselves rather to framing the best constitution that had a real chance of being adopted when submitted to Congress and the several states?[36]

Although posterity has tended to emphasize the work of the Constitution's framers in the Federal Convention of 1787, the ratification of the U.S. Constitution in 1787–1788 was a landmark in the history of government. For the first time, the people of a country took a decisive part in deciding how to govern themselves. The Constitution's ratification took place at both state and national levels, within formal institutions of government and in the realm of public opinion.[37]

On the formal level, the process unfolded as the Convention specified in Article VII of the Constitution. The Convention sent the proposed Constitution to the Confederation Congress, which debated it before sending it to the state legislatures. Congress did not endorse the proposed Constitution, as Madison and Hamilton had hoped, nor did it condemn the document, as Richard Henry Lee, Nathan Dane, and Abraham Yates had demanded. Even so, Congress's referral of the document to the states for their consideration had the practical effect of declaring the Constitution legitimate, and all but one state (Rhode Island) accepted its legitimacy and authorized elections for delegates to state ratifying conventions. These conventions then met in full view of the people and debated the Constitution extensively, in most cases clause by clause. The approval of nine states was needed to put the Constitution into effect—a supermajority difficult to achieve but easier than the unanimous consent of all thirteen state legislatures required to amend the Articles of Confederation. Beyond these practical aspects, the ratification struggle had another, cultural byproduct: it bolstered American national identity, for the people of each state knew that their decisions about the Constitution would affect their fellow citizens in other states, and that realization heightened the people's understanding of themselves as citizens of a new nation and strengthened the bonds of Union.

In each state, a furious debate raged over the Constitution, with its opponents demanding that it had to be rewritten or at least amended before they would agree to it, and its supporters insisting that it had to be accepted as it was. The principal issues dividing Americans were the proposed Constitution's lack of a bill of rights, its grants of power to Congress to regulate interstate and foreign commerce, its methods of representing the people and the states, its creation of a one-man chief executive with generous grants of power and the ability to be reelected without limit, and its creation of a system of federal courts.

The Constitution's opponents denounced its lack of a bill of rights as a threat to liberty. They worried that Congress's law-making powers were too broad and could endanger state interests, that it would not truly represent the diverse population of the United States, that the president might become a king, and that the federal courts would swallow up the state courts and restrict ordinary people's access to the courts.

The Constitution's supporters argued at first that a bill of rights was not necessary because the new federal government had no power to endanger liberty. They defended Congress's grants of powers as the minimum that could preserve the Union and defend American interests at home and abroad, and they insisted that the system of representation in Congress was adequate and even desirable. They maintained that the president would never become a king, pointing out that his powers were far less than those of any real king, and contended that a system of federal courts was needed to defend the Constitution and federal law from encroachments by the states.

After five states adopted the Constitution in late 1787 and the opening months of 1788, the sixth state convention, Massachusetts, ground to a halt, until leading politicians on both sides of the issue forged an acceptable compromise. The deadlock arose because the Constitution's opponents wanted the document revised before they would approve it and its supporters rejected the idea of any alterations. The compromise rejected either extreme; instead, the Constitution's opponents prepared a list of amendments that the convention would adopt as recommendations, and the document's supporters pledged to work to persuade the first Congress under the Constitution to endorse these amendments and propose them to the states. This device of recommended amendments prevailed in every ratifying convention that followed Massachusetts (except South Carolina); it allowed the Constitution's opponents to save face and offered the promise that at least some amendments would be added to the Constitution. Most of the recommended amendments were drafts for a federal declaration or bill of rights, the lack of which was the strongest argument against the Constitution.

The plan of recommended amendments capitalized on a key difference between the amending processes of the Articles of Confederation and the Constitution. Given that Article V required the consent of three-fourths of the states, whereas the old Article 13 required all thirteen states to agree, it was easier to amend the Constitution than to amend the Articles. The increased likelihood of amending the Constitution helped to guarantee its ratification.[38]

On June 25, 1788, the ninth state convention, New Hampshire, ratified the Constitution, putting it into effect as the new form of government for the United States. Two more state conventions, Virginia and New York, also ratified it in the summer of 1788 (though by then they faced the choice not of ratifying or rejecting the Constitution but of joining the Union under the Constitution or refusing to do so). North Carolina and Rhode Island held out, demanding a bill of rights and other amendments.

In June 1789, James Madison, now a representative from Virginia in the First Federal Congress, stepped forward as the leading advocate of amending the Constitution.[39] He distilled from the more than two hundred proposals from the state ratifying conventions a list of rights-protecting amendments that omitted any that would endanger what he and President Washington saw as the just powers of the general government. After three months of debate, Congress sent a revised and trimmed list of twelve amendments to the states, including what we now know as the Bill of Rights. This set of proposals was enough to persuade North Carolina to ratify the Constitution in November 1789. The last holdout, Rhode Island, reluctantly followed suit in June 1790. Meanwhile, the states swiftly ratified what became known as the Bill of Rights, with Virginia becoming the crucial eleventh state to ratify the first ten amendments on December 15, 1791.

Surrounding the Federal Convention, the Confederation Congress, the state legislatures, and the state ratifying conventions during the ratification controversy of 1787–1788 was a war of words and arguments. This print war, which spawned a range of publications from learned pamphlets to newspaper essays to wall posters, was decisive in illuminating the arguments for and against the Constitution and in uniting the people of the several states in a shared national argument about the Constitution and whether it should be adopted or rejected.[40]

Both the political processes of ratification and the argument in print over the Constitution expanded the set of Americans who took active part in politics. No longer was politics the sole province of the "better sort" of Americans; virtually every literate American adult had at least some role to play. States suspended their property qualifications for voting to allow every adult male otherwise qualified by age (and in some states by religion) to choose delegates to the ratifying conventions, on the theory that constituting a new government required a wider participation by the citizenry than an ordinary election would entail. The American people built on the experience of ratification. In the era of the early Republic, an increasing number of Americans beyond the conventional members of the governing elite began to take a more active part in public life, even running for and winning office under the Constitution.

In sum, whether led by or arguing with the founding fathers, Americans created the model of how to make and adopt constitutions and what they should contain. By the 1830s, when the last of the founding fathers died, state constitution-making was a settled and familiar process. On the national level, the Constitution of 1787 soon became a focus of popular reverence, with little pressure to replace it. Instead, Americans engaged in formal constitutional change—changing the Constitution's text by a procedure more exacting and formal than ordinary law-making—focusing on framing and adopting constitutional amendments. Because Article V required a consensus on the problem and the means of solving it by constitutional amendment, only two amendments became part of the Constitution between the adoption of the Bill of Rights in 1791 and the end of the Civil War in 1865. The Eleventh Amendment (1795) established a technical rule that no state could be sued in federal court without its consent, and the Twelfth Amendment (1804) provided that electoral votes be cast separately for president and vice president, seeking to prevent a recurrence of the electoral deadlock of 1800–1801.

Two other forms of constitutional change have evolved to supplement the amending process. The first, and more controversial, was judicial interpretation of the existing constitutional text—judicial review. The second was the evolution of informal methods known as custom and usage, which fleshed out the skeleton of government authorized by the Constitution.[41] This array of methods of constitutional change has helped to keep the Constitution adaptable to different times and conditions.

FEDERALISM

Modern students of the U.S. Constitution hail federalism as its most creative feature—yet federalism was a byproduct of individual decisions by the Federal Convention rather than a carefully devised system of relations between the federal government and the states. Not until the Convention had finished its work did federalism emerge, and not until the argument over the Constitution in 1787–1788 did its defenders explain and praise federalism's balancing of powers and responsibilities between the states and the federal government as a great advance in constitution-making.[42]

During the Revolution, the people of each state found it hard enough to write and adopt a new constitution. Devising a form of government to hold the thirteen states together as a firm Union was a greater and more threatening challenge. The two contrasting extremes among the possible models for such a government—allowing each state to go its own way versus fusing them into one consolidated nation—seemed equally unsatisfactory.

The thirteen states could not "go it alone," trusting that their common cause and common interests would hold them together in their efforts against Britain; this overriding truth persisted from the earliest days of American politics. In the first known American political cartoon, published in 1751 in anticipation of the last great colonial war on the North American continent, Benjamin Franklin gave the phrase "JOIN OR DIE" a memorable visual form—showing a dead snake cut into segments, each labeled to represent a different colony (except the head, which carried the label N.E., meaning New England). That symbol persisted through the next few decades, reminding Americans what they risked if they chose to let the Union fall apart either into its individual components or into two or three regional confederacies.

Although the states needed some form of overarching government to stay united, most Americans agreed that molding the states into one vast continental republic would not work, either. Classical political thought, which the eighteenth-century world treated as the distilled wisdom of the ages, taught that a republican government (the only type of government that could preserve liberty) could not work for an extensive territory. A republic that was too big would risk collapse into anarchy or tyranny—or, as history taught, into anarchy that would lead inexorably to tyranny. As the largest of the thirteen states, Virginia, was at the outside limit (either by extent or population) of the size of a polity that could support a republican government, how could the union of all thirteen states have one government?

Creating a nested set of governments in which the individual states would manage their own concerns and interests, but would defer to an overarching general or federal government on questions of shared interest, seems a natural solution two centuries later, but at the time it ran head-on into another axiom of the conventional political wisdom of the eighteenth century. Two sovereign governments cannot operate in the same territory, side by side—an idea symbolized by the Latin phrase *imperium in imperio* (an empire within an empire).[43] Designing an American republican government for an American Union became the central problem from the 1770s to the adoption of the Constitution of the United States in 1787–1788 and well into the history of the early Republic.

Americans knew three precedents for creating an intercolonial union. The first, the New England Confederation of 1643, united four colonies—Massachusetts Bay, Plymouth, Connecticut, and New Haven—as a defensive alliance against the Native American nations of the region, and it worked well for decades. Its principal organ of government was a council of eight commissioners, two from each colony, who administered a common treasury financed by contributions voted by each colony's legislature; each colony also provided militia detachments as needed for the common defense. The Confederation excluded Rhode Island because of the member colonies' suspicions of their neighbor's friendly policy toward Native American peoples and its principles of absolute religious toleration. Gradually the Confederation eroded under the pressure of external events, such as the absorption of New Haven by Connecticut. It dissolved in 1684, around the time that King James II began to take an interest in reworking the forms of government of the American colonies.[44]

Between 1686 and 1688, James II sought to impose one government on the American colonies. His ostensible purpose was to coordinate colonial defense against the French and the Native Americans, but he also had become impatient with the colonial legislatures' claims that they were the equivalent of Parliament and their campaigns of resistance against royal governors. His plan, known as the Dominion of New England, brought the New

England colonies, New York, and the two colonies comprising New Jersey under one royal governor with an appointed council; in addition, he revoked the colonies' charters to decrease their powers of self-government. Rather than breaking the colonists' spirits, however, the Dominion of New England sparked resentment and ultimately resistance. In 1689, when news arrived from England of the overthrow of James II in the Glorious Revolution, Americans rose up against the royal governor of the Dominion, Sir Edmund Andros, and arrested him. The new rulers of England, King William III and Queen Mary, restored the status quo and annulled the Dominion of New England, which was a memorable illustration of the perils of imposing intercolonial union from outside America without consulting the wishes of the American colonists.[45]

The third such scheme of intercolonial union, the Albany Plan of Union of 1754, was the product of efforts to coordinate the colonies' defensive measures against the French and their Native American allies. In 1754, the royal governor of New York, Sir William Johnson, convened the Albany Congress; New York, Massachusetts, New Hampshire, Connecticut, Rhode Island, Pennsylvania, and Maryland sent delegates, as did the Iroquois Confederacy. One delegate, Benjamin Franklin of Pennsylvania, had drafted a plan of union that he shared with his colleagues. The Albany Congress reworked this plan and submitted it to the Crown and to the colonies. It would have created a President General to be named by the Crown and a grand council whose members would be chosen by the colonial legislatures under a rule of representation to be determined by the amount of taxes that each colony would pay to the union.

Unfortunately, the Albany Plan of Union sank in a swirling confusion of objections. The British government resented any attempt to diminish its sovereignty, and the colonial legislatures resisted any plan to reduce their independent authority. Disappointed at the time by the failure of his proposal, Franklin later wrote that had the Albany Plan been adopted, it might have averted the conflicts that led to the American Revolution.[46]

Despite this inconclusive record of experimentation with union, in the 1760s and 1770s the American colonists recognized that effective resistance to British colonial policy would require collective action. The first intercolonial resistance meeting was the Stamp Act Congress, which met in New York's Old City Hall in 1765. Its successor, the First Continental Congress, convened in Philadelphia's Carpenters Hall in the fall of 1774 in response to what Americans called the "Intolerable Acts" enacted by Britain after the Boston Tea Party of 1773.

These congresses were ad hoc bodies, each of which met to respond to a specific crisis with the purpose of devising a specific response to that crisis. Even so, when the First Continental Congress neared the end of its business, it provided for the convening of a Second Continental Congress in the spring of 1775 if its boycotts proved ineffective. By the time that Congress assembled, British forces and Massachusetts militia had exchanged fire at Lexington and Concord, and at least some American politicians believed that a more permanent body should coordinate American resistance, including the assembling and commissioning of a Continental Army with a commander-in-chief.

The crisis expanded beyond the bounds of anyone's expectations, and by July 4, 1776, when Congress proclaimed the Declaration of Independence, it was a de facto American government.[47] Indeed, the Second Continental Congress, under the prodding of John Adams, authorized the colonies to write new state constitutions. Efforts to transform the Continental Congress into a true government, with legitimacy based on consent, proved difficult, however. The states, jealous of their authority, were reluctant to give up power to a central government. It took more than a year for Congress to frame the Articles of Confederation; proposed on November 15, 1777, the Articles languished in limbo until the final state, Maryland, adopted them on March 1, 1781.

The Articles of Confederation created a Confederation Congress with considerable responsibilities for American affairs but far too little power to meet those responsibilities.[48] Each state had one vote, even though the largest and most populous, Virginia, was more than two hundred times as large as the smallest, Rhode Island. The Confederation rested largely on the hope that the state governments would meet its requisitions for money and supplies and that the states would cooperate with its statements of American policy on foreign affairs. It had no power to regulate commerce among the states, nor could it make laws having direct effect on individual American citizens. And any amendment to the Articles required the consent of all thirteen states, which never was achieved.

In the years following the war's end, state governments tended to ignore the Confederation, leaving it all but powerless.[49] Politicians who thought in national terms began to wonder whether revising the Articles would ever be possible. Increasingly, the solution appeared to be not revising the Articles but replacing them with a new form of government. Most of the delegates to the Federal Convention of 1787 agreed that something had to be done, and that the states would have to cede some authority to a new general government. Many also recognized that once they decided to frame a new Constitution, one of the effects of that document would be to amend the constitutions of all thirteen states by transferring power from one level of government to another.

The challenges causing the greatest difficulty for the delegates had to do with issues of representation. Large-state delegates such as James Madison of Virginia and James Wilson of Pennsylvania pushed for a two-house legislature that would replace the Confederation Congress and that would be apportioned on the basis of population, or of wealth, or of taxes paid to the general government. By any of these standards, the large states would have greater representation than the small states. Small states such as

Delaware and New Jersey resisted Madison's and Wilson's arguments, insisting on preserving equality of representation as a central principle from the Articles.

The ultimate compromise, with one house preserving the principle of equality among the states and another based on proportional representation, may seem obvious in retrospect, but it required tough-minded political bargaining to induce the delegates from the large states to accept a compromise of what they saw as a central principle of republican government. Ironically, once the Convention adopted this Connecticut Compromise (so named because of the pivotal role of Connecticut delegates to the Convention in achieving its adoption), delegates from the small states proved willing to vest a surprising amount of authority in the general government, whereas delegates from the large states increasingly resisted attempts to expand that government's authority.

The piecemeal construction of the Constitution, and what became its central principle of dual federalism (meaning a system of two levels of government, federal and state, coexisting in the same nation), dominated the second half of the Convention. Even so, the delegates had no overarching plan of federalism in view. The shape and extent of federalism as a constitutional principle became clear only after the finished draft of the Constitution reached the public.

The nature of federalism in the Constitution became a central issue in the ratification controversy. The Constitution's defenders, some of whom had resisted the emerging scheme of federalism during the Convention, hailed it in writings and speeches supporting the Constitution. In *The Federalist No. 39*, for example, Madison pointed out that the Constitution was a successful middle ground between the pure theoretical types of national and federal government; unlike those pure forms, which would have been doomed to failure, the Constitution mixed elements of both to the American people's advantage. Madison cited such aspects of the Constitution requiring a sharing of authority between the general government and the states as the role of the Senate in approving executive nominations and ratifying treaties, the states' authority over conducing elections for federal office, and the states' role in the amending process.

Similarly, in the Pennsylvania ratifying convention, James Wilson praised the Constitution's creation of what he called "a federal republic," insisting that this new form of government represented a major advance over the old forms of confederations and federations. In a confederation or federation, Wilson noted, there was always the potential for the individual members to erode the general government's authority or for the general government to absorb and crush the independence of the individual members. In contrast, in a federal republic, the people of the United States were the ultimate sovereigns, with both the states and the general government as their servants; the people would decide which level of government would prevail in any dispute between them.[50]

Within the ranks of the founding fathers an array of often-clashing understandings of constitutional federalism emerged. Alexander Hamilton defined the extreme nationalist view. Insisting in *The Federalist No. 85* that "a NATION without a NATIONAL government" was "an AWFUL spectacle," he did everything he could to vindicate the principle of broad construction of the Constitution, under which any power of the general government that could be implied from the words of the Constitution and not specifically banned by any constitutional provision was legitimate. His goal was to win the greatest possible scope of power and freedom of action for the general government consistent with the Constitution's commands.[51]

Ironically, Thomas Jefferson at first welcomed this aspect of the Constitution; soon after he received his copy, he wrote from Paris to James Madison on December 20, 1787, "I am captivated by the compromise of the opposite claims of the great & little states, of the latter to equal, and the former to proportional influence."[52] At this time, the American minister to France was well disposed to vindicating the general government's authority and to inducing the states to cooperate with the United States in meeting American obligations to foreign creditors. After Jefferson's return home, as he pondered the development of the federal system and the federal government's power to command the states, he began to rethink his position.

From the early 1790s almost to the end of his life, Jefferson insisted that any ability of the general government to coerce the states would betray the principles of the Revolution, and he argued vehemently for a strict construction of the Constitution, under which any power not explicitly authorized by a constitutional provision was outside the general government's authority. In 1798, Jefferson even insisted that a state could use its power to nullify within its borders any efforts to enforce an unconstitutional federal law. And yet, during his presidency, Jefferson expanded the scope of federal constitutional power by negotiating the treaty for the Louisiana Purchase in 1803 and enforcing his embargo on trade with the warring nations of France and Britain in 1807–1808.[53]

Other founding fathers espoused views of federalism that fell between the polar positions of Hamilton and Jefferson. George Washington tilted strongly in Hamilton's favor on the question of national power versus state sovereignty. So, too, did John Jay until the War of 1812 filled him with doubts about the federal government because he saw the war as unfairly damaging the interests of his native New York and other northern states.[54] John Adams also tilted in the direction of national power, but Adams never showed any grasp of federalism as a constitutional principle, largely because in the late 1770s and 1780s he had been in Europe on diplomatic missions for the United States and thus had had no direct experience of the problems of balancing competing claims of federal and state authority.[55]

In contrast, James Madison became the leading American expert on American constitutional federalism. Throughout the

1780s and 1790s, his service in the Confederation Congress, the Virginia legislature, and the Congress of the United States gave him extensive experience concerning issues of federal versus state authority. As a rigorous constitutional thinker, Madison shifted his intellectual weight to oppose what he deemed to be any threat to the constitutional system, whether it was the injustice and mutability of state laws in the 1780s or the growing power of the federal government in the 1790s. Though often criticized for inconsistency, he insisted that his core constitutional values had never changed. For example, he saw no clash between his demands for limits on state law-making powers in the 1780s and his embrace of schemes of state power to check federal law-making powers in 1798. Over time, however, his understanding of the ever-shifting line between federal and state authority became so nuanced that in his old age he became a target for advocates of national power and state sovereignty alike. Each side insisted on black-and-white readings of the workings of federalism and inflexible allegiance to federal power or to state sovereignty; to Madison's distress, such uncompromising line-drawing seemed to threaten the Union's survival.[56]

Issues of federalism continued to embroil national politics well into the nineteenth century, as advocates of federal power and state sovereignty regularly struggled to push the constitutional system to an uncompromising position one way or the other. Every constitutional system includes within it gaps or abeyances— questions left to be contested on a case-by-case basis and for which any effort to force a clear and comprehensive solution might trigger conflict that could blow the system apart. Such abeyances absorb the shocks and strains that otherwise might damage the constitutional system permanently beyond all hope of repair. The danger lies in trying to force the solution to such an abeyance.[57]

Based on this view, the history of the Constitution of 1787 between its adoption and the outbreak of the Civil War in 1861 revealed increasing tension over the nature of federalism.

Although the existence of the constitutional abeyance on questions of federal versus state authority allowed for discrete compromises that averted ultimate conflict, sooner or later a controversy would arise that could not be turned aside or compromised. The series of sectional crises that arose in the 1820s, 1830s, and 1850s tested the system of federalism to the breaking point. The result, in the spring of 1861, was the shattering of the Constitution of 1787 and the Union it was designed to preserve.

The original Constitution staved off the ultimate crisis of disunion until the internal pressures became too great to contain; ironically, at the same time, that long delay of the ultimate push for disunion enabled the federal government to attain a state of constitutional authority and military and economic power sufficient to preserve the Union even in the face of a political and military attempt at secession. The cost of maintaining the Union was a bloody and terrible civil war. It is an ironic and tragic coincidence that the Battle of Antietam, the single bloodiest day of the Civil War, September 17, 1862, took place on the seventy-fifth anniversary of the signing of the Constitution.[58]

POLITICS

Constitutional structures and institutions, whatever their flaws or limitations, were remarkable achievements—but Americans also faced the challenge of making them work in the ordinary tasks of politics.[59] Here, too, they defeated conventional wisdom and devised, sometimes deliberately and sometimes by accident, new means of conducting politics, while creatively adapting existing means of political advocacy and action. This story's central theme is the evolution of a tense and often-shifting balance between leadership by enlightened statesmen and insistence by the people that they were determined to play an active role in their own governance. A byproduct of this tension was the development of the American system of political parties, which we now take for

granted and which has proved essential to the success of the constitutional system. That system of parties, paradoxically, emerged
from a far different, even antithetical world in which parties were
deemed dangerous conspiracies against the general good.

Though Americans were experienced politicians within their
individual states, they had little or no experience working together
across state lines, even in the confines of one legislative or representative chamber. Organizing the Revolution and running the
Confederation were learning experiences for these politicians, and
the Federal Convention was even more so—especially for James
Madison.[60] Though posterity has conferred on Madison the title
of "Father of the Constitution," by the Convention's end Madison
was disappointed in the proposed Constitution, in great measure
because most of his most cherished ideas—such as apportioning
both houses of Congress on the basis of population or creating a
council of revision empowered to strike down state laws—went
down to defeat in the Convention's second half. Similarly, the
most extreme nationalist among the Convention's delegates,
Alexander Hamilton, found the finished draft of the Constitution
deeply disappointing; he prepared his own mark-up of the document, bringing it into conformity with his own ideas about what
a new charter of government for the United States should look
like, and asked Madison to include that version in his notes of the
Convention's debates for the edification of posterity.

Even so, within ten days of the Convention's end, the two men,
sitting in the Confederation Congress in New York City, were
astonished by the hostility and suspicion with which some of their
colleagues viewed the proposed Constitution, and agreed to work
together to get it ratified. Likewise, many speakers during the last
day of the Convention confessed their disappointment with the
Constitution yet pledged nonetheless to work for its adoption as
the best proposal that had a chance of success.

Ratifying the Constitution blended old and new methods of
politics. For example, the tool that Madison and Hamilton used

to make their most formal and elaborate case for the Constitution was print—a central means of practicing American politics for most of the eighteenth century. In the era of the nation's founding, the most efficient way to communicate political ideas and arguments was to print them for wide dissemination. Modern readers see *The Federalist* as a coherent and polished work of constitutional argument or political theory, but it originated as a newspaper column that appeared twice a week in the major newspapers of New York City. In the ratification controversy of 1787–1788, *The Federalist* was only one (though the most detailed and elaborate) of a series of hundreds of pamphlets, newspapers essays, and other printed arguments for and against the Constitution. The flood of print had begun in the 1760s with the first stirrings of American resistance to British colonial policy; it had ebbed and flowed through the 1780s, but swelled to an amazing degree in the late 1780s, and continued well into the early nineteenth century.[61]

At the same time, ratifying the Constitution helped to rewrite the rules of American politics. The state ratifying conventions met in full view of the public, often assembling as many as two hundred delegates, with galleries for interested spectators. Printers then published, whether in newspapers or later in pamphlets, their attempts to record and disseminate those debates. The openness of the ratifying debates set a precedent for later legislative bodies to stop meeting behind closed doors and to open galleries for ordinary citizens and for journalists to attend the sessions of legislatures—the first stirrings of the public's right to know. The state ratifying conventions often resembled large popular seminars on constitutional government, with leading advocates of the Constitution acting as seminar leaders seeking to point and direct the discussion but knowing that they could not force the delegates into agreement. These conventions presaged the growing willingness of the people in the 1790s and the early nineteenth century to make their views known on political measures, to organize to advance those views, and on occasion to challenge the new nation's political leadership.

This new and turbulent political world required the new nation's leaders to practice a kind of politics both resembling and diverging from the politics of today. Given that modern Americans hate politicians and love their national icons, it is natural for them to assume that the greatest figures of American history never were and could not have been politicians. For example, they like to think that Washington never had to do any fund-raising, that Hamilton was not interested in political spin, and that Jefferson was an idealistic statesman who never soiled his hands with politics. Actually, Washington had to do emergency fund-raising in 1789, borrowing $500 from a neighbor to get himself from Mount Vernon to New York City for his inauguration. Hamilton not only was concerned with political spin—he was a ferocious and prolific writer for the public press, defending his measures and assailing his foes under a score of pen names. Finally, rather than being a retiring philosopher with no gift for politics (as he sometimes presented himself), Thomas Jefferson was a master politician by the standards of his era.

In part, this confusion comes from our failure to grasp the difference between politicians of the early republic and those of modern times. In Jefferson's era, politicians did not rely on their political careers for financial support. Washington and Jefferson were gentleman-planters who lived on the labor of slaves (though Washington supplemented that income with shrewd speculations in land and Jefferson briefly practiced law). Alexander Hamilton shuttled between his law practice and his posts in government, and it was the law practice that helped to support his growing family.

Another difference between the founding fathers' era and ours was that the calendar of public life in the early republic was not the constant, hard-driving force we know today. Jefferson could spend weeks at Monticello while he was secretary of state, vice president, or president. In the late 1790s, President Adams spent months at a time in Braintree, Massachusetts, caring for his ailing wife, while his cabinet officials secretly met with and took directions from Alexander Hamilton (then a lawyer in private practice, with no official government role). One cause of the seasonal, intermittent calendar of politics in this period was the relatively slow speed at which news traveled within the United States or across the Atlantic Ocean. Reports of events such as the fall of the Bastille, the execution of Louis XVI, or the signing of the Jay Treaty could take weeks or months to reach American shores. The speed at which news traveled within America was little better. Political news traveled no faster than a man could run, a horse could gallop, or a ship could sail—giving politicians more time to ponder, react, and decide.

The difficulties of travel and communication also cut down the number of occasions requiring oratory—as did the era's political culture. Not until the ratifying conventions of 1787–1788 did American law-making bodies meet in public view. The people's right to know was in its infancy, and most state legislatures and the Continental and Confederation Congresses met behind closed doors. After the launch of government under the Constitution in 1789, only the House held open sessions; the Senate met behind closed doors until an election dispute in 1797 forced a change in the Senate's rules. Politicians rarely had to address an audience other than their colleagues. Even at election time, in Jefferson's Virginia a candidate's willingness and ability to buy drinks for the neighborhood was more important than his ability to win votes by making speeches.[62] Few Americans ever saw their president, senators, or representatives in person. The twice-yearly circuit court sessions of the early Republic meant that the most visible public faces of the new government were federal judges.

Finally, the modern determinants and landmarks of political authority and influence did not exist in the early Republic. Under the Articles of Confederation, term limits turned delegates to the

Confederation Congress out of office after three years, giving no chance for a seniority system to develop; seniority did not matter in the Congress of the United States until decades after its creation in 1789. There were no organized political parties as we understand the term—just loose, unstable coalitions of shared interests or partisan alliances that could dissolve and recombine with a change in measures or in men. Neither the state legislatures nor Congress had a system of institutionalized legislative committees with powerful chairmen controlling the legislative agenda. Almost every committee was an ad hoc creation, dealing with its own piece of legislation or other business. The rules of procedure governing national bodies such as the Confederation Congress and the Congress of the United States took similar form and produced similar results in the state legislatures.

How was politics practiced in this period? It consisted for the most part of groups of politicians working together in legislative chambers and committee rooms, debating and arguing and listening and seeking to forge a mutually acceptable consensus, or waiting on the writing efforts of a single man working by himself with paper, ink, and a quill pen. It also entailed, sporadically at first but with increasing frequency and regularity, politicians communicating not just with one another but with members of the general public. Politicians sought both to explain public policy and to influence the electorate's acceptance and support of either that policy or the officials identified with that policy. Politicians also sought to influence the political population's perceptions and opinions of themselves, their allies, and their adversaries. But the process did not work all one way. Elite national politicians had to pay close attention to the ways in which the people thought about politics and politicians. The currents of public opinion often posed unpleasant surprises for the so-called governing class.

Thomas Jefferson is a valuable case study in the remarkable world of politics in the early Republic.[63] In this complex system of interactions between governors and governed, and interactions within the ranks of the executive, legislative, and judicial branches, he was a master of the game.

The first of Jefferson's great political abilities was his skill with his pen. John Adams deemed Jefferson to have "a happy talent for composition" and a "peculiar felicity of expression."[64] Not only did he have these abilities—his colleagues knew that he had them, and regularly relied on them. Legislatures in the late eighteenth century did not have the army of legislative assistants, administrative assistants, or staff attorneys that we know today. If a legislator wanted a bill drafted, he had to do it himself—or to find a colleague who agreed on the need for the bill and was willing and able to draft it for him. This was an ideal environment for Jefferson.

In every legislative body in which Jefferson served, he soon and justly won the reputation for being a skilled, eloquent draftsman. This ability was one key reason that he was chosen to draw up the Declaration of Independence. Throughout his career, he never used a speechwriter or aide; instead, he did the work himself and consulted with colleagues to secure their advice. In one case, he was not happy with the revision of his handiwork. As late as 1821, he insisted on juxtaposing in his "Autobiography" his draft of the Declaration of Independence with the official text, convinced that any reasonable reader would prefer his version.

Jefferson was that rare president who always was his own speechwriter—but, in one notable case, he was willing to accommodate revisions suggested by his colleagues. In October 1801, the Baptists of Danbury, Connecticut, sent him a frantic appeal for moral support from a religious minority in their battle with a hostile Federalist and Congregationalist majority. Jefferson therefore prepared and circulated a draft response to his cabinet, paying especially close attention to the views of Postmaster General Gideon Granger and Attorney General Levi Lincoln, both New Englanders and shrewd politicians who knew their region and its politics well. Then Jefferson revised his letter, which he finally sent on January 1, 1802, to make it a statement of his constitutional principles and a careful endorsement giving the Danbury Baptists the moral support they sought without committing his administration to any concrete action on their behalf.[65]

Throughout his political career, Jefferson sought to order the world with words. Not just in his time, but in the span of years from his time to ours, Americans have argued about the character of America, the nature and destiny of the American republic, the shape of the good society, and the meaning of liberty and equality, within the intellectual matrix established by his written words. As Abraham Lincoln wrote in 1859, "the principles of Jefferson are the definitions and axioms of free society."[66]

Jefferson's political mastery had to do with more than political draftsmanship. Politics is a matter of the human equation as much as it is one of abstract contests of political principle. For the most part, eighteenth-century politics was a face-to-face affair between individual politicians. In those settings, personal skills such as affability, a willingness to listen and to appear to listen, an ability to hold one's tongue, and a gift for forging personal relationships were integral to political success. Jefferson had these skills in ample measure. As a member of the House of Burgesses, he soon won the trust and respect of much older colleagues, and not just because he had distinguished mentors such as George Wythe and Governor Francis Fauquier to vouch for him. So, too, as a member of the Second Continental Congress, he won his colleagues' respect—even though, as John Adams observed, Jefferson was the most close-mouthed man in that body. In dealing with members of the House and the Senate while he was secretary of state, he drew on the skills he had honed in five years of representing the United States in France. And, as president, one of Jefferson's greatest achievements was his deft management of the pro-administration majorities in both houses of Congress.

The elderly John Adams suggested another reason for Jefferson's political success. In a letter to his old friend Benjamin Rush, a fellow signer of the Declaration of Independence and a friend of

Jefferson, Adams reflected on the great men he had known. He concluded, with a typically Adamsian mix of insight, envy, and resentment, that Washington, Franklin, and Jefferson all had a gift integral to their reputation as great men, a gift that Adams himself did not have: the gift of silence.[67] Adams complained that the ability to keep silent conferred on the person possessing that gift a false reputation for profundity, for others would fill that silence with deep and extraordinary meanings that he might not have intended or imagined. Jefferson knew when to keep his mouth shut, and he used that knowledge to great advantage.

Jefferson hated confrontation. For this reason, in a trait that was not peculiar to him but that he developed perhaps to extreme lengths, he crafted a series of public faces or personae to show to various people—to President Washington, to his ally and partner in politics James Madison, to adversaries such as Alexander Hamilton and Aaron Burr, and to those whose support he wanted to win or whose opposition he wanted to blunt. The purpose of this chameleon-like behavior was simple—to persuade the person sitting opposite him that he agreed with that person or at least was willing to accept that person's views of a given matter. By the end of a given conversation, anyone sitting across the table from Jefferson, unless naturally wary and suspicious, would be convinced that Jefferson was on his or her side and was grateful for that support. Even with that wary and suspicious person, Jefferson would use every last iota of his conversational brilliance, learning, and capacity for collegiality to fend off confrontation.

Of course, it is not always possible to escape confrontation. In cabinet meetings in the Washington administration, Hamilton tended to orate as if addressing a jury, while Jefferson would sit largely silent, occasionally inserting a sarcastic comment to puncture the flow of Hamilton's words. When confrontation seemed unavoidable, Jefferson would stage a tactical or even strategic withdrawal, as when in late 1793 he stepped down from his post in the Washington administration to return to Monticello. This pattern recurs throughout his public life, from his earliest days as a colonial legislator to his leadership of the struggle to found and organize the University of Virginia.

Further, Jefferson was an astute student of public opinion. In his time, currents of ideas, information, and what we would call gossip passed between elite politicians, and from elite politicians to the general public and back again through middlemen. For example, James Madison had a good friend in Virginia, George Lee Turberville, who regularly sent him letter after letter packed with political information about the views prevailing at home, and to whom Madison sent letter after letter detailing the doings in the center of American public life, where Madison tended to be. So, too, Madison served as one of Jefferson's chief informants and his most trusted advisor. Similarly, Abigail Adams was her husband's chief advisor and political informant, though John Adams had a few close friends home in Massachusetts who also sent him news from home.

What kind of news passed back and forth and around in these circles of friends and allies, these informal partisan alliances? One kind of news had to do with the substance of political measures— such as proposed amendments to the Constitution, the federal assumption of state debts, American foreign policy, the administration of government, and the organization of executive departments and federal courts. A second kind had to do with who was allied with or opposed to whom, who was in and who was out, and who had power and influence and who did not. A third kind enabled the listener or reader to form a clear picture of the character of an individual politician. Did he walk to work or ride his own horse? Was he drawn in a carriage? If so, how many horses drew the carriage? Did he powder his hair or not? Did he wear ostentatious clothing or plain, simple republican garb? Did he bow or shake hands? It was best to conduct yourself in as plain, simple, and republican a manner as possible—ostentation was a sign of potential aristocracy or even leanings to monarchy.

Washington and Jefferson paid close attention to such aspects of the politics of self-presentations and proved themselves among the greatest masters of the art. When the first president-elect of the United States arrived at his inauguration in New York City on April 30, 1789, people were surprised and pleased to see that he was wearing not his old Continental Army uniform, but a plain brown woolen suit of American manufacture. This choice of attire said three important things: "I take office not as General Washington but as George Washington, Esq., a civilian"; "I take office as a committed republican"; and "Buy American, as I do." Similarly, when in his diary entry for May 24, 1790, Senator William Maclay of Pennsylvania described Secretary of State Jefferson's testimony before a Senate committee, he noted that Jefferson's clothing seemed rumpled and not quite tailored to fit, and that Jefferson lounged in his seat. Here, as at other times in his life, Jefferson dressed and carried himself as a silent republican reproach to any kind of monarchic or aristocratic fashions or habits, for fashions and habits are the symptoms of underlying social and political ailments that can afflict a republic—or the symptoms of underlying social and political views that can cure those ailments.

Sometimes the way a politician dressed or behaved could be misread. Many criticized Vice President John Adams in his first years in office because of the opulence of his attire. In response, he complained that he was wearing the only clothes he had, the clothes that he had worn while he was American minister in Britain in the 1780s; he could not afford a new wardrobe. In sum, because he had to wear his old fine clothing instead of spending money he did not have to buy plain new clothing, he got the unfair reputation of being aristocratic when he was merely being economical.[68]

Gossip focused not just on observations of dress and behavior but also on reports of toasts offered at banquets or who conversed with whom and about what. Such political gossip was the raw material on which politicians and ordinary citizens relied to assess the fitness or republican-ness of those aspiring to leading roles in the nation's public life. Knowing that gossip helped to shape the public character and reputation of those who would lead the nation, politicians had to ensure that their characters and reputations were worthy—and that their foes' characters and reputations were not.

A remarkably detailed and intricate grammar of political combat prevailed in the early Republic, and Jefferson was an expert in this method of political fighting.[69] Throughout his public life, he collected reports, rumors, anecdotes, and gossip, scribbling them down on separate scraps of paper often within minutes of hearing something worth recording. Eventually, he gathered these scraps into what he called "three volumes bound in marbled paper"—an account that he intended later readers to treat as a true documentary history of the political life of the early American republic to combat the pro-Federalist version appearing in Chief Justice John Marshall's *Life of George Washington* (first published in 1804 and issued in various editions thereafter).[70] Juxtaposing official opinions and memoranda with these crabbed and hasty notes of gossip and innuendo, Jefferson wanted his readers to understand that American politics was operating on two levels, and that at the hidden level of gossip and innuendo, a titanic struggle was going on for the soul of the United States. If in a political world lacking formal determinants of status, leadership, affiliation, and allegiance the key determinant of politics was the character of the individual politician, then shaping how character is perceived became a vital political battleground. Jefferson was brilliant at keeping track of how characters were or ought to be perceived, and at working with those who thought as he did to encourage proper perceptions among the people.

Grasping the values governing late eighteenth-century American politics, Jefferson also was adept at guiding himself by those values. One central value was the dangerousness of political ambition. Men should not seem to want power; they should present themselves as accepting power only with great reluctance and as yearning for the chance to lay the burden aside and to return home. George Washington presented himself this way throughout his career. When the Second Continental Congress convened in early 1775, Washington arrived as a Virginia delegate wearing his old uniform as a colonel of the Virginia militia—reminding the other delegates that he had served in the armed forces and was ready to do so again should his country call on him. But when Congress chose him to be commander-in-chief of the Continental Army, Washington bemoaned his lack of qualifications for the job, regretted the necessity of accepting it, and began his yearning for retirement that he kept up in public and private for eight long years. He meant it—but he also knew that it was vital for him to be seen and heard meaning it.

So, too, throughout his political career Jefferson expressed reluctance to assume the burdens of office, yearned for retirement, reminded others of his unhappiness in public life, and invoked his desire to return to his family, his plantation, and his books. Again, though he meant every word of it, he also knew that it was vital to his success as an elite national politician for him to be seen and heard meaning it. Like Washington, Jefferson had a stern sense of the public good and a conviction that if he could further the public good by assuming office, duty and civic virtue required him to do so. But unlike Washington, Jefferson had an ideological reason beyond his sense of the public good. He had a vision of the good society, and he had become convinced not only that he had the proper vision of the good society but that he was the best man to help his country achieve that vision. Jefferson's ambition was not for himself pure and simple. Rather, he sought to win authority so that he might use it to secure and vindicate his vision of the good society.

Jefferson's vision of a good society emerged from the Declaration of Independence, from his revision of Virginia's laws (including his bills for religious freedom, public education, and "the proportioning of crimes and punishments"), from *Notes on the State of*

Virginia, from his inaugural addresses and presidential messages, and from his myriad of political letters. Its foundation was a society devoted to agriculture as practiced by a nation of yeoman farmers, though with room for the grander plantations of people such as Jefferson. Cities, trade, and commerce were at best necessary evils. His watchwords were republican simplicity and virtue, insulated from the corruption that would lead to aristocracy and monarchy. Religion, he thought, should also be pure, republican, and free, not coerced by government or religious hierarchy, and purged of the corruptions imposed by generations of priestcraft.

One key element of Jefferson's vision of a good society that has not been sufficiently appreciated is its contrast with another vision of society that haunted him for much of his life. The specter that preoccupied Jefferson was not Hamilton's vision of a great nation built on a three-legged stool of agriculture, manufacturing, and commerce. Instead, it was what Jefferson confronted in 1784 when he arrived in Europe to begin his service as an American diplomat. Jefferson lived in France, with visits to Britain, Italy, the Netherlands, and the German Rhineland. During his travels he took attentive notes of life in these nations, and he wrote home regularly about his impressions. What stands out most strongly in his letters about Europe is his horror at the corruption, decadence, and waste that monarchy and aristocracy inflicted on great nations and peoples—a state of affairs most painfully evident in France.

Lurking behind these impressions is the belief that Jefferson shared with many other Americans: monarchic and aristocratic corruption in Great Britain had led to the corruption of British constitutional liberty in the former mother country and to its attempts to undermine British constitutional liberty in America. Jefferson's European travels and observations only intensified these convictions. Linked with this belief is another belief, part of the intellectual furniture of any well-stocked mind in the Atlantic civilization: that similar corruption taking similar forms had brought down the Roman Republic and had led to the tyranny of the Caesars, as recounted by Sallust, Tacitus, and Suetonius. As a result, when Jefferson returned to the United States, he was primed to react to anything that reminded him of European corruption as a harbinger of American corruption that he had to fight with all his might and soul and heart.

These preoccupations and perceptions provide a key to what some scholars have dismissed as Jeffersonian fanaticism. Jefferson held these views strongly, and he applied them almost with cookie-cutter rigidity to what he saw in America. Thus Hamilton's fiscal policy reminded him of the policies of Sir Robert Walpole, with their attendant corruption and undermining of English liberty in the early eighteenth century. Hamilton's design to strengthen the executive branch reminded him of monarchic corruption in Britain and France, and the dangers to liberty and democracy that those measures posed. Using a standing army to suppress domestic revolt in agricultural western Pennsylvania, as Washington and Hamilton did in 1794 against the Whiskey Rebellion, seemed to Jefferson yet another step to bringing tyranny to America.

Throughout his presidency, Jefferson practiced the same republican politics of self-presentation, of collecting and disseminating the right forms of political intelligence (or gossip), and the use of well-chosen words to order the world. He hated speechmaking, one likely reason why Adams (who was good at oratory and enjoyed it) noted Jefferson's being so close-mouthed in Congress. Jefferson ended the annual practice of appearing before a joint session of Congress to deliver a presidential address on the state of the Union. Not only did this decision spare him an annual public ordeal—more important, it abolished what he saw as a quasimonarchical practice (echoing the British "speech from the throne" that opens sessions of Parliament) that had no place in the American constitutional system. He used letters to inform the public of his views and policies and those of his administration, knowing that a letter from a political leader on a great public question would soon become public property. This is why so many of his private letters warn the recipients not to show them around; he knew that a letter from his pen, unless explicitly safeguarded from public view, would not stay private for long.

Jefferson used customs of dress and etiquette in the same way. His "pele-mele" seating at presidential dinners, in which people seated themselves at will, was a direct blow at the European custom of seating people at such occasions according to their political or social status. So, too, his willingness in 1803 to receive the British ambassador Sir Anthony Merry while clad in his dressing-gown and carpet slippers was neither a mere affectation nor an expression of absent-mindedness; rather, it was his explicit rejection of the quasimonarchic and aristocratic ceremonies and customs in diplomacy that he abhorred as threats to republican virtue.

Jefferson said that he hated being president, calling the office a "splendid misery," and there is little reason to doubt that he meant what he said. He served two terms and, at the close of his second, chose not to seek a third. Returning to Monticello, he never left Virginia again. Even so, he remained a notable public figure, and he took great pains to work with his friends and colleagues and with the people to shape a new role in the constitutional realm—that of ex-president.

In a sense, Jefferson was the first to have a chance to do this task. George Washington was unique in American public life; he was the American Cincinnatus, who had made a profession not just of holding and wielding great executive power, but of setting it aside and returning to the ranks of the people out of his own inclination and, just as important, out of a sense of duty to the republic. John Adams had been defeated at the polls when he sought a second term—though, as recent scholars have concluded, his defeat was not the flat-out repudiation he felt it to be. Wounded by what he deemed an unjust rejection at the people's hands, Adams withdrew into himself for years after his defeat, not reemerging as an active participant in public life until after the close of Jefferson's presidency. Jefferson was the first man voluntarily to assume the role of an ex-president and to work to shape that role in American public life.[71]

Even the major role that Jefferson assumed in his later years— "the sage of Monticello"—had a political cast. In thousands of letters, he sought to influence American cultural, scientific, intellectual, and political development—fostering political principles close to his heart and encouraging the writing of American history and biography and the collecting and preservation of primary sources to aid those efforts. His greatest retirement project, however, took up a cause that he had cherished for decades— educational reform in Virginia. Both as a discontented alumnus soured on his old College of William and Mary and as an exponent of an enlightened citizenry as a bulwark of a democratic republic, Jefferson committed himself to founding a new kind of university, one allied with no religious denomination or sect, welcoming students from everywhere, and devoted to the life of the mind. His founding of the University of Virginia—designing the buildings, choosing the faculty, drawing up the curriculum, assembling lists of textbooks and library books—was a political act as much as anything else in his life.

CHURCH AND STATE

For centuries, European nations and peoples had struggled to resolve the problems of the proper relationship between church and state. To what extent were alliances between religion and government necessary to promote social and political stability, to choke off potentially disastrous contests over religious issues, or to secure the promotion and dissemination of religious truth? Would any alliance between religion and government produce only strife and bloodshed of the sort that had plagued Europe for hundreds of years? Americans, who were all too familiar with the savage record of Europe's religious wars, were determined to guard against similar carnage and misery breaking out in their new nation.

In the eyes of posterity, one of the proudest achievements of the founding fathers was the invention of a peculiarly American solution to these questions. In retrospect, we can see that this solution combined matters of constitutionally protected rights, applications of federalism, and the political temperament needed to recognize that some ambiguities were best left unresolved. This solution was not instantly or easily achieved. Rather, the era of the American Revolution was an era of experimentation in relations between church and state, as it was for so many other major issues of governance.

The background for this experimentation extends back nearly 175 years, to the founding of the first colonies. Each of the thirteen colonies that formed the original United States was founded at a different time and for an array of different reasons. Some were founded as havens of religious liberty for those who founded them—though not necessarily for others who chose to believe differently. Other colonies were founded either as business ventures or as political experiments in which religious issues were of secondary concern. In all thirteen colonies, some form of alliance between religion and government held sway. One key source of dispute that helped to fuel what became the American Revolution was the concern of Protestant sects or denominations such as Presbyterianism or Congregationalism that the British Crown was about to establish the Church of England as the sole legitimate church throughout British North America. Even the efforts of the Anglican Church to secure the appointment of a bishop for the colonies seemed to threaten the legitimacy or even the existence of non-Anglican churches.[72]

In the first days of the Revolution, opponents of the radical case against British colonial policy sought to use the American colonists' religious diversity as a political tool. For example, at the opening of the First Continental Congress in Philadelphia in 1774, John Jay of New York and John Rutledge of South Carolina noted that it was unlikely that the assembled delegates could agree on any coherent policy of resistance, pointing out that perhaps they were so religiously diverse that they could not even agree on the choice of a clergyman to lead them in prayer. At this, the radical delegate Samuel Adams of Massachusetts proposed that the Philadelphia minister Jacob Duche, known to be a very conservative divine of the Anglican Church, be asked to lead Congress in prayer. Adams's motion defeated the efforts of Jay and Rutledge to frustrate the business of Congress; Adams knew that the goodwill symbolized by a radical Congregationalist's willingness to hear prayers led by a conservative high-church Anglican minister would help other delegates to see the Massachusetts men as reasonable colleagues with reasonable grievances deserving a fair hearing. The Adams–Duche incident is noteworthy for two points: as proof of the general recognition throughout the American colonies of the religious diversity of the American people, and of the conflicting ways that politicians could use that religious diversity as a political weapon.[73]

The coming of the Revolution not only shattered the colonial structures of political authority and legitimacy—it also weakened whatever authority and special legal status the Anglican Church (renamed the Episcopal Church) could wield in the new American states. Many Anglican clergymen had sided with the Crown and Parliament in the 1760s and early 1770s, and after 1776 found it prudent to leave America or to make public apologies for their former loyalties. Further, the denominations that had resisted Anglican claims of authority saw new opportunities to vindicate their own legitimacy and perhaps even to claim authority for themselves by allying themselves with new state governments. At the same time, even more radical denominations such as the Baptists began to argue, on both religious and secular grounds, that churches were best served by being on their own, with no ties to the state. They were joined in these arguments by liberal thinkers who maintained for a variety of reasons that separating church and state was not the problem but the solution.[74]

Modern controversies over issues of church and state, taking place in the arena of the courts, foster arguments that only one way of interpreting the church–state question in the era of the American Revolution is correct. Either the founding fathers intended strict separation of church and state or they intended that government be free to foster the cause of religion as opposed to the cause of atheism or agnosticism. Stark choices of this kind are false choices when applied to the past, however, and never more so than in the area of religious liberty and issues of church–state relations. The real history is far more complex and diverse. Not one but two distinct lines of thought and argument emerged from the era of the Revolution, each prevailing in a different set of states and each having a different but complementary set of arguments and justifications.

One model of church–state relations, usually called separationist, had at its core the principle that religion and the secular realm of politics and government should be separate; in particular, the state should have no power to coerce religious belief, to force an individual to worship against his or her conscience, or to pay to support religious institutions in which he or she does not believe. This separationist model is usually associated with Virginia, as codified in Article 16 of the Virginia Declaration of Rights of 1776, drafted by George Mason with assistance from the young James Madison; this provision emphasized the right of individuals to worship in any manner they deem fit so long as they do so peaceably.

In 1779, as part of his efforts to revise the laws of Virginia, Thomas Jefferson drafted a bill for religious freedom. Jefferson's bill went further than the Mason–Madison provision of the Declaration of Rights, arguing that because "almighty God hath created the mind free," it was impossible and impious to coerce any form of religious belief or observance. Jefferson argued that strict separation of church and state was needed to protect the secular realm of public life and the mind of the individual from the corrupting and coercive alliance of religion and government.

Jefferson's bill, like the rest of his project for revising the state's laws, languished in neglect until Madison revived the report of the committee of revisers in 1785–1786. Madison acted in response to the efforts of more conservative Virginians, led by Patrick Henry, to secure public funding for "teachers of the Christian religion," by which Henry meant Protestant Christian ministers. In response to Henry's efforts, Madison framed a "Memorial and Remonstrance Against Religious Assessments," which has become the greatest single presentation of the case for strict separation of church and state. On matters of religious freedom, Madison agreed with Jefferson, but in the "Memorial and Remonstrance" he added a vital element to the argument—that the alliance between religion and government also would threaten the purity of the religious sphere by introducing the corrupting influences of the secular world. Thus, for Madison, the argument took the form of a triangle of mutually supporting principles. Though there is no evidence that Madison was aware of any precedent for his arguments, his line of reasoning paralleled arguments made more than a century before by Roger Williams, the great Puritan religious thinker and founder of Rhode Island.

In a titanic political struggle, Madison and his backers defeated Henry's bill, after which Madison revived Jefferson's measure on religious freedom and rammed it through the state legislature (though the legislators edited Jefferson's draft to remove the radical Jeffersonian stress on the uncontrollable nature of the human mind). When news of this victory reached Jefferson in Paris, he proudly publicized it, and soon the news of the Virginia Statute for Religious Freedom spread through western Europe, winning acclaim for Jefferson and for Madison as enlightened statesmen.[75]

It would be a mistake, however, to take the Virginia experience or the ideas of Jefferson and Madison as a distillation of the American people's views on the proper relations between church and state. Most other states in this period followed a different model. This nonpreferentialist, or accommodationist, model taught that an alliance between religion and government was necessary to preserve the virtue and morality of the people, because that virtue and morality was vital to the preservation of liberty and republican government. There were two variants of this model. In one, which briefly held sway in Virginia and persisted for a time in the Carolinas and some of the middle Atlantic states, only one sect or denomination of Protestant Christianity, the Episcopal or Anglican Church, was "established" as the state's official religion; that sect's churches received support from taxes to pay for ministers and church buildings. Those who belonged to dissenting sects—that is, sects other than the one established by law—could still worship but could not expect to receive state support for their ministers or churches. The other variant, which prevailed in the New England states other than Rhode Island, created multiple establishments, in which not one sect but a range of sects or denominations of Protestant Christianity was established by law and entitled to receive public moneys for their support. The classic formulation of this model appears in Articles II and III of the Massachusetts Declaration of Rights of 1780, which emphasize individual duties of worship and the power of government to levy taxes for the purpose of supporting religious institutions.

These two models of church–state relations coexisted uneasily in the several states from the 1780s through the first decades of the nineteenth century. Gradually, various states that had adopted either single or multiple establishments abolished them, whether by statute or by revising their state constitutions. By 1833, when Massachusetts abolished the last vestige of its multiple establishments, it appeared that the United States as a whole had embraced the Jefferson–Madison model of strict separation. This turns out not to be the case, for some states still imposed religious tests on voting and holding public office, reserving such privileges for members of favored religions and excluding members of other, disfavored religions. Pennsylvania, for example, required any candidate for office to swear to or affirm his belief in the divine inspiration of the Old and New Testaments. In other words, the American consensus on church–state relations shifted from accepting two divergent models to embracing a generally separationist model within a larger context in which most Americans assumed the existence of a consensus on religious values informed by Protestant Christianity.

Some scholars have suggested that the leading founding fathers were more willing to accept diversity of religious belief and more skeptical of alliances between religion and government than most Americans were. This may be the case, but the founding fathers' struggles with the issues of church and state teach two enduring lessons: that they were engaged with their countrymen in a great political experiment and that this experiment was not the achievement of some set of Platonic philosopher kings but rather the product of a creative argument between leaders and people that took place in all thirteen states and that required years or decades to achieve final results.

Even after the fall of the last system of established churches in 1833, Americans continued to argue about the proper role of religion in American public life. The development of new public institutions, such as public schools, became focal points of public controversy over church–state relations. At the same time, the American people's religious diversity expanded exponentially due to immigration and the explosion of denominationalism in the history of American religion. To this day, issues of church–state relations continue to rage in American politics and law, and advocates on both sides invoke the founding fathers to support their views.

EQUALITY

Posterity has judged the founding fathers most harshly on the gap separating their words about equality from their actual practice. Despite the stirring proclamation of the Declaration of

Independence, "We hold these truths to be self-evident, that all men are created equal," the American Revolution left many issues of equality largely unresolved. Instead, the founding fathers and their contemporaries often had to grapple with conflicting ideas about equality. George Washington, for example, had to struggle to overcome his initial exasperation with New England soldiers who persisted in electing their own officers and who refused to abide by a more hierarchical form of military discipline. At the Revolution's height, John Adams had to contend with his wife Abigail's eloquent plea that the constitution-makers and law-makers of the new nation "remember the Ladies" as they fashioned the new political institutions and laws of an independent America. In the 1780s, as Thomas Jefferson wrote his only full-length book, *Notes on the State of Virginia*, he sought to rationalize the existence of chattel slavery in his native land by making conflicted, deeply disturbing arguments for the inferiority of those of African descent, while conceding that slavery was monstrously unjust.

Despite the founding fathers' successes in solving so many of the political and legal problems confronting them and the nation they worked so hard to create, they did not solve—nor did they even make a serious attempt to solve—these problems of inequality. And yet, though the modern indictment of the founding fathers rests on the bedrock principle of equality before the law, we may well have more in common with them in their responses to the challenges of equality that we might want to admit.[76]

Of all the issues of equality that confronted the founding fathers, the most serious proved to be that of slavery. Although historians still disagree about how slavery was introduced into the American colonies, by the dawn of the eighteenth century it was present in the British colonies on the North American continent, and throughout Britain's Caribbean possessions. Slavery had become essential to the agricultural economies of the southern colonies—tobacco in Virginia and North Carolina and rice and indigo in South Carolina and Georgia—but slavery was recognized and protected by statute from New England to Georgia.[77]

The American Revolution's rhetoric of liberty and equality was the catalyst for Americans in various states to reexamine the institution and to ask whether it was consistent with the libertarian ideology animating the revolution against British authority. Some younger politicians and military men, such as Colonel John Laurens of South Carolina, argued that the states should bring slaves into their armed forces, promising them their freedom if they would fight for the American cause—but American politicians were not ready to heed the urgings of Laurens and those who argued as he did.

Similarly, British officers made promises of freedom to any slaves who would desert their owners and enlist in British units—but these promises were a tactic to undermine American resistance rather than expressions of antislavery principles, and the British did little to honor their promises to those slaves who accepted the offer of freedom in exchange for military service. In 1781, in one of the war's most horrifying episodes, the British army besieged at Yorktown decided that they could not share supplies with the runaway slaves and their families who had flocked to British lines. They drove these refugees—men, women, and children alike—into the "no man's land" between the two armies. Artillery fire by both sides pulverized that land and slaughtered the unfortunate former slaves.

Even after the war ended, the states were slow to act on the issue of slavery. In 1780, Pennsylvania enacted a gradual-emancipation statute that provided that people of African descent who were born after the date the law was enacted would be freed but only after they had turned twenty-eight. Pennsylvania did not fully end slavery till 1847. In 1787, a series of lawsuits known collectively as the "Quock Walker" case ended when Chief Justice William Cushing of the Massachusetts Supreme Judicial Court held that under the state's 1780 constitution, slavery no longer could exist within the state. In 1799, New York enacted a gradual-emancipation statute similar to Pennsylvania's, with slavery ending in 1827. These and other states acted not necessarily because of the principles of liberty and equality invoked to support the Revolution, but at least as much because slavery was of diminishing importance to those states' economies. In states in which the owning of slaves and the use of slaves to farm were powerful economic factors, slavery was entrenched by law and public opinion.

Abolitionism did not exist in the era of the Revolution and the early Republic, though considerable antislavery sentiment existed, principally in the northern states. Many Americans, including influential figures such as Benjamin Franklin, Alexander Hamilton, and John Jay, belonged to antislavery societies; these groups advocated an end to slavery, but they stressed that individual slaveowners should free their slaves (a process known in the law as "manumission") rather than calling for any sweeping use of government power to end slavery, the hallmark of abolitionism.

The American Revolution did raise questions that few colonial Americans had even thought of raising about slavery and the position of African Americans. And as the contrast between an ideology of liberty and the reality of slavery became starker, a growing number of Americans began to express distaste, moral qualms, and even outright revulsion toward slavery. Nonetheless, the record of slavery's history in the era of the Revolution is one in which a widespread but mild antislavery sentiment failed to overcome a tough-minded, determined resistance by those with a vested stake in the institution. Further, politicians such as John Adams and Benjamin Franklin, though expressing opposition to and criticism of slavery, chose to tolerate slavery's existence rather than risk the achievement of goals such as declaring American independence or framing and adopting the Constitution.

The most controversial example of the founding fathers' failure to confront slavery is the making of the Constitution by the Federal Convention.[78] The Virginia Plan, put forth by the Virginia and

Pennsylvania delegations as the basis for the Convention's first stage of work, used a system of proportional representation based on each state's number of free inhabitants. On June 13, 1787, an amendment added a clause including three-fifths of "other persons," a euphemism for slaves. This three-fifths clause found its way into the Connecticut Compromise on representation and taxation that became a core component of the Constitution. The system of representation in the Constitution gave southern states extra weight in the House and in the Electoral College, and thus entrenched slavery in the document—though without a specific use of the word.

The slavery question arose again in August. Delegates from the slave states of the deep South such as Charles C. Pinckney of South Carolina opposed the effort to give the federal government power to regulate international trade, particularly the slave trade. Though Virginia delegates James Madison and George Mason and delegates from northern states such as Rufus King of Massachusetts and Gouverneur Morris of Pennsylvania resisted this effort, the southerners proved obdurate. Indeed, they criticized their adversaries as hypocrites, arguing that a ban on importing slaves from the Caribbean or Africa closed the slave market to all suppliers of slaves except slave-producing states such as Virginia. In the face of their determination the Convention adopted another compromise, under which the federal government could not ban the overseas slave trade for twenty years, until January 1, 1808, but could, within limits, tax the importation of slaves. In return, the South Carolinians conceded that a simple congressional majority would be enough to enact general laws regulating foreign trade. Another component of this compromise on slavery was the inclusion in the Constitution of a fugitive-slave clause borrowed from the Northwest Ordinance of 1787, providing that a slave escaping across state lines to a free state still could be captured and returned to his master.

Many later politicians and historians have condemned what they see as the Federal Convention's failure of nerve, moral courage, and ingenuity in dealing with the problem of slavery.

The delegates were fully aware of the southern states' commitment to slavery, and they believed the threats voiced by delegates
such as Pinckney that South Carolina and the other deep southern
states would leave the Union unless the Constitution contained
some protection for slavery. (It is also possible that these concerns
kept the delegates from adding a declaration or bill of rights to the
Constitution; most state declarations included language that recognized liberty and human equality before the law, and in
Massachusetts such language had prompted the state's highest
court to declare slavery unconstitutional that very year.) Facing
what they saw as a choice between striking a blow against slavery
and holding the Union together, the majority of delegates chose
to preserve the Union.

At the same time, recognizing the growing antislavery sentiment in the northern states, the Constitution's framers took care
to omit the words "slavery" or "slaves" from the document. On
August 22, 1787, the day the Convention appointed a Committee
of Eleven to deal with slavery and the issue of regulating overseas
trade, Elbridge Gerry of Massachusetts sketched the Convention's
approach to the issue. As Madison recorded his words, "he thought
we had nothing to do with the conduct of the States as to Slaves,
but ought to be careful not to give any sanctions to it."[79] In accom-
modating the interests of northern and southern states, the delegates gave greatest weight to the goal of framing a Constitution
that would work on a practical level, and tiptoed around issues of
political and moral principle that would blow apart their fragile
consensus if confronted.

Later generations quarreled over the words and deeds of the
founding fathers with respect to slavery. The institution's defenders
insisted that the compromises protecting slavery were integral to
the Constitution and could not be disturbed to even the slightest
degree without threatening the Union. For their part, critics of
slavery divided on the Constitution and the founding fathers, with
some radical abolitionists, such as William Lloyd Garrison and

Wendell Phillips, denouncing the document as "a covenant with death" and "an agreement with hell," while others, such as Frederick Douglass, insisted that the founding fathers had created a "liberty document" that could be purged of the taint of slavery if the quest for that purge combined political creativity with political will and resources.[80]

Issues of equality raised by the slavery dispute penetrated the rest of American political culture as well. In some ways, it had the most durable effect on one feature of the founding fathers' approach to constitution-making, their deference to state governments in regulating elections and access to the vote. Differing ideas of social and political equality reigned in the various states and sections of the nation, from New England to the deep South. The result was a spectrum of individual states' standards for exercising the vote. The principle of federalism militated in favor of preserving this spectrum, as did the lack of political and governmental technology for enforcing a uniform national standard for voting. Ultimately, however, the greatest constraint on imposing uniform national standards on any issue such as voting was the fear of the consequences of such a national standard for the issue of slavery.

For all these reasons, therefore, the Convention left voting what it had been before the delegates met and what it would continue to be to this day—a matter left to the state governments to regulate. In 1870, 1919, 1964, and 1971, amendments added to the U.S. Constitution imposed federal limits on what the states could do about access to the polls—barring discrimination based on race, sex, nonpayment of a poll tax, and age (for those eighteen and over). The factor making the first of these amendments, the Fifteenth (1870), possible was the Union victory in the Civil War and the framing and adoption of two previous amendments dismantling the various arrangements and provisions in federal and state constitutions and laws growing out of the demolished institution of slavery. Even these amendments, framed as federal standards governing state discretion, leave undisturbed the Convention's central decision on voting—that it was a matter best left to the states.[81]

AMERICA IN THE WORLD

Modern Americans tend to forget that the United States of America, for all its modern military, economic, and cultural might, began as a fragile confederation of former colonies on the fringes of the Western world, regarded by the powers of Europe as at best an entertaining distraction and at worst an annoyance. Rich in natural resources yet plagued by enduring problems of governance, the United States seemed adrift in the turbulent waters of great-power politics. Further, as Americans had to do for generations, the founding fathers also faced Native American nations with whom they coexisted in uneasy peace punctuated by bitter military conflicts.

Independence gave Americans added reason to worry about the rest of the world. Because they no longer were under British rule, they could not look to a distant, powerful mother country for protection. In response, some of the founding fathers, such as John Adams and Alexander Hamilton, sought to develop a neutral stance toward Europe, though pursuing commercial opportunities with European nations, and worried about the effects of European interference and European wars on America. Others, principally Thomas Jefferson, argued that the existence of a great ocean as a buffer against European interference meant that America could turn its back on the old world.[82]

Those who spent time in Europe displayed contrasting reactions to the experience on their return. Benjamin Franklin had crossed the Atlantic several times in his life and had lived in Great Britain for nearly two decades; he thus was more seasoned in exposure to Europe and its values than were his younger colleagues John Adams, John Jay, and Thomas Jefferson. Franklin thus took Europe in stride, made gentle but pointed fun of Europeans' snobbery and pretentiousness, and always took every opportunity to extol American virtues, natural resources, and achievements.

In contrast, both Thomas Jefferson and John Adams were traumatized by their years in Europe, though by some measures those years were among the happiest of Jefferson's life. Jefferson reveled in the literature and music available in Europe and went out of his way to study surviving examples of classical architecture, but he had no liking for European decadence, and he was aghast at the exploitation and corruption that he saw in France. In letters to his friends and colleagues, he argued that a great nation was letting itself be destroyed by the evils of monarchy, aristocracy, and an established church, all these forces combining to exploit and oppress the people. Thus, Jefferson's vehemence in supporting the French Revolution and his casual acceptance of its horrors are byproducts of what he saw during his time observing the old regime. Though Jefferson knew that Europeans saw him as a provincial, he refused to see himself that way. Rather, Jefferson saw America and Europe as equal in stature and significance to the world, and he concluded that America had far more to teach Europe than Europe had to teach America.

In contrast to Jefferson, John Adams came to Europe seeing himself as a provincial making the long and difficult journey from his beloved farm in Braintree to the center of the western world. At once awed and disgusted by what he found there, Adams experienced deep inner conflicts about European manners, politics, and customs. Unlike Jefferson, he had almost no inclination to admire the fine arts or architecture of France, Britain, or the Netherlands. At the same time, he felt almost as much distaste for Old World snobbery as Jefferson did, but somewhere deep inside himself he wondered whether the Europeans were right about the awkward provincialism of America—and he secretly suspected that they were right about his own awkward provincialism.

These experiences left both men out of sync with things in America. On his return, Jefferson found his countrymen entranced by trade, commerce, and the quest for luxury goods, and eager to embrace policies of public finance and customs of hierarchy and deference. To his eyes, such things were symptoms of incipient monarchy and aristocracy, the political equivalent of smallpox and the plague, and he responded with all the vehemence, eloquence, and horror of which his humorless, thin-skinned soul was capable. For his part, Adams found his countrymen entranced by what he saw as fantasies fueled by the grand delusion of the French Revolution. The symptoms that terrified him were the casual optimism with which so many Americans welcomed the turbulence convulsing France and the democratic heresies he associated with Franklin and Paine (and ultimately with Jefferson). Whereas Jefferson feared the emergence of an American monarchy and aristocracy, Adams feared the emergence of a vengeful American mob bent on tearing down all good order in society. Both men agreed, however, on the source of the divergent problems they perceived— the influence of Europe had baleful effects on the new republic.

In contrast to these two veteran diplomats, most Americans had little or no experience of Europe. Even so, they realized that the convulsions of Europe could span the Atlantic to embroil America. For these reasons, the place of America in this new and dangerous world gave new importance to key issues of constitutional design having no precedent in the Americans' experiments with state constitution-making or the origins of the Articles of Confederation. Who would control foreign relations and issues of war and peace? Under the Articles of Confederation, a secretary for foreign affairs coordinated the activities of American diplomats abroad and negotiated with foreign diplomats stationed in America, but he had little independent authority to act. The Jay–Gardoqui controversy is a case in point.

In 1785, John Jay, the Confederation's secretary for foreign affairs, met with the Spanish envoy Don Diego de Gardoqui and learned that Gardoqui was prepared to negotiate a commercial treaty with the United States that would significantly boost American trade with Spain—on the condition that the Americans forgo their claims to navigate the lower Mississippi River and use the port of New Orleans. Jay, who had little understanding or sympathy for American settlers along the lower Mississippi, favored the deal. Not only would the trade flowing from the treaty be good for the nation (specifically states such as Massachusetts, Pennsylvania, and his own New York)—he also thought that the increase of the American population ultimately would force the Spanish to recognize American interests in the southwest and reopen the Mississippi to American use. He asked Congress for authority to negotiate a treaty on that basis.

After bitter debate over Jay's proposal, Congress voted to approve it—but by a vote of only eight states to five. The five southernmost states (Georgia, North and South Carolina, Virginia, Maryland, and Delaware) made it clear that they had enough votes to block the ratification of any treaty by the two-thirds vote the Articles of Confederation required, and that they would never consent to Jay's proposal to abandon American claims to access to the Mississippi River. The result was that negotiations would be pointless; further, southern politicians such as James Madison and James Monroe formed an abiding suspicion of John Jay that dogged him for the rest of his political career.

Incidents such as the Jay–Gardoqui controversy combined with the other pressures on the United States from former allies and former foes to stress the need for a sensible system of dealing with issues of foreign affairs, war, and peace. The delegates to the Federal Convention gave priority to giving the new government the power to defend American interests in a hostile world, yet they also were realistic enough to know that the United States was too weak to engage in a direct conflict with Britain or France. Further, the Constitution's framers balanced the need for creating a vigorous, flexible, and effective executive with their commitment to republican government and their lingering suspicions of executive power.

The only model they knew well in this sphere was that of the unwritten British constitution, which gave the king control over issues of war, peace, and foreign relations. Such matters seemed peculiarly suited to executive institutions and executive power, and yet the delegates did not want to recreate an elective version of the British Crown. For this reason, they politely listened to but rejected out of hand Alexander Hamilton's proposal that a single chief executive, indirectly elected to serve during good behavior, hold principal power over issues of war, peace, and diplomacy.

The Constitution they framed created what the eminent political scientist Edward S. Corwin called an "invitation to struggle" between Congress and the president.[83] It assigned the president the role of commander-in-chief of the armed forces of the United States, yet gave Congress the power to declare war, while some delegates also observed that the president retained power to repel sudden attacks on the United States. It also gave a shared power and responsibility for making treaties to the president and the Senate: the president might negotiate a treaty, but the Senate had to ratify it by a two-thirds vote.

The Constitution left unclear what independent authority the president had over foreign relations. As a result, when in 1793 the United States had to decide whether to remain neutral in the war between Revolutionary France and the conservative European monarchies led by Great Britain or to honor its 1778 alliance with France, President Washington and his cabinet concluded (though Jefferson dissented) that the president had independent authority to decide the question and to issue a proclamation of neutrality having the force of law. In 1798, facing a crisis in relations with France, President Adams worked with a cooperative Federalist majority in Congress to rescind American treaties with France and to authorize American naval vessels to attack French vessels. By 1800, Adams decided that a war with France was unnecessary and undesirable; he invoked his independent authority to send a diplomatic mission to end hostilities with France, despite opposition from Federalists in Congress and his own cabinet. As a result, Adams invoked his presidential authority to force Secretary of War James McHenry to resign; when Secretary of State Timothy Pickering refused to resign, Adams fired him. These actions established precedents governing presidential authority to remove officials of the executive branch. They also ended the quasiwar with France, but because the Federalists divided on supporting Adams for reelection, he narrowly lost to Jefferson.[84]

President Jefferson's efforts to use presidential power creatively and effectively resulted in an unusually successful first term.[85] His two great accomplishments were the acquisition of Louisiana from France and the fielding of the Lewis and Clark expedition to survey the territory, blending scientific inquiry with a projection of American military power into the heart of the North American continent. Jefferson's second term was more troubled and disappointing.[86] His efforts to use American trade as a weapon to compel the warring powers of Britain and France to cease hostilities failed, inflicting more damage on the American economy than on Britain or France. And when President James Madison asked Congress for a declaration of war against Great Britain in 1812 to oppose British attacks on American shipping, the war was largely an embarrassment for American arms until the titanic and unexpected victory of General Andrew Jackson and his small army over a larger British army at New Orleans.[87]

By the end of the War of 1812, the presidency had established an independent and active role for itself within the Constitution's arrangements for dealing with issues of war and peace. Two clusters of factors explain this result. First, as Alexander Hamilton argued in *The Federalist No. 70*, a single chief executive brings the valuable qualities of "decision, activity, secrecy, and dispatch" to exercises of the executive power, and these are peculiarly applicable to issues of diplomacy, war, and peace. Second, the part-time nature of American government in this period contributed to the elevation of the presidency. Congress was not in constant session, whereas either the president or key members of the executive branch nearly always were available to meet whatever foreign crisis presented itself. At the same time, the relatively slow pace of events in the era of the early Republic meant that there was more time for debate of the kind usually associated with Congress. Both in theory and in fact, therefore, during the early national period there was less occasion for a free-wheeling president and more opportunity for executive–legislative cooperation and consultation and shared action.

THE CONSTITUTION AS EXPLODING CIGAR

As Jefferson complained in 1816, later generations have ascribed to the founding fathers "a wisdom more than human" and have treated their handiwork with "sanctimonious reverence."[88] This attitude disregards one central fact that Jefferson recognized and stressed—that the Constitution was and remains a human artifact that human beings made and that human beings must make work, and one consequence of its being a human artifact is that it includes imperfections. Some of these imperfections were deliberate compromises between seeking to create the best possible constitution and seeking to create a constitution that had the best chance of winning adoption by the people of the several states. Other imperfections were the product of fear lest attempts to solve quandaries such as slavery or to define a national qualification for the right to vote exacerbate sectional and other tensions that might blow the fragile Union apart. Still others were the result of the founding fathers being subject to the same human frailties that bedevil all human beings in all societies—lapses of creativity or imagination and failures of care or foresight. As John Adams warned his cousin Samuel in 1784, "Our Country, My Friend, is not yet out of

Danger. There are great Difficulties in our Constitution and Situation to reconcile Government, Finance, Commerce, and foreign affairs, with our Liberties.—The Prospect before Us is joyfull, but there are Intricacies in it, which will perplex the wisest Heads and wound the most honest hearts and disturb the coolest and firmest Tempers."[89]

The years between the launching of the Constitution in 1789 and the inauguration of Thomas Jefferson in 1801 show that, time and time again, the workings of the new Constitution raised problems that its framers and ratifiers did not anticipate or had sought to defer: problems that cast new and disturbing light on some of their most cherished ideas and that caused their expectations and understandings and intentions about the Constitution to blow up in their faces, like an exploding cigar.

For example, in the spring and summer of 1789, during the first session of the first Congress under the Constitution, the House of Representatives was writing the legislation that would create the executive departments of government under the Constitution, in particular the departments of state, war, and treasury. Each would be headed by a single officer with the title of secretary. They knew that these officials would be named by the president with the advice and consent of the Senate. Who, the question naturally followed, should have the power to remove a head of an executive department, such as the secretary of state? The Constitution's text provides no clear answer to the question, nor did any discussion during the debates on framing the Constitution produce clear guidance that the Representatives could recall. Instead, they began to approach the question as if they were charged with a responsibility that the Constitution's framers and ratifiers had not met.

Four positions emerged from the House's debates. First, the only way to remove an executive branch official was by impeachment; second, if the official was to be named by the president with the advice and consent of the Senate, that was how he should be removed; third, if Congress could devise an office, Congress also could specify in the statute creating that office the means for removing the holder of that office; and, fourth, the president had the constitutional power, exercisable at will, to fire an executive-branch official. Congress decided on the fourth position, which might seem to settle the issue. Yet in a political crisis in 1868 and in cases that the U.S. Supreme Court decided in the 1920s and the 1930s, the matter recurred. In fact, in 1868, the issue led to the impeachment of President Andrew Johnson.[90]

Also in the summer of 1789, the Senate confronted the question of the meaning of the phrase "the advice and consent of the Senate." President George Washington, accompanied by Secretary of War Henry Knox, came to the Senate, presented to the senators his proposed terms for a treaty to be negotiated with the Creek Indians, and asked them for their advice and consent to the same. As the Senate's secretary read the proposed terms aloud, with Washington seated in the president's chair and Knox standing by his side, the senators were alarmed and dismayed by what one of them, Senator William Maclay of Pennsylvania, called "his attempt to overawe us." Despite Maclay's general reverence for President Washington, he was determined to maintain the independence of the Senate. Maclay therefore took the floor and asked that the president leave the proposed terms of the treaty for the senators to discuss, and that they would send him their response later. The senators gratefully followed Maclay's lead, and Washington left "in a violent fret," growling, "This defeats every purpose of my coming here." Washington, who had sat through every day of the Convention, had one idea of "advice and consent," but the Senate, six of whose members were framers, had a very different idea of the matter.[91]

In the fall of 1789, Congress created the Treasury Department, to be headed by a Secretary of the Treasury. The statute assigned him the responsibility of meeting the requests of Congress to provide reports on the public credit. Congress thought that it was

Because the founding fathers sought to order the world with words, printing became an essential tool. Benjamin Franklin, who began as a printer, used print all his life to achieve political goals. Even while serving as American minister to France, he used his own press to print his own writings, ranging from humorous bagatelles to political arguments. *Library of Congress LC-USZ62–90299.*

In this 1751 woodcut, the first American political cartoon, Benjamin Franklin urged the colonies of British North America to unite against the French and their Native American allies. A generation later, this symbol became a rallying cry for the founding fathers and those they led to win the war for American independence from Great Britain. *Library of Congress LC-USZC4–5315.*

This map, published in Philadelphia at the time of the Federal Convention, illustrates the sheer size of the nation the founding fathers sought to create—and thus the scope of the political challenge facing them. *Library of Congress.*

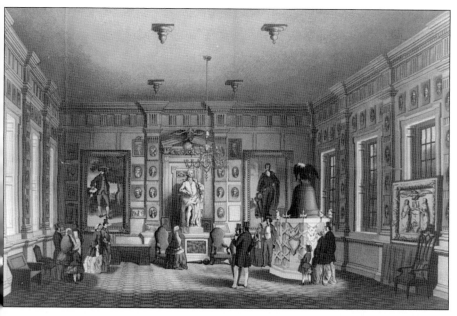

The main chamber of the Pennsylvania State House, now called Independence Hall, was the birthplace of the Declaration of Independence in 1776 and the Constitution of the United States in 1787. This room has long been the secular equivalent of a sacred shrine of American national identity. *Library of Congress LC-USZ62–2357.*

War as well as words helped to create the American nation. In this painting, now hanging in the U.S. Capitol, John Trumbull depicts the 1781 surrender of Lord Cornwallis to a combined French-American force led by George Washington. *Library of Congress LC-USZ62–78307.*

The founding fathers took active part in the debates and arguments characteristic of the Age of Enlightenment. In his lifetime, Thomas Jefferson used his library as an intellectual toolbox for his part in the work of founding the American republic. This book stand, which allowed him to display up to five books at a time, helped make possible his skilled synthesizing of different ideas and arguments, a hallmark of Enlightenment thought. *Thomas Jefferson Foundation/Monticello.*

President Warren G. Harding coined the phrase "founding fathers" in a series of speeches he delivered between 1916 and his inauguration in 1921. On May 30, 1922, in a speech dedicating the Lincoln Memorial, he reminded his audience that republics and empires are founded not by demigods but rather by fallible human beings. *Library of Congress LC-USZ62–75612.*

In 1932, a blimp laid a wreath at the base of the Washington Monument in Washington, D.C., to mark the bicentennial of George Washington's birth. Americans often use such anniversaries to reconnect with the founding fathers and the history they made—and they often use their era's cutting-edge technology to link past and present. *Library of Congress LC-USZ62–91908.*

In the 1930s and 1940s, American fascination with the founding fathers reached new heights, mainly because of the resonances between issues from the nation's founding and constitutional controversies during the administration of President Franklin D. Roosevelt. This poster, published in the late 1930s by the Federal Arts Project of the Works Progress Administration, dramatizes those links. *Library of Congress LC-DIG-ppmsca-18562.*

In 1943, President Franklin D. Roosevelt dedicated the Jefferson Memorial in Washington, D.C., to mark the two hundredth anniversary of Jefferson's birth. A Marine honor guard stands before Rudolph Evans's statue of Jefferson installed at the heart of the Memorial. *Library of Congress LC-USZ62–47142.*

The original Declaration of Independence, Constitution of the United States, and Bill of Rights have long been patriotic icons, the ultimate symbols of the work of the founding fathers. In 1953, accompanied by a full military escort, these unique, fragile documents were moved to their present home at the National Archives in Washington, D.C. *Library of Congress LC-USZ62–136106.*

Representative Barbara Jordan was a skilled legislator and one of the most powerful orators in American history. In 1974, during the televised hearings of the House Judiciary Committee on the impeachment of President Richard Nixon, she declared her faith in the Constitution of the United States. *Texas Christian University, Barbara Jordan Collection.*

imposing a duty on the secretary of the treasury to keep him under their thumb. Instead, Alexander Hamilton, the first secretary of the treasury, used the writing of reports on the public credit as the means to set the agenda of American politics, and to shift the initiative of policy-making from Congress to the executive branch.[92]

The Electoral College, the mechanism used to choose presidents and vice presidents every four years, had a checkered history before it was altered by constitutional amendment in 1804. When the Federal Convention built it into the Constitution, the delegates expected it to thin the herd of prospective candidates, leaving the House to select the president and vice president from the top five candidates. George Mason of Virginia predicted that this would happen in nineteen out of twenty elections. It did not work out that way.[93]

In 1789, the Electoral College made George Washington its unanimous first choice for president, giving the runner-up, John Adams, a plurality of 34 of the 69 electoral votes. Federalists led by Alexander Hamilton rigged this result (persuading some electors to scatter their second votes among a host of contenders while ensuring that Washington received all the first votes) to make sure that Adams did not have ground to challenge Washington for primacy in the eyes of the people, something that Adams would not have done. When the vice president discovered that (as he saw it) his reputation had been damaged by Hamilton, he harbored a growing resentment of the New Yorker that lasted the rest of his life and, in 1800, helped to destroy his bid for a second term as president. In 1792, the Electoral College again made Washington its unanimous first choice with 132 electoral votes, with Adams (at 77 votes) doing much better than he had in 1789. In 1796, the first contested presidential election, Adams beat Thomas Jefferson by 71 to 68 votes.

By 1800, the Electoral College had selected the president and vice president three times out of three, without any need for recourse to the House of Representatives. This string of results ended in 1800. In that year, the tie between Jefferson and Aaron Burr at 73 electoral votes apiece led to the kind of unsettled election that George Mason had predicted would happen nineteen times out of twenty. By 1800, however, the people and the politicians had grown so used to the electoral college's selecting of presidents, and the partisan strife dividing Federalists from Republicans had grown so bitter, that the deadlocked 1800 election touched off a major crisis.

As ballot after ballot in the lame-duck House (dominated by the Federalists) failed to break the deadlock, Federalists sought to strike a deal with Burr, who declared that he was willing to defer to Jefferson but was insulted by the insistence of Jefferson's backers that he declare himself unworthy to compete with Jefferson for the presidency. In response to growing rumors that the House would thwart what Republicans deemed the wishes of the people, either by striking a deal with Burr or by asking Adams to continue in office until the electoral deadlock was resolved, Governor James Monroe of Virginia threatened to march his state's militia on the nation's capital unless the House selected Jefferson. Jefferson maintained outward calm but seethed at what he regarded as Burr's treachery; even the usually even-tempered James Madison gave way to anger and frustration. Finally, only three weeks before inauguration day, the House chose Jefferson as president on the thirty-sixth ballot, and only after enough Federalists cast blank ballots to allow Jefferson to be elected by those willing to vote. Within four years, Congress devised the Twelfth Amendment to prevent a repeat of the 1800 deadlock, by directing electors to cast separate ballots for president and vice president.[94]

One final example of a flaw in the original Constitution of 1787 did not crop up in the era of the founding fathers, but almost happened in 1973. Under Article I, section 3, clause 6, the chief justice of the United States presides over the impeachment trial of a president, and the vice president presides over the impeachment trials of federal judges and other executive-branch officials. Who presides over the impeachment trial of a vice president of the United States? The answer is the vice president of the United States. The framers of the Constitution may have intended to have the chief justice preside over impeachment trials of presidents *and* vice presidents, once they made their last-minute addition of the vice presidency to the Constitution, but they never made the needed change to the provision governing who would preside over impeachment trials in the Senate. In the case of the 1973 resignation of Spiro Agnew, the vice president insisted that his indictment on federal charges of bribery and corruption (stemming from his conduct as governor of Maryland but including his taking of bribes while vice president) could not go forward unless and until Congress launched a full impeachment inquiry. Fearing that this process would delay or even derail the ongoing investigations of charges that President Richard M. Nixon had committed impeachable offenses, the House leadership refused to launch an impeachment inquiry and deferred to the ordinary processes of criminal law. Forced to accept a deal requiring him to resign his office and then to plead *nolo contendere* (no contest), Agnew never got his own impeachment trial—let alone the chance to preside over it.[95]

Each of these case studies represents a failure of insight, a failure of foresight, or an instance in which those who made the Constitution fell prey to Robert K. Merton's law of unintended consequences.[96] And each of these case studies puts into question the general tendency of Americans to venerate the founding fathers for their omniscience or their peerless political and constitutional wisdom.

This discussion of constitutional exploding cigars does not, however, pose a false choice between unreflective praise and unreflective censure of the founding fathers. Rather, it suggests that we ought to recognize them as human beings who dared greatly and achieved greatly, but who were beset by all the flaws and failings common to the rest of humanity. This nuanced view of the founding fathers has another, equally useful and welcome consequence. Just as it allows the founding fathers to step down from the pedestals to which they have been elevated by a worshipful succession of later generations, so also it allows later generations to stop abasing themselves before the idols of the founding fathers. Their humanity, with its complementary components of human greatness and human frailty, allows us to reclaim our humanity as well.

CHAPTER 4

Legacies

What History Has Made of the Founding Fathers

N APRIL 26, 1777, WHILE SERVING IN THE Continental Congress, juggling committee assignments, and fretting over the war, John Adams stole some time to write to his wife, Abigail. Both Adamses excelled at the art of writing letters—partly by necessity, as it was their only way of communicating when separated by his service in Congress or on diplomatic missions, and partly by inclination. Adams used letter writing to ease his soul and to commune with his "dearest friend," who was his wisest advisor and staunchest supporter. Now, after pouring out his concerns, ranging from his shaky health to the lack of news from Europe to the puzzling failure of Massachusetts soldiers to arrive to replenish General Washington's army, he exploded in frustration:

> Is it not intollerable, that the opening Spring, which I should enjoy with my Wife and Children upon my little Farm, should pass away, and laugh at me, for labouring, Day after Day, and Month after Month, in a Conclave, Where neither Taste, nor Fancy, nor Reason, nor Passion, nor Appetite can be gratified?
>
> Posterity! You will never know, how much it cost the present Generation, to preserve your Freedom! I hope you will make a good Use of it. If you do not, I shall repent in Heaven, that I ever took half the Pains to preserve it.[1]

In this eloquent, angry passage, Adams spoke not just for himself but for all the founding fathers. Posterity preoccupied them, and often haunted them. Would posterity "make a good Use" of the liberties and forms of government that they had established? Would posterity remember those who had given them those legacies and be grateful? Though Adams may have been more voluble and candid than most of the founding fathers, his concerns animated them all.

At a distance of more than two centuries, it remains difficult to disentangle the founding fathers from their principal achievements—the creation of an independent nation, with a vigorous and adaptable form of government and a body of liberties that, they hoped, would be a model for the world. Because these achievements were the products of collective deliberation, we remember the founding fathers as a group; many historians, politicians, and jurists have praised them as the most creative and learned gathering of statesmen in American history, among the greatest such gatherings that the world has ever seen. At the same time, especially beginning in the second half of the twentieth century, we have come to recognize the founding fathers' limitations and failings, and we have struggled to balance gratitude with recrimination in assessing them.

Within this legendary collection of nation builders and constitution-makers, posterity chose individuals to revere as heroes or to chastise in absentia. The reputations of some founding fathers (George Washington and Benjamin Franklin) have remained consistently high—so high that their mythic images occasionally eclipse their humanity. The reputations of others (Thomas Jefferson and Alexander Hamilton) have risen and fallen almost in complementary historical cycles, suggesting that their struggles with one another when alive continue by proxy long after their deaths. Still others (John Adams, James Madison, and John Jay) have languished in neglect for decades, only to be rediscovered and restored to the national pantheon. Tracing these individual threads in the tapestry of American historical memory illuminates our stormy and inconsistent relationship with our past in general and with the founding fathers in particular.

One battle over the founding fathers has always raged, and continues to rage, because so much is at stake—the battle to interpret the Constitution of the United States and the Bill of Rights by reference to the "original intent" or "original understanding" or "original meaning" that we can identify in the words and deeds of the founding fathers. This constitutional controversy seeks to conscript the past in the service of the present, in ways and with a passionate intensity seemingly without parallel in any other nation. Understanding this controversy challenges us to strike a balance between mechanical deference to the founding fathers and equally mechanical rejection of taking the past into account in solving modern constitutional problems.

ANCESTOR WORSHIP?

Unlike so many nations with origins lost in the distant past, the United States began as a political entity in a specific time and place, as the handiwork of specific individuals. In other words, the United States is a nation because it chose to be, and the American people continue to reserve for those who created the nation the cultural roles and reverence associated with biblical patriarchs or patron saints. Thus, the founding fathers have taken on roles in the nation's cultural life reminiscent of those of ancestors in cultures such as Confucian China or Republican Rome.

What history has made of the founding fathers as a group has unfolded on two tracks—one being their developing role in the American people's historical memory and the other being their evolving place in history as interpreted by successive generations of historians as an American historical profession emerged in the nineteenth and twentieth centuries.[2] Increasingly, these tracks have diverged, opening a gap between the general public, who seek reassuring narratives presenting role models to guide posterity, and historians, who seek to understand the past on its own terms.

A crucial fact often missing from "the legend of the founding fathers" is that at first they did not realize that they were becoming founding fathers. Rather, joining in opposition to what they deemed tyrannical measures that Great Britain sought to impose on them, they saw themselves only as British subjects seeking to defend their English rights. They were not interested in independence from Britain; indeed, British politicians and polemicists were far quicker to charge Americans with scheming to claim independence than Americans were to contemplate that step. Not until early 1776, when war was under way and the Second Continental Congress had begun to debate the measure, did its members, and the people whom they sought to represent, accept that they were founding a new nation.

The experience of the Revolution, and the efforts to secure a new government for a new nation, helped to fix the idea of founding in American political thinking. In the new nation's first decades, as Americans grappled with the challenges of nation building and constitution-making, the founding fathers helped to create a national mythology that they hoped would advance political goals. In *The Federalist No. 2*, for example, John Jay reimagined the Federal Convention's purposes and deliberations:

> This Convention, composed of men, who possessed the confidence of the people, and many of whom had become highly distinguished by their patriotism, virtue and wisdom, in times which tried the minds and hearts of men, undertook the arduous task. In the mild season of peace, with minds unoccupied by other subjects, they passed many months in cool uninterrupted and daily consultations, and finally, without having been awed by power, or influenced by any passions except love for their Country, they presented and recommended to the people the plan produced by their joint and very unanimous councils.[3]

Historians will recognize the omissions and distortions in Jay's account—it is silent about the delegates who dropped out, walked out, or refused to sign the finished document, or about the bitter disputes that brought the Convention to the brink of dissolution.[4] Jay was not writing history, however. Rather, he sought to evoke a pleasing vision of wise founders animated by disinterested patriotism, with the aim of persuading his readers to ratify the document produced by that (partly fictitious) disinterested patriotism.

The theme persisted throughout the ratification controversy, as supporters and opponents of the Constitution told competing stories about the document's origins and the ideas and motivations of those who framed it. In *The Federalist No. 37*, James Madison outlined the difficulties that the Convention faced in writing a constitution, including the range of interests to be accommodated, the novelty and difficulty of the problems confronting the framers, and the daunting challenges presented by using language as a means to order the political world. Madison drew on Benjamin Franklin's closing speech to the Convention—one of the few episodes of the gathering's otherwise-secret debates made public during the ratification controversy—to show that a perfect Constitution was not to be expected from an imperfect gathering of noble but imperfect men wrestling with imperfect tools to solve seemingly intractable problems. In sum, Madison, like Jay and Franklin, sought to promote a positive image of the Constitution's framers that would legitimize the Constitution and make it palatable to the people.[5]

By contrast, the Constitution's opponents focused on the Constitution rather than on the Convention that proposed it, treating with nervous care the loaded political question of criticizing a gathering of men including George Washington and Benjamin Franklin. Even the acidulous Luther Martin of Maryland, a nonsigning delegate to the Convention, took care not to assail his former colleagues with inflammatory rhetoric. In the *Genuine Information*, a lengthy defense of his refusal to sign the Constitution serialized in a Maryland newspaper, Martin wrote of the Convention:

> Mr. Speaker, I revere those illustrious personages as much as any man here. No man has a higher sense of the important services they have rendered this country. No member of the convention went there more

disposed to pay a deference to their opinions; but I should little have
deserved the trust this State reposed in me, if I could have sacrificed its
dearest interests to my complaisance for their sentiments.[6]

Martin's attempt to side-step the Convention's high reputation
among the American people failed. Primed in part by energetic
printers and writers for the press who did their work even before
the gathering convened, the people in 1787 were favorably disposed to the Convention, however they might divide over its
handiwork, the Constitution.[7]

The oft-invoked image of unity among the Constitution's
framers was an early casualty of the process by which the
Constitution became the new nation's form of government. In the
1790s, a series of domestic and foreign issues gave rise to bitter
disagreements over the Constitution's meaning, dividing the electorate and the founding fathers. Some of these controversies not
only split the founding fathers politically but tore apart personal
friendships. Madison and Hamilton, who had collaborated so well
during the 1780s, each accused the other of betraying his trust.
Adams and Jefferson, who had labored together in Congress in the
1770s and as fellow diplomats in the 1780s, also parted ways, and
the political friendship that Madison had forged with George
Washington was a third casualty.[8] Other breaches paralleling these
opened up throughout American society, and for a time Madison's
gloomy diagnosis in *The Federalist No. 10* that factionalism was the
bane of all republican government threatened to become a predic-
tion of the Constitution's future.

Each side charged the other with having betrayed the nation's
founding and the Revolution's true principles—thereby drama-
tizing how bitter these divisions had become. The escalating
series of attacks and counterattacks culminated in the election of
1800, pitting incumbent President John Adams, running under
the Federalist banner, against Vice President Thomas Jefferson,
the Republicans' nominee. Jefferson and Aaron Burr narrowly
defeated Adams and Charles C. Pinckney, but Jefferson and Burr

tied in the electoral vote, leading to another fraught political episode that did not end until a few weeks before Inauguration Day, when the House of Representatives finally chose Jefferson over Burr after thirty-six ballots. Once the crisis had been resolved, Jefferson proclaimed his victory a revolution equal in significance to that of 1776, declaring that all Americans were reunited in their fealty to principles of republicanism and federalism.[9]

Partisan rancor abated in the nineteenth century's first decades, due in part to the encroachments of mortality on the founding fathers. The survivors, aware that they faced a last battle to define their places in history, sought to leave posterity their version of events, and in many cases, albeit with uneven success, to abandon their old animosities.

This campaign for vindication in the eyes of history preoccupied former President John Adams. Though he spent the first years of his involuntary retirement brooding in his home in Quincy, he roused himself in early 1809, beginning a stream of essays for the *Boston Patriot* newspaper that lasted three years. Adams was writing to answer a pamphlet, long forgotten by others but still fresh in his own mind, that Alexander Hamilton had published against him in 1800, with the goal of undermining his chances for a second term. Adams also started his *Autobiography*, but left it unfinished, breaking off in the midst of his diplomatic service in the early 1780s. A voracious reader, Adams pored over his old friend Mercy Otis Warren's 1805 *Rise, Progress, and Termination of the American Revolution*, one of the first great American works of history. Hurt and infuriated by Warren's treatment of him, Adams wrote her letter after letter protesting that she had caricatured him and misrepresented his record and his political philosophy. In her own defense, Warren argued that Adams had given her ample reason to write as she did, but the old man remained unconvinced.[10]

Adams sought solace in correspondence with an old friend and fellow signer of the Declaration, Benjamin Rush. Both men felt that they had been cast aside by an ungrateful nation despite

extensive service to its interests. They exchanged eloquent rumi-
nations about the Revolution and their parts in it, each seeking to
soothe the other's wounded feelings. How, they wondered, would
posterity remember them? Would it ever be possible to recover the
fragmentary, eroding truth about the Revolution? Determined to
get his views into the historical record, Adams answered questions
from a younger generation of writers hoping to recapture the past;
his letters presented colorful, dramatic, and sometimes inaccurate
reminiscences of the events he had seen or helped to shape.[11]

At Rush's urging, Adams reached out to Jefferson. The letters
that the two men exchanged between January 1, 1812, and their
deaths on July 4, 1826, are among the great monuments of
American literature. That correspondence's recurring themes
include the need to educate future generations about the Revolution's origins and course, the credit to be given to its true leading spirits, and the meaning that it should have for posterity.
Though they agreed on how hard it would be to grasp the Revolution's history, Adams and Jefferson diverged on its meaning for
the future. Adams never could accept Jefferson's view that the
American Revolution inaugurated a great democratic revolution
that would sweep the globe; he insisted that the Revolution was
an American event, with lessons mostly for America rather than
for the rest of the world.[12]

Like Adams, Jefferson had been working to set his historical
reputation in order; he was as eager and industrious as Adams in
his efforts to define the past that he wanted posterity to remember. He answered hundreds of inquiries from biographers and
historians, giving vivid reminiscences and valuable biographical
sketches of men such as George Washington, Benjamin Franklin,
and his beloved mentor George Wythe.[13] Jefferson also wrote,
ostensibly for his family but with an eye to a wider readership, an
Autobiography that got as far as his return to America in 1789. In
addition, he prepared "three volumes bound in marbled paper," a
compilation of official papers interwoven with private notes that,

he hoped, would present a reliable Republican account of the early Republic.[14]

More engaged with the visual arts than Adams was, Jefferson advised his former secretary, the painter John Trumbull, on his project of painting key scenes from the Revolution such as the presenting of the Declaration of Independence, the surrender at Yorktown, and Washington's resignation of his commission in 1783. Congress and President James Madison tendered the official invitation to Trumbull in 1816, with the goal of adorning the rotunda of the U.S. Capitol, but for decades before the official invitation, Trumbull had traveled widely to paint life portraits of as many of the Declaration's signers as possible, with the goal of incorporating those likenesses into a grand canvas. Recognizing the power of images, Jefferson offered Trumbull shrewd marketing advice, suggesting that the painter commission engravings in a range of grades and prices so that not only the wealthy but every American home could have a Trumbull hanging on the wall.[15] He then displayed one of Trumbull's engravings on the wall of Monticello. (Despite his grumbling that Trumbull's painting fictionalized the history it purported to present, Adams hung a copy of the engraving on the wall of his home, Peacefield.)

James Madison also arranged his papers for posterity and answered hundreds of letters inquiring about the making of the Constitution; the roles of men such as Jefferson, Washington, and Hamilton; and the proper workings of the constitutional system. (One historical dispute that preoccupied him was his effort to deny the charge that Hamilton had mockingly dismissed Franklin's call for prayers in the Convention because "we have no need of foreign aid!")[16] Most important, Madison oversaw a careful transcription of his *Notes of Debates in the Federal Convention of 1787*, which, honoring the oath of secrecy sworn by the Convention's delegates in 1787, he kept confidential until his death in 1836. Madison hoped to enlighten future readers about the difficulties and challenges of constitution-making and to provide his widow with a valuable source of income in the form of publication rights to his manuscript *Notes*.

Those founders no longer available to craft their place in historical memory often had descendants, relatives, or protégés eager to do the work for them. Alexander Hamilton's sons, led by John Church Hamilton, determined to erect a bulwark against the rising tides of Jeffersonianism, published a multivolume selected edition of their father's papers prefixed by an adulatory, uncritical biography. Similarly, Thomas Jefferson Randolph, Jefferson's favorite grandson, prepared a four-volume edition of Jefferson's writings that sparked furious political controversy when it appeared in 1829—in part because Randolph disclosed Jefferson's private doubts about George Washington and other contemporaries.[17]

Chief Justice John Marshall, who idolized his old commander from their time together at Valley Forge, wrote the first major life of Washington (1804), abridging it to one volume "for use in schools."[18] Marshall's biography, with its staunch allegiance to the Federalist agenda, revived political controversy in the new nation and spurred Jefferson to prepare his own account of Washington's administration. In 1829, John Quincy Adams began writing a biography of his father as the first step in preparing an edition of the senior Adams's papers; he undertook this project to distract himself after his humiliating defeat by Andrew Jackson in 1828, but in 1830 his own election to the House of Representatives opened a new chapter in his political career that forced him to set this project aside. After Adams died in 1848, his son Charles Francis Adams completed his father's plan, publishing a ten-volume edition of *The Works of John Adams*, the first two volumes being a *Life of John Adams* incorporating the opening chapters prepared by his father.[19] Senator William Cabell Rives of Virginia, a protégé of James Madison, began a biography of his mentor. Unfortunately, Rives died before he could complete the work, leaving three massive volumes ending with Madison's retirement from the House in March 1797.[20]

Other writers took note of the ever-increasing American appetite for reading about the nation's formative years and the lives of the founding fathers and sought to satisfy that burgeoning demand. Some, such as Abiel Holmes and Charles Goodrich, were clergymen who prepared chronicles of American history for use in schools, seeking to inculcate patriotism and public service in the schoolchildren who were their intended audience. A new generation of aspiring historians joined these pious chroniclers in seeking to teach the lessons of the past for the edification of posterity. The most industrious was Jared Sparks, a professor at Harvard who eventually became the university's president. Sparks was acclaimed for his multivolume editions of the papers of Washington and Franklin, but his aim was adulation, not disinterested scholarship; he abridged or even destroyed original documents that he deemed damaging to his heroes' reputations. In addition to his editing labors, he launched and edited a long-running series of short biographies of leading American historical figures, the *Library of American Biography*, writing many of the volumes himself.[21]

In the 1820s and 1830s, armed with a growing historical and biographical literature focusing on the founding fathers, Americans began to practice their own form of ancestor worship. This development coincided with and was accelerated by the gradual passing of the founding fathers. The result was an increasing tide of anxiety among later generations of citizens and politicians. Those who had created the nation's constitutional and political order no longer would be present to guide its development. Their deaths closed the heroic age of American history. Those addressing this theme often used the words "founders" or "fathers" to describe those whose lives they were honoring and whose deaths they were mourning.

In many ways, George Washington's death in late 1799 was a catalyst of this process, so it is fitting that in 1800, in probably the most famous example of this trend, Henry Lee delivered an eloquent eulogy for Washington (written for him by John Marshall) dubbing his fellow Virginian "the father of his country." This phrase, which instantly became synonymous with Washington, had deep roots in the political culture of the Roman Republic, a central inspiration for Washington and his peers. Given the abiding popularity of Plutarch's *Lives of the Most Noble Greeks and Romans* as a source of moral exemplars, inspiration, and self-understanding, it was not surprising that Americans adopted a Plutarchian perspective on the founding fathers—using their lives and careers as a series of moral exemplars supplementing those from the classical past.

The key chronological landmarks following Washington's death were the deaths of Alexander Hamilton (1804, of a mortal wound resulting from his duel with Aaron Burr), former presidents John Adams and Thomas Jefferson (1826), former president James Monroe (1831), Charles Carroll of Carrollton (the Declaration's last signer, in 1832), Chief Justice John Marshall (1835), and former president James Madison (the last of the Constitution's framers, in 1836). Some veterans of the Revolution persisted into the 1840s and even the 1850s, but they were stragglers behind the wave of a major demographic shift.

Of all these deaths, the most dramatic were those of Adams and Jefferson, who both died on July 4, 1826, the fiftieth anniversary of Congress's adoption of the Declaration of Independence. Though some diehard Federalists muttered their suspicions that Jefferson had taken poison to ensure his death on the fated day, most Americans had far different views of the matter. Orators across the nation commemorated the passing of the two great patriots, making eloquent analogies with the deaths of biblical patriarchs and insisting that the events of the fiftieth anniversary of the Declaration signaled divine favor for the new nation and its constitutional experiment.[22]

Responding to these momentous events, statesmen and orators expressed the anxiety of children bereft of their parents. For so long, the burden of these speeches ran, the founders had walked among them, always available to provide sage counsel to the rising generation. Somehow the United States had survived the ordeal of the Revolution, the no less painful ordeal of replacing the Articles of Confederation with the Constitution, the agonizing decade of the 1790s, and the "second War of Independence" in 1812–1815—including the burning of the new nation's capital in 1814. But through all of those difficult crises, the founders had been there to help the nation weather the storm. What would happen now—what would the nation do—now that they were gone?

Few captured the unease of the generations succeeding the "founders" or the "fathers" better than Abraham Lincoln, who in January 1838 delivered his first major political address, "The Perpetuation of Our Political Institutions," before the Young Men's Lyceum of Springfield, Illinois. Lincoln, not quite twenty-nine years old, was a self-taught lawyer and member of the Illinois legislature just beginning his second term; but even then he felt the stirrings of grander political ambition. In his lecture Lincoln challenged his audience to preserve the free government created by those whom he hailed as "a once hardy, brave, and patriotic, but now lamented and departed race of ancestors," whom he dubbed "our fathers." Lincoln urged that "reverence for the laws" become "the *civil religion* of the nation"; further, he warned his countrymen against those of "towering genius" who would not be content to labor to preserve the founders' legacy but instead, hungering for eternal fame, would sweep that legacy aside to create one of their own.[23] By contrast, in 1836, two years before Lincoln's address, the young Ralph Waldo Emerson opened his little book *Nature* with the following lament:

> Our age is retrospective. It builds the sepulchres of the fathers. It writes biographies, histories, and criticism. The foregoing generations beheld God and nature face to face; we, through their eyes. Why should not we also enjoy an original relation to the universe? Why should not we have a poetry and philosophy of insight and not of tradition, and a religion by revelation to us, and not the history of theirs?

On the issue of the founding fathers and their place in American history and culture, Emerson's was a minority view, however influential it was as a core text of the emerging Transcendentalist movement. In this context, Lincoln best grasped the spirit of the times.

Reverence may have attached to the country's laws, as Lincoln preached, but it also attached to those who laid the constitutional and legal groundwork for the new nation. Recognition that the United States had a defined set of origins in historical time made it easier for this newest and most fragile of nations to begin to create a usable past.[24] Throughout the nineteenth century, commemorations of the nation's origins in the Revolutionary War, including anniversaries such as the Declaration of Independence, the launching of government under the Constitution, and the anniversaries of the births or deaths of figures such as Washington, Franklin, and Jefferson, helped to fix these revered figures in the nation's historical memory.

Succeeding generations lacking any direct personal experience of the founding fathers still engaged in a complex and turbulent relationship with them. The dominant theme of that relationship changed from period to period, depending on the political context. From the 1820s through the 1850s, a mood of anxious veneration reigned, as Americans tried to live up to the standards they associated with the founding fathers and to heed the warnings and counsel that the founding fathers left for posterity. A disturbing undercurrent of this historical mood was a new contentiousness over which of the great regions of the nation, North and South, could rightly claim to be the legatee of the founding fathers; this quarrel over the heritage of the founding fathers was both an expression and an accelerant of the growing sectional crisis.

In the years preceding and during the Civil War, a bitterly fought tug-of-war over the American historical memory eclipsed the anxious veneration of the earlier period. Contending sides in the sectional crisis of the 1850s that exploded into war in 1861 insisted that theirs was the one true expression of the founding fathers' hopes and intentions; they portrayed their adversaries by contrast as betrayers of the founding fathers in particular and American principles and hopes for the future in general. Thus, for example, the great seal adopted by the government of the Confederate States of America in 1861 had at its center General George Washington mounted on a horse, and that government's constitution was a slightly revised version of the U.S. Constitution of 1787, with the material variations from the original text designed to make explicit the rebels' understanding of the nature of the Union, the centrality of state sovereignty, and the legitimacy of slavery. In contrast, President Abraham Lincoln repeatedly insisted that he was defending the experiment in government launched by the founding fathers; most memorably, in 1863, in the Gettysburg Address, Lincoln tied the Union's cause to the Declaration of Independence and the founding fathers' creation of "a new nation, conceived in liberty and dedicated to the proposition that all men are created equal."[25]

From the end of Reconstruction in 1877 into the early twentieth century, modern America emerged from the shadow of civil war. Relieved that they had weathered the ordeal of the Union, the reunited American people regarded the founding fathers and their time with a veneration that now seemed self-satisfied, almost smug. Not only had Americans weathered disunion and civil war, thus overcoming the greatest fears felt by the founding fathers—they had solved the problem of slavery, one that the founding fathers either could not solve or did not dare to try to solve.

Complacency pervaded the centennial anniversaries of the Declaration (1876), the Constitution (1887), and Washington's inauguration (1889). Taking the founding fathers and their achievements for granted—a remarkable contrast with the feelings prevailing before the Civil War—became so widespread that in 1888 the poet and essayist James Russell Lowell warned that the Constitution was not "a machine that would go of itself," counseling against airy nonchalance about the American experiment.[26]

Yet another reason underlay the shift in American views of the founding fathers and their achievements. The national trauma of the Civil War became the central episode in American historical memory, supplanting the American Revolution and the making of the Constitution. That the war happened at all signaled the failure of the founders' experiment in government, requiring what Lincoln called in the Gettysburg Address "a new birth of freedom." That the generation of the Civil War had survived such a ghastly ordeal while preserving the Union and freeing the slaves eclipsed the founding fathers' achievements. In particular, Lincoln's martyrdom at the war's close vaulted him to a posthumous stature equal to that of Washington. Thereafter, Americans gave Lincoln and Washington equal status as central heroes of the American story.

At the same time that native-born Americans ignored warnings such as Lowell's, celebrations of national anniversaries became opportunities for immigrants to the United States to lay claim to the nation's history as part of their own heritage. Learning how to be American meant learning the nation's civic and patriotic rituals and stories, including familiar myths such as George Washington and the cherry tree and Betsy Ross and the creation of the American flag. The founding fathers became central to this use of American history as a vehicle for instilling civic commitments in the millions of immigrants to American shores.[27]

The era of urbanization, industrialization, and immigration that transformed the face of American life in the late nineteenth century posed new problems of law and policy.[28] To what extent could federal or state governments use their lawmaking and regulatory powers to counter economic ills, to enforce safety standards in the nation's factories and workplaces, and to regulate the quality of goods such as foodstuffs and drugs? Many of these disputes generated lawsuits that found their way to the highest reaches of the federal judicial system. In adjudicating these disputes, lawyers and judges often invoked the values and teachings of the founding fathers as authority to strike down such measures as unconstitutional.

When lawyers and courts used the founding fathers as a collective authority to justify invalidating taxation and economic regulation, they sparked a vehement reaction that seeped beyond the austere world of constitutional argument and historical scholarship into the wider political culture. Younger political scientists and historians disputed such instrumentalist readings of the nation's past with vehemence, though sometimes the alternative interpretations they proposed seemed just as much to enlist the past in the service of the present. Their aims were not only to refute legal and constitutional appeals to original intent but to raise new questions about the nature of the American founding.

Charles A. Beard, who began his historical career at Columbia University but then became an independent scholar, was the central figure in this reexamination of the founding fathers and the Constitution. In three landmark works, *The Supreme Court and the Constitution* (1912), *An Economic Interpretation of the Constitution of the United States* (1913), and *The Economic Origins of Jeffersonian Democracy* (1915), Beard argued that the founding fathers split along economic and class lines—much like the America of his own time—and that the Constitution's framers were motivated less by disinterested patriotism than by the desire to protect their own economic interests. Beard's arguments shaped the assumptions of two generations of historians while continuing to fix the founding fathers at the center of the controversy over interpreting the Constitution. They fostered a skeptical, iconoclastic view of the founding fathers clashing with the veneration that had prevailed before he wrote, and with the arguments of those who still chose to see the founding fathers as high-minded patriots, such as President Warren G. Harding, who in the midst of this period coined the phrase "founding fathers."[29]

The clash over the founding fathers reached its high-water mark in the 1930s, during the presidency of Franklin Delano Roosevelt. In part, this was the result of an ironic coincidence juxtaposing the sesquicentennials of the Constitution's framing and adoption and the launching of government under its authority with the constitutional battles of the New Deal era. The Roosevelt administration's experiments with creative uses of government power to remedy the damage that the Great Depression wreaked on the American economy, to tend to the needs of the American people, and to guard against a future catastrophic economic collapse collided with the fierce opposition of conservative politicians and scholars who insisted that these experiments violated the original intent of the Constitution as expressed by the founding fathers. In response, not only Roosevelt and his supporters but a host of scholars and journalists reinterpreted the Constitution's origins, stressing the founding fathers' creative experimentation, which they sought to foster in the new nation.[30] In one key respect, however, Roosevelt did not follow the path marked out by progressive historians who insisted on placing Jefferson and Hamilton in eternal opposition. Rather, Roosevelt argued (following the progressive journalist Herbert Croly) that Americans should use Hamiltonian means, a vigorous national government with sweeping economic powers, to achieve Jeffersonian ends, liberty and democracy for the American people.[31]

World War II continued to rework public perceptions of the founding fathers. The confrontation with the ideologies of fascism and Nazism spurred Americans to devise a countervailing ideology based on liberty, democracy, and equal rights, rooted in a usable past of increasing democracy. The founding fathers became central figures in that ideology and that usable past, with Jefferson as the personification of American democratic values. In 1943, when Roosevelt, who claimed Jefferson as his intellectual hero, dedicated the Jefferson Memorial to mark the bicentennial of the Virginian's birth, Jefferson received his own personal pantheon in the nation's capital. So, too, Jefferson and Monticello displaced the American Indian and the buffalo on the nickel and Gutzon Borglum carved a portrait of Jefferson, along with Washington,

Lincoln, and Theodore Roosevelt, into Mount Rushmore in the Black Hills of South Dakota.

Roosevelt's synthesis triumphed during the first decades of the Cold War, when scholars, politicians, and journalists joined to adapt World War II's American ideology of liberty, democracy, and equal rights to the exigencies of the ideological battle with communism. The lives, words, and deeds of the founding fathers remained central to this emerging American ideology, which within the historical profession acquired the label "consensus history" because it stressed those areas in which historical actors agreed rather than those areas in which they might have disagreed.

For example, Daniel J. Boorstin of the University of Chicago offered in his 1952 book *The Genius of American Politics* a celebratory vision of the founding fathers as supreme pragmatists unencumbered by any ideology. Their calm practicality, Boorstin declared, was a key reason why Americans had managed to resist the seductive pull of Marxist ideology.[32] In contrast, the cool, ironic views of Richard Hofstadter of Columbia University, distilled in his influential *The American Political Tradition: And the Men Who Made It* (1948), presented a reading of American history that criticized its constricted vision of politics and its failure to consider solutions to enduring national problems falling outside the limits of liberal capitalism.[33] Hofstadter and Boorstin might have disagreed vehemently about their respective views of the consensus uniting the founding fathers—but they would have agreed that the founding fathers remained a crucial part of that history.

At the same time, other domestic developments with international implications and consequences shone a bleaker, more uncompromising light on the founding fathers and their world. The pivotal set of events was the civil rights revolution spanning the decades from the 1940s through the 1960s. In its first stage, focusing on litigation over federal protection for African Americans' constitutional rights, litigants and judges looked closely at issues of slavery and equality both in the time of the founding fathers and in the era of the second founding of the United States, as embodied by the framing and adoption of the Civil War Amendments to the Constitution. These amendments, which formed the constitutional settlement of the Civil War and Reconstruction, invalidated the compromises concerning slavery that the founding fathers had made in framing and adopting the Constitution. In the process, those amendments—and renewed judicial interest in their meaning and effect—highlighted the failures of the founding fathers in wrestling with issues of slavery and equality.[34]

Historians responding to this changing world revived the study of the Revolution and the making of the Constitution and probed anew the compromises at the heart of the Constitution over slavery, representation, the slave trade, and the issue of fugitive slaves. No longer as understanding and sympathetic as previous scholars had been, these historians asked uncomfortable questions about whether the founding fathers had shown a failure of moral nerve, courage, and creativity in accepting the compromises over slavery demanded by a vehement Southern minority.[35]

Changes of personnel and research strategies expanded the historical profession's inquiry into the founding fathers. Increasingly, social history took center stage, in particular the histories of women, ethnic and racial minorities, Native Americans, and ordinary white Americans who were not part of the governing class. Juxtaposing these groups with the founding fathers transformed the writing of American history—and the ways that historians and their readers saw the former stars of the story. At their best, the products of this new historical scholarship opened new vistas into the American past in general and the era of the nation's founding in particular. By expanding the range of historical subjects deemed worthy of study and analysis, they reshaped the nation's past and supplanted the old narrative of ever-constant progress from the great days of the founding fathers to the present with a complex, nuanced account that made room for acknowledging historical actors' shortcomings even by the standards of their own time. The excitement that this kind of scholarship engendered among historians had an unintended consequence, however—it implied that older, more conventional subjects and methods of doing history should be set aside as outmoded or even reactionary.[36]

Still other changes in the historical profession transformed scholarly and popular understandings of the founding fathers and their world by greatly expanding the range and availability of primary sources. Formerly, those who worked on the founding fathers either had to travel widely to libraries, historical societies, and archives to consult primary sources or had to rely on a narrow range of relatively primitive, unsatisfactory published compilations. Published versions of the papers of the founding fathers existed in one of two forms—an early edition, sponsored by the federal government or by the family, that presented modernized texts purged of "embarrassing" or "private" material, and a later edition, prepared by a trained scholar on commission from a leading publisher, presenting more careful and accurate transcriptions of a more generous but still highly selective portion of the individual's papers.[37]

Beginning with the launch of *The Papers of Thomas Jefferson* in 1950, a documentary-editing revolution transformed American historical scholarship. These comprehensive multivolume editions, prepared by trained historians and published by university presses, present exact transcriptions of the fullest possible range of primary sources annotated to elucidate obscure or cryptic material; they include not just the letters and other documents that the subject prepared but also letters that others wrote to him.[38] Closely related to these "statesman's papers" projects are the "documentary histories"—equally rigorous, multivolume editions of the full range of papers relating to events and processes such as the ratification of the Constitution, the first federal elections, the First Federal Congress, and the early years of the Supreme Court and the federal judiciary.[39]

Though requiring decades to complete, these projects have made possible a new comprehensiveness and depth of research, analysis, and interpretation in examining the nation's past; they also have enriched American literature by rediscovering some of the finest writing in American history. In the case of the American founding, these projects have illuminated a complex series of political events integral to the origins of the Constitution yet undeservedly obscure in the nation's historical memory.

Sometimes a modern edition can rescue a key historical figure from the shadows and launch a process of popular acclaim and lionization. Such was the effect of the publication in 1961 by Harvard University Press of the opening installment of *The Adams Papers*, the four-volume *Diary and Autobiography of John Adams*. Adams's writings were serialized in a profusely illustrated series of articles published by *Life* magazine, and the *American Historical Review* invited President John F. Kennedy to review the Harvard edition of Adams's *Diary and Autobiography*.[40]

Documentary editors also can present a more ambiguous, conflicted picture of a founding father, as has been the case with *The Papers of Thomas Jefferson*. Despite the efforts of its founding editor, Julian Boyd, to fix at its core an uncompromisingly Jeffersonian vision of its subject's career and the political history of the early Republic, the Princeton edition has spawned a rich body of historical literature portraying Jefferson as a sometimes devious, manipulative politician and a deeply conflicted man who shielded himself from conflicts between his professed views and his actual conduct.[41]

One unusual byproduct of the documentary-editing revolution was the unlikely success of the Broadway musical *1776*. Written by Sherman Edwards and Peter Stone, *1776* reworks in musical-comedy form the Second Continental Congress's struggles with the issue of independence in June and July of 1776, featuring a singing and dancing cast including John and Abigail Adams, Thomas and Martha Jefferson, and Benjamin Franklin.

The play premiered on Broadway in 1969 and ran for three years, winning the Tony award for best musical and spawning a 1971 film version with the original cast (edited by its producer, Jack Warner, at the urging of President Richard Nixon, to remove the play's criticism of political conservatism). A 1997 revival ran at New York's Roundabout Theatre for nearly a year. (*1776* brought a remarkable number of younger historians into the profession, including the present writer.[42])

By contrast with the transformative effects of the documentary-editing revolution, official commemorations of recent national anniversaries related to the founding fathers have distorted and caricatured the history that they were intended to commemorate. These commemorations differed starkly from the commissions organized to mark the sesquicentennials of the American Revolution and the Constitution in the 1920s and 1930s. During the disappointing bicentennial of the American Revolution from 1974 to 1983, historians found themselves shunted to the sidelines in favor of spectacles such as a parade of tall ships in New York harbor and obligatory shows of fireworks.

Seeking to avoid a similar fate for the Constitution's bicentennial in 1987–1988, the American Political Science Association, led by James MacGregor Burns of Williams College, joined with the American Historical Association, led by Richard B. Morris of Columbia University, to found a joint initiative. The purpose of this initiative, Project '87, was to encourage reflection and scholarly and public discussion of the ideas at the core of the Constitution. Despite the fine work done by Project '87, its efforts proved the exception rather than the rule. As in the 1970s, the Commission on the Bicentennial of the Constitution, led by former chief justice Warren E. Burger, marginalized the scholarly community, preferring to sponsor reenactments of events such as George Washington's inauguration.[43]

Ignoring the official bicentennial events, historians reexamined the era of the Revolution and the making of the Constitution, continuing to ask uncomfortable questions about "excluded groups" and the failures of the founding fathers' vision. As a publishing counterpoint to this interpretative enterprise, a new genre of historical writing—though to many historians it had a familiar flavor—emerged in the 1990s and early 2000s. Dubbed "Founders Chic" by *Newsweek* magazine, this cascade of books for general audiences presented comforting, celebratory portraits of the founding fathers and the history they helped to make, while brushing past difficult, uncomfortable questions about the founding fathers that academic historians chose to pursue. The controversy that this genre sparked within the academic community has had little effect on the readership targeted by these books. Indeed, the most widely read example of "Founders Chic," David McCullough's 2001 biography *John Adams*, inspired a popular and acclaimed 2008 HBO miniseries starring Paul Giamatti and Laura Linney as John and Abigail Adams.[44]

At the same time that Founders Chic books dominated the nation's bookstores, historians and constitutional theorists began to reconsider the centrality of the founding fathers—both to the era in which they lived and worked and to succeeding generations' attempts to understand their past and shape their future. The continuing popularity of social history, with its attention to the social, economic, and private lives of ordinary men and women, helped to redirect the profession's former preoccupation with "great white men." So, too, growing attention to the histories of Native American nations and peoples and the history of free and enslaved African Americans cast in a disturbing light the founding fathers' lives and achievements. Some historians have taken this matter to extremes, rejecting as reactionary any attempt to write history or biography focusing on the lives, thoughts, and deeds of the founding fathers. Constitutional theorists, reacting against the popularity of original-intent analysis among conservative and right-wing jurists, lambaste the founding fathers for failures of creativity, short-sightedness, and misperceptions of the future development of the constitutional system.[45]

By contrast, some historians studying men such as Adams, Jefferson, Washington, Hamilton, and Burr have sought to restore them to their historical and political contexts. These figures, they argue, did not act in isolation, but rather within a shifting field of expectations by and reactions from the people; they operated in the political realm in large part by reference to what they hoped or feared popular reaction to their policies and conduct might be. In many ways, therefore, this nuanced and thoughtful modern scholarship reconsidering the nation's origins cuts against the dangers inherent in the phrase "founding fathers."

Ironically, the man who coined the phrase "founding fathers" gave us sage counsel on how to undertake such enterprises of historical reconsideration. On May 30, 1922, in the middle of his dedicatory remarks at the Lincoln Memorial, President Warren G. Harding declared: "Abraham Lincoln was no superman....Lincoln was a very natural human being, with the frailties mixed with the virtues of humanity. There are neither supermen nor demi-gods in the government of kingdoms, empires, or republics. It will be better for our conception of government and its institutions if we will understand this fact."[46]

WHICH FOUNDING FATHER ARE YOU?

Several websites offer readers the opportunity to assess their characters or personalities and determine which of several founding fathers they most resemble.[47] Such websites translate into a form comprehensible to twenty-first-century websurfers an enduring question that has preoccupied historians and ordinary citizens alike—the competing claims of individual founding fathers for an honored place in American memory. Tracing these shifting patterns of individual reputations' development illuminates the

American people's evolving relations with their past and what they understand their past to mean.

As a group, the founding fathers have merged in American memory into a disinterested, bloodless, statesmanlike collective being whose authority has become more and more nonpolitical, impartial, even godlike. Within this group, however, the historical reputations of individual figures have risen and fallen with the changing fortunes of American politics and the ideas and principles with which they were identified.

The most closely studied example is the posthumous career of Thomas Jefferson. From his death in 1826 until the outbreak of the Civil War in 1861, Jefferson was as controversial as he had been in life. Some extolled his commitment to liberty, equality, and the rights of man, whereas others denounced him as the intellectual godfather of nullification, secession, and disunion. Still others spurned his commitment to rights and equality and embraced his rigid states'-rights constitutional theory, taking it further than he would have done. From the end of the Civil War in 1865 until the era of the Great Depression, Jefferson's reputation fell to its lowest ebb. Many Americans outside the South had come to believe that Jefferson bore a great measure of responsibility for the Civil War. Further, historians and biographers exploring the vast corpus of Jefferson's papers for the first time discovered many inconsistencies between his public and private writings; the number and scope of these inconsistencies persuaded many scholars of Jefferson's dishonesty. From the 1930s through the late 1960s, by contrast, Jefferson achieved apotheosis as a symbol of human rights, religious freedom, separation of church and state, and democratic revolution—values and principles given new value and urgency by the amassed experiences of the Great Depression, World War II, and the Cold War. Beginning in the late 1960s, however, Jefferson's historical stock started to fall once again. New historical and public attention to issues of race, slavery, and civil rights, along with Jefferson's conflicted and appalling views on the nature of race in general and African Americans in particular, have helped to foster a more troubled and ambivalent view of Jefferson, a process accelerated by the remarkable shift of historical and public opinion on the vexed question of his relationship with his slave Sally Hemings.[48]

As Jefferson rose, Alexander Hamilton fell, and as Jefferson fell, Hamilton rose, their reputations waxing and waning as functions of partisan, sectional, and ideological conflict. Though he was all but forgotten in the years before the Civil War (except as the leading author of *The Federalist*), Hamilton's historical reputation rose spectacularly in the late nineteenth century, as many politicians and scholars hailed him as the father of modern industrial, urban America and as the uncompromising advocate of constitutional Union, an intellectual precursor of the beloved Abraham Lincoln, who also was a martyr to political violence. The first decades of the twentieth century rocketed Hamilton to new heights as the most admired founding father after George Washington; devotees of national economic and industrial development claimed Hamilton was a prophet of modern America. The New Deal brought a dramatic reversal of fortune for Hamilton, for many stigmatized him as an apologist for wealth, power, privilege, and the laissez-faire capitalism that had brought about the Great Depression. Yet again, as Jefferson fell in the 1990s, Hamilton rose anew, as historians and journalists rediscovered him as a consistent and coherent advocate of vigorous national constitutional power and a tough-minded realist at home and abroad; further, they contrasted his distaste for slavery (sometimes exaggerated into proto-abolitionism) with Jefferson's status as a slaveholder who fathered children by the enslaved Sally Hemings.[49]

Still other founding fathers vanished from view or suffered eclipse by contrast with the great antagonists Jefferson and Hamilton. Though venerated between 1836 and 1861 as perhaps the greatest of the founders after Washington and Franklin, James Madison languished for nearly a century. At first, like Jefferson, Madison suffered in the decades following the Civil War, misrepresented as an advocate of state sovereignty and even as an ally of the alleged prophet of secession, Jefferson. Although Jefferson's historical stock rose in the 1930s, most treatments of Madison depicted him merely as Jefferson's loyal protégé, with few claims to independent status as a constitutional and political thinker. Despite a flurry of attention surrounding the 1937–1939 sesquicentennials of the Constitution and the Bill of Rights, it was not until the 1950s that posterity, encouraged by the scholarship of the historian Douglass G. Adair and the journalist and biographer Irving N. Brant, rediscovered Madison as a major constitutional theorist. Oddly, this rediscovery occurred all over again in 1987–1989, during the bicentennials of the Constitution and the Bill of Rights.[50]

John Adams's bitter prophecies that posterity would forget him achieved almost complete fulfillment for more than a century—though the coincidence of his death with Jefferson's on the same day linked the two men in national memory. In part, Adams owed this unfortunate fate to the tight control that his descendants retained over his papers from the 1820s until the 1950s. Not until 1954, when the Adams family deposited the cache of Adams papers with the Massachusetts Historical Society and agreed to open them to researchers and permit the Society to launch a modern scholarly edition, did John Adams reemerge in the popular imagination—a process that received periodic boosts due to John Adams's unlikely emergence as an icon of popular culture.

George Washington and Benjamin Franklin have long held sway as the two gold-standard founding fathers, by most measures impervious to changing historical trends and popular whims. Even so, many scholars have complained that public veneration has obscured rather than enhanced public comprehension of Washington and Franklin. Here, too, the documentary editing revolution subverts this tendency, presenting these men in their own words and allowing us to understand them in the full scope of their humanity.

Of those usually identified as first-rank founding fathers, only John Jay continues to languish in popular esteem or even popular knowledge. The sources of Jay's undeserved obscurity are mostly accidents of history. First, Jay was not present in the Second Continental Congress to sign the Declaration of Independence, having returned to New York to help form that state's independent government. Second, the New York legislature refused to send him to the Federal Convention of 1787, and thus Jay missed the chance to take part in the framing of the Constitution. Though Jay may be best known as a coauthor of *The Federalist* with Alexander Hamilton and James Madison, a bout of illness sidelined him before he could write more than four essays, and he managed to add one final essay in early 1788; that last essay, on the Senate's shared treaty power with the president, was the only one of Jay's essays to address an enduring constitutional question. Finally, Jay's brief and frustrating tenure as the new nation's first chief justice under the Constitution was eclipsed by the far longer, more eventful, and more creative tenure of the fourth chief justice, John Marshall.[51]

THE DEAD HAND OF THE PAST? ORIGINAL INTENT

Given that the American constitutional system has at its core a written document of political foundation, it was only natural that arguments over how best to interpret that document would become central to American politics, governance, and law. Though the people of the several states adopted the Constitution in 1788, that victory did not end controversies about the Constitution or its meaning. Rather, it began "the shared conversation about the Constitution that has become central to American government and politics."[52]

Because we can trace the Constitution's origins to a particular time and place, as the handiwork of a specific—and venerated—group of politicians and statesmen, it also was inevitable that arguments about what the founding fathers did or did not intend, understand, or expect the Constitution to mean would remain at the core of interpreting it. These arguments embody the challenge of reconciling the need to apply the Constitution to changing times and circumstances with the need, real or perceived, to honor the intentions, understandings, and meanings that the founding fathers gave to the document—or might have given to the document. The wide-ranging, complex controversy created by these arguments is usually known by the shorthand term "original intent."

No modern constitutional democracy has focused so intensely on the intentions of their constitution's framers or ratifiers as has the United States. A key cause of this difference is that the American original-intent controversy grows out of the difference between the origins of the United States and the origins of most other nations. In addition to the ease with which we can date the new nation's origins and identify those who created it, the United States was and still is held together by its shared constitutional and political values rather than by any commonalities of race, ethnicity, or religion. Questions of the nation's origins and purposes therefore are bound up with matters of constitutional and political choice. Recognizing that we are a nation because we chose to be, we must then ascertain what kind of nation we chose to be. That step requires us, in turn, to examine what kind of constitution and constitutional system we chose to have, which then confronts us with the question whether we should defer to the choices the founding fathers made and or challenge, even set aside those choices to take account of changing conditions and needs.

Those who insist that original intent is the key to interpreting the Constitution cite, among other justifications, this interpretative method's real or perceived ability to restrain judicial discretion. In their view, original-intent interpretation erects a valuable bulwark against the risk that federal judges will write their own private preferences into the nation's fundamental law. Judges, they insist, must be reined in by certainty—and the certainty of history's command is the most reliable restraint.

The idea that federal courts pose dangers to constitutional democracy has roots in the 1787–1788 controversy over ratifying the Constitution itself; many Americans, including leading advocates such as George Mason of Virginia and Melancton Smith of New York, opposed the Constitution because of their fear that federal judges would usurp power both from state courts and from the other branches of the federal government. That fear has echoed through the more than two centuries of the Constitution's history—both from the left, as when late-nineteenth-century and early-twentieth-century federal courts struck down federal and state legislation regulating the economy as violating the framers' intentions with respect to the Constitution's contracts clause, and from the right, as when mid-twentieth-century federal courts seeking to enforce the Fourteenth Amendment's equal-protection clause allegedly invaded the sacred sphere of "states' rights."[53]

Though the particular threat posed by federal courts changes from controversy to controversy and era to era, one idea stands out as this controversy's most consistent theme over time—that the American commitment to constitutional democracy rules out federal courts as focal agencies of constitutional change. Transformations in the ways that we interpret the Constitution, this argument runs, must be the work of democratic institutions such as Congress, state legislatures, or the presidency—not unelected judges. If an issue poses the need for changing how we interpret the Constitution, these critics conclude, that change would be best achieved by amending the Constitution by the method set forth in Article V, which entrusts the task to the people's elected representatives in Congress and the state legislatures—not by decisions handed down by judges who are not directly responsible to the electorate.

Opponents of original-intent jurisprudence reject these arguments on two grounds. History, they insist, is at best a flawed restraint on judges. Instead of providing certainty and clarity, history all too often can support a broad spectrum of ways to interpret a given constitutional provision. If there is a wide range of different readings of the Constitution, each grounded in a plausible historical argument, history exerts no restraint worthy of the name.

Dozens of major Supreme Court decisions present combative readings by majority and dissenting justices, equally learned and equally inconsistent with each other, of the original intent underlying contested provisions such as the "necessary and proper" clause of Article I, the religion clauses of the First Amendment, or the equal-protection clause of the Fourteenth Amendment. Moreover, even if the Court rallies behind one historical interpretation, critics of the Court's decisions will offer contrasting interpretations to impeach that adopted by the Court, using the time-honored way of disputing legal precedents based on history. Thus, for example, Chief Justice Roger B. Taney built his pro-slavery opinion for the Court in *Dred Scott v. Sandford* (1857) on a stark originalist argument that the framers did not intend to give the federal government the power to limit slavery's spread; three years later, in his 1860 Cooper Union speech, Abraham Lincoln made an equally uncompromising, learned, originalist argument that the framers did intend to give the federal government power to restrict the spread of slavery.

When competing advocates lay on the judicial table diametrically opposed readings of original intent, the result is to undermine the history offered by the Justices. If judges build a judicial interpretation of a constitutional text on a historical argument, knocking the props out from under that historical argument also knocks away history's support for the judicial interpretation. Building on bad history is like building on sand.

Further, the critics maintain, original-intent jurisprudence abandons arguing the merits of a constitutional dispute in favor of shifting responsibility. Those who interpret the Constitution by reference to original intent speak, or purport to speak, for safely-dead founding fathers, putting the burden of the decision on the shoulders of those no longer around to answer for it. Original-intent jurisprudence thus decays from being a restraint on judicial discretion to becoming a cloak for judicial discretion; judges mold history as they choose to support their interpretation and then impose the onus for an unpopular decision on the dead past. A further consequence of using original-intent jurisprudence is to abandon the merits of a given constitutional problem in favor of focusing on the history that supports or challenges the Court's reading of the Constitution. Critics and defenders of the Court argue about whether the justices have got the history right or wrong—not about the actual issue posed by the case in question.

On this critical view, originalist judges use the founding fathers for political cover in two mirror-image ways. Either they shift to the founding fathers the blame for an unpopular decision forcing a change that might offend a significant part of the electorate, or they shift to the founding fathers the blame for an unpopular decision that preserves an institution or practice coming under severe criticism.

A useful example of blame-shifting as the basis for a controversial change in constitutional law is the set of cases decided by the Supreme Court between the late 1940s and the early 1960s in which the justices began to interpret the religion clauses of the First Amendment to require strict separation of church and state. In this effort, the majority justices repeatedly invoked Thomas Jefferson, James Madison, and the Virginia disestablishment experience as historical and constitutional authority for this step. Facing critics who argued that strict separation of church and state would undermine the republic's moral integrity, these justices insisted that they were giving effect to the enlightened views of the revered founding fathers of that republic.

The classic example of blame-shifting as the basis for the defense of a controversial constitutional arrangement is, once again, *Dred Scott*. Seeking to shield slavery from the forces of political and constitutional change, Chief Justice Taney took cover behind the founding fathers in construing slavery's legitimacy as part of the original constitutional design.

In either case, the intended result is the same—the Court uses the past to shield its interpretation of the Constitution from present criticism. And, either way, the result is the same: critics of the Court's decision offer their own version of the past to sap the historical foundations of the Court's decision. In the end, critics of original-intent declare, nothing is gained and much is lost by conscripting the past in the service of the present.

Issues of historical method swirl around original-intent jurisprudence, the most important of these being questions of evidence and intention. Are the sources that most judges, litigants, and scholars sift to determine original-intent reliable enough for that purpose? And did the founding fathers themselves intend that their expressions of intent be binding on posterity?

The evidentiary focus of original-intent jurisprudence is James Madison's *Notes of Debates in the Federal Convention of 1787*. As a Virginia delegate, Madison made sure that he had a front-row seat, providing him with the best possible chance to see and hear the debates. Using a system of shorthand that he devised himself, he recorded each day's proceedings, never missing a session, and he spent two or three hours each night transcribing and editing his shorthand notes. Later scholars have hailed Madison's work not only as the most comprehensive account of the Convention's proceedings but also as the finest example of parliamentary reporting in his generation—though, in 1986, a test of their reliability (reading them aloud while timing the reading with a stopwatch) established that Madison at his best managed to record only 5 to 10 percent of what was said in a given session of the Convention.[54]

Though we might think that the author of a primary source who worked so hard to create it would see his handiwork as the first resource for understanding the Constitution, Madison himself insisted instead that the intent of the Constitution's ratifiers, as found in surviving records of the state ratifying conventions, was the soundest reference point for interpreting the Constitution. Madison based his preference for the ratifying debates on ideas of authority and publicity. The delegates to those conventions were elected to choose to adopt or reject the document, and thus exercised the authority to constitute a government, known as the constituent power. For this reason, they were the true founders of the Constitution, and their intent should be dispositive where it could be ascertained. Further, the ratifying conventions met in full view of the public, making a full range of arguments for and against the Constitution, specifically including arguments for and against clashing readings of the constitutional text. Thus, for Madison, the ratifying debates were the crucial sources for defining the Constitution's original intent because they were both accessible and authoritative. By contrast, he viewed his own notes on the debates on framing the Constitution as of value mainly to future constitution-makers, who would learn from them the challenges of framing a constitution.

Madison's argument is historically vulnerable, however. One such Achilles' heel is the problem of availability and reliability of evidence. For many years, the fragmentary records of the ratifying conventions were widely scattered, remaining largely unavailable for generations. Not until the twentieth century did historians attempt a comprehensive, rigorous edition of this priceless historical evidence, *The Documentary History of the Ratification of the Constitution and the Bill of Rights, 1787–1791*, launched in the 1960s by Merrill M. Jensen of the University of Wisconsin and continued by his students.[55] Until then, historians and constitutional scholars had relied on an incomplete, unreliable edition by Jonathan Elliot, *Debates in the Several State Conventions on the Adoption of the Federal Constitution*, launched in 1827 and reprinted in revised and expanded editions over the next three decades.[56]

The other vulnerability, ironically, resulted from two decisions made by Madison himself—to prepare his own shorthand record of the Federal Convention's debates and to leave the manuscript to his wife as a legacy to ensure a living income after his death. The publication in 1840 of Madison's *Notes*, in an edition prepared by Attorney-General Henry D. Gilpin, and their superficial appearance of comprehensiveness focused the attention of constitutional interpreters on Madison's record of the Federal Convention rather than on the surviving evidence from the state ratifying conventions.[57] In all, four editions of Madison's *Notes* and of other surviving evidence from the Federal Convention appeared between 1894 and 1927. All these editions, reprinted by a host of publishers, have kept historians and constitutional scholars focused on the framing debates and have eclipsed ratification.[58] (Even Madison, who usually stressed ratification evidence as opposed to framing evidence, was not above hinting in congressional debate that his notes of the Federal Convention's debates on *framing* the Constitution would support a given reading of the document if he were not bound by oath to keep them secret.)

Besides principled and methodological arguments, there are historically grounded arguments against original intent—that the debates over the Constitution's framing and adoption never envisioned that the document would continue in force for more than two centuries, and that the efforts to put the Constitution into effect generated issues that the debates over framing and ratification either did not resolve or did not address or foresee.

Whatever the merits of the controversy over original-intent interpretation of the Constitution, arguments over the point arose as early as the debates over ratifying the document in 1787–1788, and they cropped up anew as Americans were preparing to set the new government in motion in 1789. Memories of ratification were still fresh in Americans' minds. Not only had many founding fathers taken part in that political conflict—they were also prominent in all three branches of the new government. In that government's early years, the founding fathers and the people whom they aspired to lead divided, often bitterly, about a wide array of political issues having constitutional significance.

The Constitution's opponents, though resigned to their defeat, were still determined to continue the larger battle over the nation's future; they sifted the debates and polemics generated by the ratification controversy and often took the Constitution's supporters to task for diverging from what they had told the people about what they intended or understood the Constitution to mean. One focus of this scavenger hunt was *The Federalist*, the series of eighty-five newspaper essays written by Alexander Hamilton, James Madison, and John Jay. By the end of 1789, Jay was the new nation's first chief justice, Hamilton was the first secretary of the treasury, and Madison was a U.S. representative from Virginia in the First Congress who acted as floor leader for the Washington administration. Thus, *The Federalist* became for those on both sides of any given issue an armory of arguments by three leading spirits behind the push to adopt the Constitution.

With vigor blended with cynical glee, critics of the Constitution used the arguments of "Publius" as benchmarks to evaluate Hamilton's claims for federal constitutional power; in their hands, *The Federalist* became not an authority for a strong general government but a means to test—and find wanting—arguments made by Hamilton and his allies for a government stronger than that described in *The Federalist*.[59] Defenders of federal power fought back using the same tools; at least once those who sought to overturn Madison's arguments against reading the Constitution to include not only expressed but implied powers ambushed him by citing his own words in *The Federalist No. 44* to support their position.[60] These debates may seem academic and abstract from the vantage point of two centuries, but at the time they were pragmatic and deadly serious.

The first issues to divide the nation and raise issues of original intent were domestic. The fiscal policies of Treasury Secretary Alexander Hamilton put into question the Constitution's grants and restrictions on federal power, and thus the founding fathers' intentions as to the kind of nation the United States would become and the kind of government, politics, and economy it would have.[61] Hamilton and his supporters maintained that the new nation's credit had to be strong to bolster the nation's reputation in the world economy. Achieving that goal required interpreting the Constitution broadly, giving the federal government generous grants of power—not just those powers expressly granted in the document but all powers that could be reasonably implied from its provisions and not explicitly barred by them. Seeking to link themselves to the Constitution's great victory in 1787–1788, they claimed the name Federalists.

Rallying behind Secretary of State Thomas Jefferson and Representative James Madison, Hamilton's opponents demanded that the Constitution be interpreted narrowly; any power that it did not authorize expressly was unconstitutional. On this theory, they insisted that Hamilton's policies exceeded the Constitution's limits on federal power. The purpose of his scheme to violate the Constitution, they charged, could not be more clear—to favor the interests of those interested in commerce, trade, and speculation over those of the people, who were mostly small farmers with little or no interest in the world economy. Such policies would corrupt American politics, turning the United States into Britain's economic vassal; destroying American political, social, and economic independence; and ultimately undoing the American Revolution. To reinforce their conception of themselves as defenders of republican government, the only true guarantor of the liberties won by the Revolution, Jefferson, Madison, and their allies dubbed themselves Republicans.[62] (The other major domestic issue—choosing the site of the permanent national capital—had at best an indirect relevance to issues of original intent, in that the choice of the site for the capital would determine which social, economic, and regional interests would first be able to influence the making of law and public policy.)[63]

In the 1790s, domestic disputes gave way to the cluster of issues raised by the French Revolution. The linkages between the fates of the French Revolution and the American Revolution (and in particular the handiwork of the founding fathers) became focal points of political disagreement and constitutional argument. At first, as France seemed to make a peaceful transition to a constitutional monarchy built on principles of constitutionalism and rights with recognizable American roots, Americans hailed this historic effort. When in 1792, however, France tried and executed Louis XVI and then plunged into revolutionary violence, Americans generally and the founding fathers in particular divided not only on the French Revolution but also on how the United States should treat its ally from the War of Independence. That policy choice had unnerving implications for the new constitutional system.

The policy choice was between preserving the French–American alliance created by the treaty of 1778 and adopting a position of American neutrality as to the wars about to convulse the European continent. The United States, Federalists insisted, could not maintain a common cause with the French, for such a choice would plunge America as well as Europe into chaos, anarchy, and war. They favored either strict neutrality, the position adopted by President Washington, or even an alliance with Great Britain, leader of the conservative monarchies opposing Revolutionary France. However, Republicans insisted that the cause of the French Revolution was identical to that of the American Revolution; if the United States were to remain neutral or side with Britain, it would violate the 1778 treaty with France, break faith with the nation's oldest ally, and undermine the integrity of the American Revolution.

The constitutional questions evoked by the policy controversy over the French Revolution focused on the powers of the president over issues of diplomacy, war, and peace, as defined by the open-ended language of Article II. The neutrality crisis of 1793 brought those issues to a head. After extensive debates in his cabinet,

Washington asserted his power as president to proclaim neutrality despite the 1778 treaty of alliance between France and the United States. Writing for the newspapers as Pacificus and Helvidius, respectively, Hamilton defended and Madison attacked Washington's claims of sole constitutional power to issue that proclamation, each making an original-intent case for his position.[64] These arguments continued in 1794–1795, when Washington sent Chief Justice John Jay as a minister plenipotentiary to negotiate a treaty with Great Britain. When Jay returned with a controversial treaty that seemed to the Republicans to concede far too much to Britain, the House of Representatives under Madison's leadership vainly sought a constitutional role in that debate. Even though the Constitution assigned the treaty-making power to the president with the advice and consent of the Senate, Madison and his allies in the House insisted that as the House had sole authority to propose bills for raising and spending government revenue, the House should have its own say on the Jay Treaty. Again, controversialists on both sides sought to invoke the Constitution's original intent on the matter, with inconclusive results.

In 1797–1798, relations between France and America worsened to the point of war on the high seas. Responding to this first national-security crisis under the Constitution, Congress enacted and President John Adams signed into law sweeping legislation limiting the rights of foreigners residing in the United States as well as the right of anyone, citizen or alien, to speak or write words critical of the government or of specified officials of that government. These hotly contested Alien and Sedition Acts once again sparked controversy over the federal government's constitutional powers, augmented by arguments over the scope and limits of the "free speech" and "free press" guarantees of the First Amendment. Kentucky and Virginia each adopted resolutions (the former set drafted by Jefferson and the latter by Madison) denouncing these Alien and Sedition Acts as unconstitutional, and the other states adopted sets of resolutions rejecting the arguments of Kentucky and Virginia. All of these arguments spiraled back to invocations of what the framers and adopters of the Constitution would or would not have intended the correct interpretation of that document to be. Federal judges not only interpreted the Constitution by reference to issues of original intent—they saw challenges mounted to their own powers based on claims that they were exceeding their grants of constitutional power as originally intended.[65]

Even events that in retrospect seem unexceptional raised issues of constitutional power and original intent. In 1803, for example, when President Thomas Jefferson had the opportunity to buy the Louisiana Territory from France, he felt conflicting emotions— excitement and eagerness at the chance to supplant the French and establish American hegemony over the western part of the continent, and uncertainty that the Constitution permitted the United States to enter into a treaty for the purchase of land. He even framed several versions of a proposed constitutional amendment to remedy what he saw as a lack of federal constitutional power. Finally he abandoned the effort, explaining to dubious political allies that he believed the cause was good and that the country would approve his exercise of federal power even if it technically exceeded the Constitution. He invoked the lawyerly theory of trusteeship: he and Congress were trustees for the American people of the constitutional powers associated with their offices, and if a trustee technically exceeds his grant of power but does so in ways that benefit those to whom the trustee is responsible, the beneficiaries can ratify the trustee's exercise of power and thus silently extend after the fact the powers granted to the trustee.[66]

The Louisiana Purchase sowed the seeds of a much more intractable disagreement—one that, in the end, shattered the fragile consensus holding the Union together under the Constitution of 1787. As the nation expanded westward, issues of federal constitutional power entwined with other questions of public policy: governing the western territories; designing and building "internal improvements" such as roads, bridges, and canals to knit the nation together as a single economic and political unit; and—most ominously—the place of slavery in American life. All these matters raised issues of constitutional power and limitations, linked to questions of how properly to interpret the Constitution, and ultimately to questions of the founding fathers' institutions about the Constitution and the American future.

Controversy reigned over whether the founding fathers had intended to tolerate slavery or to embrace it, or had hoped that future generations would find a way to abolish it. Beginning in 1820 with the Missouri Compromise, Americans sought to forge a series of regional and sectional compromises that would govern the expansion of the Union and regulate the spread of slavery within the growing United States. Defenders of these compromises invoked precedents set by the founding fathers, such as the Northwest Ordinance of 1787, which barred the spread of slavery to federal territory north of the Ohio River. Their opponents insisted that the Constitution gave the federal government no power to limit the spread of slavery, adding that the right to own slaves was a special case of the right to own private property that the Fifth Amendment protected against interference by the government.

At the same time, a growing movement against slavery offered a range of readings of the nation's origins supporting a spectrum of antislavery positions.[67] Radical abolitionists such as William Lloyd Garrison and Wendell Phillips denounced the Constitution as "a covenant with death" and condemned the founding fathers for making compromises with slavery, protecting its existence, and fostering its development. To dramatize their rejection of a revered national symbol, they staged public burnings of the Constitution.

Other antislavery advocates, rejecting the Garrison–Phillips position, argued that the freedom principles at the core of the Constitution justified reading the document as essentially antislavery, with its proslavery provisions capable of being repealed without damaging the original charter. The founding fathers, they insisted, foresaw the ultimate extinction of slavery and expected that a later generation would devise a solution to the problem that they could not solve themselves. The abolitionist Alvan Stewart, in an 1836 polemic, declared:

> [The Constitution's] silence in the use of the word *slave* is a rebuke louder than a thunder peal, telling the world [that] slavery should never exist by its authority,...that...the absence of the word "*slavery*" was a protest against the offense, and an everlasting acknowledgment of the shame the instrument would have felt by its insertion.[68]

Seeking to counter these various forms of antislavery argument, proslavery advocates asserted (ironically, in terms echoing the arguments made by Garrison, Phillips, and their allies but for diametrically opposed reasons) that the compromises protecting slavery were integral to the Constitution's existence, the price of Union. Indeed, as later scholars pointed out, Jonathan Elliot, whose *Debates in the Several State Conventions* remained for more than 150 years the authoritative documentary history of the Constitution's adoption, edited the ratification debates to emphasize that the Constitution was a proslavery charter.[69]

In this controversy, the most notorious example of original-intent argument was Chief Justice Roger B. Taney's opinion in *Dred Scott v. Sandford* (1857).[70] Dred Scott was a slave who sued in federal court to obtain his freedom because his former owner, who had traveled as a government official throughout the midwestern and western United States with his family and his slaves, had lived in free states and in a free territory before returning to the slave state of Missouri. After his former owner's death, Scott, aided by antislavery activists, filed suit against his former owner's executor, John F. A. Sanford (misspelled as Sandford in reports of the case). The case rose slowly through the federal courts during the 1850s. When it arrived at the Supreme Court, six justices were ready to reject Scott's lawsuit on technical grounds of jurisdiction and standing; two others were willing to vote to uphold Scott's claim of freedom.

Understanding the case differently from his colleagues, Chief Justice Taney saw a chance to dispose of a divisive political issue by issuing a definitive decision by the Court. He therefore penned a long, seemingly authoritative opinion, which in the nation's eyes became the opinion for the Court even though Taney wrote for himself alone. Having served as chief justice for nearly twenty years, Taney had won acclaim as a worthy successor to John Marshall; for these reasons, Taney's views had greater visibility and greater persuasive effect than those of any or even all of his colleagues.

Taney insisted that the intent of those who framed and adopted the Constitution was and should be dispositive, no matter what anyone else (including, Taney seemed to imply, himself) might think. That intent was that the federal government had no power to limit the spread of slavery in any way; thus, the long-dead Missouri Compromise of 1820 was unconstitutional, and any attempt to cite it as precedent for congressional power to limit the spread of slavery was invalid as well. (The six other justices filed a narrower opinion concurring in the result, on the ground that under Missouri law Dred Scott, as a slave, had no right to sue for his freedom in federal court.)

Two days before the Court delivered its opinions in *Dred Scott*, James M. Buchanan of Pennsylvania was inaugurated as the fifteenth president of the United States. The controversy over slavery haunted Buchanan, a veteran Democratic politician and former secretary of state. As a so-called "doughface" Democrat, Buchanan was also a northerner who sympathized with the interests of the slave states, where the Democratic Party had its greatest strength. In his inaugural address, Buchanan told his audience—and, through telegraph reports of his speech, the nation—that in a few days the Supreme Court would decide a case that would resolve the issue, and called on all Americans to obey the Court. When the justices handed down their decision in *Dred Scott*, infuriated opponents of slavery charged that a conspiracy of proslavery Democratic politicians (including former President Franklin Pierce, President

Buchanan, Chief Justice Taney, and Senator Stephen A. Douglas of Illinois) was bent on spreading slavery through the nation and besmirching the founding fathers.

The most eloquent, well-reasoned denunciations came from Abraham Lincoln, who in 1838 in his first important speech had described the founding fathers as "a once hardy but now lamented and departed race of ancestors." In 1858, in accepting the Republican nomination as candidate for the U.S. Senate from Illinois, Lincoln asserted the existence of that proslavery conspiracy in one of his greatest speeches, the "House Divided" speech. He continued this theme through the Illinois Senate campaign in his landmark debates with Stephen A. Douglas—but he also recognized that he had to mount a direct attack on the historical foundation of Taney's decision in *Dred Scott v. Sandford.*

In 1860, as he worked hard to persuade snobbish Eastern politicians that he was worthy of the Republican presidential nomination, Lincoln traveled to New York City to speak at the city's great school of engineering and architecture, Cooper Union. Grounding his Cooper Union Address on careful and extensive historical research to ascertain the "original intentions" of "our fathers, who framed the Government under which we live," Lincoln made a powerful case that the founders not only had envisioned but had welcomed congressional power to limit the spread of slavery in the federal territories. At Cooper Union, Lincoln shattered the credibility of Taney's pro-slavery reading of original intent under which the federal government lacked any power to restrict the spread of slavery.[71] Lincoln's speech pioneered a form of legal–historical argument that has become a standard in disputes over original-intent analysis of the Constitution. If the Court bases its decision on its reading of history, a skillful and persuasive critique of the decision's historical basis can undermine by implication its legal legitimacy and force.

With his Cooper Union address, Lincoln persuaded Republicans that he was a plausible and worthy presidential candidate, but southern politicians and controversialists remained unconvinced, clinging to the logic of Taney's opinion in *Dred Scott* and its original-intent defense of slavery's legitimacy and the protection it received from the Constitution. During the Civil War, those who sought to create the Confederate States of America claimed that they were seceding from the Union in large part to give effect to the original vision of the Constitution as promulgated by the founding fathers. Even the Confederacy's seal made this argument, presenting at its center an image of George Washington mounted on horseback. Not to be outdone, President Lincoln deliberately tied the Union's cause to the Declaration of Independence and the founding fathers' creation of what he called, in his Gettysburg Address, "a new nation...conceived in liberty and dedicated to the proposition that all men are created equal."[72]

The Union victory in 1865 left one-fourth of the nation devastated, prostrate, and under military occupation. Following the end of the Civil War, the nation launched an agonizing process of reconstructing the Union, and worked to amend the Constitution to adapt it to the nation that the war produced. Three times between 1865 and 1870, Congress used Article V's amending process to add new provisions to the Constitution's text. Underlying each amendment was the hope that it would require no sequel; the Southern response to the first and second of these amendments made clear that further use of Article V was necessary. Amendment XIII (proposed and ratified in 1865) abolished slavery throughout the Union. Amendment XIV (proposed in 1866 and ratified in 1868) gave national citizenship primacy over state citizenship, built equality into the Constitution as a fundamental principle, and subjected state and local governments to the commands of the federal Constitution, including the Bill of Rights. Amendment XV (proposed in 1869 and ratified in 1870) forbade the states from denying access to the vote based on race, color, or previous condition of servitude.

Opponents of each of these amendments insisted that the original intent of the Constitution prohibited them. Slavery's legitimacy, they argued, was part of the original conditions under which slave states had consented to the Constitution, and abolishing slavery also would deprive slaveowners of private property without just compensation. States' rights, they urged, were also part of that original compact, and any attempt to rework the Constitution to give primacy to national citizenship and national power would violate states' rights. Finally, they maintained, because the Constitution's framers and ratifiers had viewed control of the franchise as solely within each state's discretion, the proposed Amendment XV violated the original compact. Though unavailing, these arguments testified to the continuing power of original intent.

After Reconstruction, other controversies over original intent continued to ebb and flow. Through the last half of the nineteenth century and into the early decades of the twentieth century, conservative jurists used original-intent arguments to block measures such as federal regulations of manufacturing and labor relations and a federal income tax. In response, some historians, legal scholars, and political scientists criticized what they saw as the antidemocratic cast of thought of the framers of the Constitution, arguing that they devised the document primarily as a means to protect their own economic interests rather than as a high-minded exercise in constitutional statesmanship.

This interpretation of the founding fathers was a driving force behind the historical scholarship of Charles A. Beard, whose pathbreaking monographs on the founding period and the political and economic views of the founding fathers influenced two generations of historians, political scientists, and legal scholars. Beard and his followers sought to undermine the uncritical reverence for the founding fathers prevailing in American culture. Achieving this goal, they hoped, would undercut the original-intent arguments that conservative jurists invoked to overturn experiments in government.

History repeated itself. In the first decades of the twentieth century, known as the Progressive era, and then in the 1930s, during Franklin D. Roosevelt's New Deal, parallel battles over constitutional interpretation raged. Conservative jurists invoked their version of original intent, citing the founding fathers as barriers to new and creative uses of government power. The founding fathers, they insisted, had intended to create only a limited general government with narrow, defined powers. Liberal scholars and polemicists countered with their diametrically opposed version of the Constitution's origins; they cited the founding fathers as exponents of creative uses of government power to solve national problems. Both sides drew on the same sources and the same history, but each was guided by its own interpretative framework.

In particular, Franklin D. Roosevelt, who embraced a pragmatic, experimental approach to the problems of government, regularly sought to align himself and his administration with the founding fathers. Roosevelt recognized that winning the battle for the warrant of history was an essential precondition to victory in the political battles of his own time. For these reasons, he insisted that he was merely being true to the founding fathers' commitment to pragmatic experimentation.

Roosevelt's greatest defeat as president came when he lost a key battle over which side was truer to the Constitution and the founding fathers. In 1937, after his landslide reelection, he decided to move against the one institution that continued to threaten the success of the New Deal—the Supreme Court. Roosevelt proposed to reorganize the Court. Claiming that the justices were old, tired, and overworked, he offered legislation permitting him to appoint one new justice for each sitting justice over the age of seventy years, up to a maximum of a fifteen-member Court. The plan sparked a firestorm of criticism and controversy. Was Roosevelt seeking to undermine the principles of separation of powers and checks and balances that the founding fathers installed at the core of the Constitution? Or were the justices' assertions of such principles as reasons to strike down New Deal legislation distortions and caricatures of the founding fathers' original intent? One factor exacerbating the controversy's intensity was that it coincided with the sesquicentennial of the framing and adoption of the Constitution, which focused popular and political attention on the Constitution's origins and the views of those who framed and adopted it. Ultimately, public opinion and the growing skepticism even of many of Roosevelt's allies in Congress doomed the Court-packing plan. To many Americans, it appeared that Roosevelt had challenged the founding fathers, and lost.

Roosevelt's rebuff coincided with a gradual and growing shift by the Justices toward accepting government regulation of the economy. These momentous events seemed to settle the battle between the president and the Court. Even so, controversies over original intent shifted their polarity radically in the late 1930s and 1940s. Liberal jurists such as Justices Hugo L. Black, Felix Frankfurter, and Wiley B. Rutledge and constitutional scholars and historians, who formerly opposed the jurisprudence of original intent when used to challenge federal regulation of economic life, now found new value and persuasiveness in original-intent jurisprudence when used to interpret rights-protecting provisions in the Constitution, the Bill of Rights, and other amendments. Their antagonists followed suit, devising or recovering contrasting versions of the past to undermine the historically based jurisprudence of the present.[73]

The leading example of this tendency was the jurisprudence of issues of church and state. Beginning in 1947 with *Everson v. Board of Education*, the U.S. Supreme Court declared that the proper interpretation of the First Amendment's religion clauses must begin with the origins of those provisions, then focused its inquiry into those origins on the Virginia disestablishment struggle of the 1770s and 1780s, and concluded that the views of Jefferson and Madison articulated the applicable lessons of that struggle for interpreting the religion clauses in modern times. The justices thus endorsed strict separation of church and state and invoked Jefferson's Virginia Statute for Religious Freedom and Madison's

"Memorial and Remonstrance against Religious Assessments" as guideposts for interpreting the First Amendment.

In response to these decisions, a diverse array of scholars and controversialists insisted that the tradition that should guide interpretation of the religion clauses was not the strict separationist vision associated with Jefferson and Madison. Instead, they espoused the nonpreferentialist or accommodationist vision articulated in the New England states, under which government could not choose among religious sects or denominations but could prefer the general cause of religion as opposed to the cause of atheism or irreligion.

The argument continues to this day. Some advocates focus on what they deem to be inconsistencies in Jefferson's and Madison's practices to undermine their perceived commitment to separation of church and state; others even attempt to read the separationist position out of existence altogether. Still others note the presence of *both* interpretations of the religion clauses and seek to reconcile them with the growing religious pluralism of the American people by adopting a generally separationist reading of the amendment.

Ironically, the principal consequence of original-intent battles from the 1940s through the 1970s was to raise questions about the use of original-intent jurisprudence. Most constitutional scholars and historians coalesced around a position recognizing the usefulness of the method of original-intent as a persuasive factor in constitutional interpretation but rejecting it as a dispositive factor.

In the 1980s and early 1990s, the forces of conservatism associated with the administration of Presidents Ronald Reagan and George H. W. Bush sought to revive original-intent jurisprudence as a means to rein in irresponsible judges and to restore the Constitution to its intended form. In 1985, in a lecture at Tulane Law School, Attorney General Edwin Meese III rocked the American legal world by calling for a "jurisprudence of original intent" that would anchor judges to the text of the Constitution interpreted solely in the light of its origins. In the process, Meese cited *Dred*

Scott as an example of the kind of jurisprudential disaster that can result when a judge writes his own preconceptions into the Constitution—despite Chief Justice Taney's deliberate, explicit framing of his opinion as an original-intent interpretation of the Constitution. Under Meese's leadership, the Justice Department began to advocate the uses of original-intent jurisprudence in modern constitutional adjudication; the department's Office of Legal Counsel issued a series of studies presenting a wide array of originalist constitutional arguments. In addition, the Federalist Society, a conservative legal organization that formed chapters in law schools throughout the nation, promoted Meese's arguments and those of his intellectual and political allies. Finally, the appointments of Justices Antonin Scalia in 1986 and Clarence Thomas in 1991 added two vigorous, vehement advocates of original-intent interpretation to the Supreme Court, ensuring that arguments about original-intent will continue to dominate constitutional interpretation for decades to come.

In response, historians and constitutional scholars such as Martin S. Flaherty, H. Jefferson Powell, Jack N. Rakove, and James H. Hutson challenged original-intent jurisprudence on grounds of evidentiary analysis and historical context. They argue that original-intent jurisprudence does not acknowledge the inadequacies of the historical evidence of original-intent. Further, they maintain, it fails to consider the historical and intellectual contexts of the Constitution's origins and the ways in which those contexts differ significantly and often radically from today. In addition, the early years of the constitutional system show that the workings of the new constitutional system repeatedly surprised and dismayed those who framed, adopted, or supported the Constitution in 1787–1788. Given the Constitution's tendency to diverge from the expectations and understandings of those who framed or adopted it, a tendency emerging as early as 1789 and persisting throughout the Constitution's first decade, and given the repeated outcropping of problems that the framers and ratifiers never anticipated, a rigid fealty to the jurisprudence of original-intent makes little or no sense.

Even so, critics of original-intent argued, there is no need to abandon inquiries into the Constitution's origins as a means to assist modern interpretation of the document. Jack Rakove identified two persuasive reasons—"firstness" and persuasiveness—why we should consider the views of those who framed the Constitution, argued over its adoption, and put it into effect. Because the framers were "present at the creation," their debates and arguments have much to teach us about that process of constitutional creation and creative adaptation, both of which shaped the origins of the constitutional system. Moreover, because the founding fathers were among the most learned and profound political and constitutional thinkers that this nation has produced, we need not sacrifice the persuasive value that their arguments and debates possess even if we reject the binding force of original-intent jurisprudence. Indeed, we ought to treat the amassed historical, political, legal, and constitutional wisdom that they left to us as a resource on which we can draw in solving the puzzles posed to us by the operations of the Constitution and by attempts to apply its principles and provisions to new problems and controversies.[74]

At the same time, though we may want to start with the founding fathers, we should not stop there—and they themselves would counsel us not to stop there. On April 12, 1790, in his first charge to a federal grand jury as Chief Justice of the United States, John Jay addressed the recent and momentous events in constitution-making of which he had been a part:

> The Institution of General and State Governments, their respective Conveniences and Defects in Practice, and the subsequent Alterations made in some of them, have operated as useful Experiments, and conspired to promote our Advancement in this interesting Science. It is pleasing to observe that the present national Government already affords advantages, which the preceding one proved too feeble and ill constructed to produce. How far it may be still distant from that Degree of Perfection to which it may possibly be carried Time only can decide.

It is a Consolation to reflect that the good Sense of the People will be enabled by Experience to discover and correct its Imperfections; especially while they continue to retain a proper Confidence in themselves, and avoid those Jealousies and Dissensions which often springing from the worst Designs frequently frustrate the best Measures.[75]

In many cases, attempts to seek guidance from the making of the Constitution are unavailing—because we seek to apply the ideas of framers or ratifiers to questions that they could not have foreseen or failed to resolve in their time, or because we take them out of context, or because we forget that, like us, they could not predict the future. When we contemplate that record, we should recall the warning that the great constitutional theorist and historian Alexander Bickel of Yale Law School issued in his book *The Least Dangerous Branch*: "No answer is what the wrong question begets."[76]

Epilogue

The Founding Fathers, History, and Us

AMERICANS' CONTENTIOUS RELATIONSHIP WITH the founding fathers has unfolded within and been shaped by a pair of linked questions. How much do the founding fathers resemble us and how much do they differ from us? To what extent are we obliged to keep faith with them, and to what extent must we challenge them or set them aside in the face of changing conditions and problems? That the American people still govern themselves under a written constitution framed by the founding fathers, albeit with a series of amendments adopted between the early 1790s and the early 1990s, gives these questions urgency and bite.[1]

The Preamble's statement that the primary purpose of the Constitution was "to form a more perfect Union" offers a way to find answers to these perennial and perennially troubling questions. In particular, the phrase "a more perfect Union" suggests the framers' recognition that the Constitution not only was improving on the Union as defined by the Articles of Confederation but that both it and the Union were capable of further improvement. Indeed, during the ratification controversy many supporters of the Constitution invoked the amending process codified in that document's Article V as a mechanism for repairing defects in the original Constitution. With this remedy available, and more workable than the comparable system codified in Article 13 of the Articles of Confederation, the Constitution's backers described the choice before the American people as between the hope of future good and no hope at all.[2]

The idea of perfecting the Union has been a vital but until recently unappreciated feature of American political and constitutional culture.[3] In particular, perfecting the Union has been a key theme of African American constitutional thought. Several African American activists, orators, politicians, and jurists, all of whom have played vital roles in the ongoing American constitutional experiment, have offered a series of revealing variations and developments of this theme, in the process illuminating the complex relationship between the founding fathers and posterity. All sought to engage with the lives and words of the founding fathers, and all blended clear-eyed criticism of the founding fathers' greatest failures with hopeful invocations of their political and constitutional principles as a means to set those failures right—to perfect the Union defined by the Constitution and preserved in the centuries that followed. Given the centrality of the African American experience for American history in general and the struggle over slavery and the Constitution in particular, the pattern of thought traced by these thinkers has urgent relevance for the evolving American relationship with the founding fathers.

On July 5, 1852, Frederick Douglass gave an Independence Day address to an audience of more than five hundred abolitionists in Corinthian Hall in Rochester, New York, in an event sponsored by the Rochester Ladies' Anti-Slavery Society.[4] Their choice of speaker was inspired: Douglass had already won international fame with his 1845 *Narrative of the Life of Frederick Douglass* and a series of lectures and addresses on slavery, abolition, and emancipation. Thirty-four years old, tall, and strongly built, with a powerful voice and a mesmerizing delivery, Douglass was a rising star of the national abolitionist movement. Standing at the podium

in Corinthian Hall, Douglass did not mince words for his genteel
audience:

> What to the American slave is your Fourth of July? I answer, a day that
> reveals to him, more than all other days in the year, the gross injustice
> and cruelty to which he is the constant victim. To him, your celebration
> is a sham; your boasted liberty, an unholy license; your national greatness,
> swelling vanity; your sounds of rejoicing are empty and heartless; your
> denunciations of tyrants, brass-fronted impudence; your shouts of liberty
> and equality, hollow mockery; your prayers and hymns, your sermons and
> thanksgivings, with all your religious parade and solemnity, are to him
> mere bombast, fraud, deception, impiety, and hypocrisy—a thin veil to
> cover up crimes which would disgrace a nation of savages. There is not
> a nation on the earth guilty of practices more shocking and bloody, than
> are the people of these United States, at this very hour.

This passage introduced the best-remembered feature of Douglass's widely reprinted address, his indictment of American hypoc-
risy; he pointed out that on the Fourth of July white Americans
thanked Heaven for their freedom while either enslaving African
American men, women, and children or ignoring the ghastly spectacle of slavery.

Unlike so many of his allies in the abolitionist movement,
Douglass refused to fix the blame for slavery on the founding
fathers. Instead, he argued that they were the victims of gross mis-
representation by his era's defenders of slavery: "*It is a slander upon
their memory,* at least, so I believe." Insisting that the Constitution
was a "GLORIOUS LIBERTY DOCUMENT," Douglass refused
to despair, pointing out that the Constitution's text nowhere
explicitly mentioned slavery. Douglass took this omission as a positive statement by the Constitution's framers that the American
nation's future would have no room for slavery. Even in the face
of many Americans' hypocritical tolerance of slavery while celebrating freedom and independence, he concluded that the words
of the core American document of political foundation combined
with the changing attitudes of his fellow citizens gave him hope
for the future: "While drawing encouragement from 'the

Declaration of Independence,' the great principles it contains, and the genius of American Institutions, my spirit is also cheered by the obvious tendencies of the age."

One hundred and eleven years after Douglass's oration, the Rev. Dr. Martin Luther King, Jr., another young African American leader, addressed a national audience.[5] An organizer of the 1955 Montgomery, Alabama, bus boycott and a leader of the Southern Christian Leadership Conference, King helped to plan the March on Washington for Jobs and Freedom. On August 18, 1963, several hundred thousand demonstrators, white and black alike, marched through the city of Washington, D.C., from the Washington Monument to the Lincoln Memorial. Gathered before the Memorial, they then heard a series of speeches and musical presentations. In the event's closing speech, Dr. King invoked the origins of the American republic:

> In a sense we've come to our nation's capital to cash a check. When the architects of our republic wrote the magnificent words of the Constitution and the Declaration of Independence, they were signing a promissory note to which every American was to fall heir. This note was a promise that all men, yes, black men as well as white men, would be guaranteed the "unalienable Rights" of "Life, Liberty and the pursuit of Happiness." It is obvious today that America has defaulted on this promissory note, insofar as her citizens of color are concerned. Instead of honoring this sacred obligation, America has given the Negro people a bad check, a check which has come back marked "insufficient funds."
>
> But we refuse to believe that the bank of justice is bankrupt. We refuse to believe that there are insufficient funds in the great vaults of opportunity of this nation. And so, we've come to cash this check, a check that will give us upon demand the riches of freedom and the security of justice.

Like Douglass, King pointed out that the founding fathers' words challenged America's failures, and he urged African Americans to invoke the best aspirations of the founding fathers as authority to confront and overcome the failures of the American experiment.

On July 25, 1974, Representative Barbara Jordan followed in the rhetorical footsteps of Douglass and King.[6] Though only a first-term Democratic member of the House, Jordan brought to Congress a distinguished record of achievement as a Texas state senator. In the tumultuous summer of 1974, as a member of the House Committee on the Judiciary, Jordan was one of those members of Congress who first had to consider whether the alleged misdeeds of President Richard Nixon required the use of the Constitution's mechanism for presidential impeachment. When she delivered her opening statement on the first day of the committee's nationally televised hearings, Jordan invoked the origins of the Constitution and the fraught relationship between that document and African Americans:

> Earlier today, we heard the beginning of the Preamble to the Constitution of the United States, "We, the people." It is a very eloquent beginning. But when the document was completed on the seventeenth of September 1787 I was not included in that "We, the people." I felt somehow for many years that George Washington and Alexander Hamilton just left me out by mistake. But through the process of amendment, interpretation and court decision I have finally been included in "We, the people."
>
> Today, I am an inquisitor; I believe hyperbole would not be fictional and would not overstate the solemnness that I feel right now. My faith in the Constitution is whole, it is complete, it is total. I am not going to sit here and be an idle spectator to the diminution, the subversion, the destruction of the Constitution.

Yet again, Jordan sounded the central theme that despite the taint of slavery and racism, the principles at the core of the Constitution of the United States, expanded and applied over the course of American history, were common property of all Americans; yet again, she challenged all Americans to defend and vindicate those principles.

Thirteen years after Jordan's eloquent statement, the nation commemorated the bicentennial of the framing of the U.S. Constitution. Dissenting from the bland celebratory tone of the planned commemorations, Associate Justice Thurgood Marshall of the U.S. Supreme Court delivered an address reprinted by law reviews across the nation. In the 1940s and 1950s, as lead counsel for the NAACP's Legal Defense Fund, Marshall had waged a brilliant and hard-fought legal campaign against segregation and racial discrimination, battling to make the guarantees of the Thirteenth, Fourteenth, and Fifteenth Amendments legal realities rather than empty promises. In 1967, after Marshall had served first as Solicitor-General of the United States and then as a federal appellate judge in New York, President Lyndon B. Johnson appointed him an associate justice of the Supreme Court; Marshall thus became the first African American member of the High Court.[7]

In his 1987 address, Marshall challenged the bicentennial celebrations then under way, focusing on the nature of the "more perfect Union" that the Constitution created. He protested what he saw as the "complacent belief that the vision of those who debated and compromised in Philadelphia yielded the 'more perfect Union' it is said we now enjoy." In measured rhetoric barely concealing his scorn, Marshall declined to share that "complacent belief":

> I do not believe that the meaning of the Constitution was forever "fixed" at the Philadelphia Convention. Nor do I find the wisdom, foresight, and sense of justice exhibited by the Framers particularly profound. To the contrary, the government they devised was defective from the start, requiring several amendments, a civil war, and momentous social transformation to attain the system of constitutional government, and its respect for the individual freedoms and human rights, we hold as fundamental today. When contemporary Americans cite "The Constitution," they invoke a concept that is vastly different from what the Framers barely began to construct two centuries ago.

Here, Marshall diverged from the path marked out by Douglass while echoing the arguments made by King and Jordan. He too insisted on "the evolving nature of the Constitution." After sketching the many battles by which successive generations of Americans forced the nation to live up to the principled promises of its founding documents, Marshall concluded:

> We will see that the true miracle was not the birth of the Constitution, but its life, a life nurtured through two turbulent centuries of our own making, and a life embodying much good fortune that was not.

Thus, in this bicentennial year, we may not all participate in the festivities with flagwaving fervor. Some may more quietly commemorate the suffering, struggle, and sacrifice that has triumphed over much of what was wrong with the original document, and observe the anniversary with hopes not realized and promises not fulfilled. I plan to celebrate the bicentennial of the Constitution as a living document, including the Bill of Rights and the other amendments protecting individual freedoms and human rights.

Wearied by his decades of service on the Court and his growing frustration with his colleagues' failure to understand the history he had endured and had helped to shape, Marshall was more dismissive of the founding fathers than Douglass, King, or Jordan had been—but he was equally committed to the power of the words they had shaped and the need to give those words real meaning in the world.

On March 16, 2008, more than two decades after Justice Marshall's controversial lecture, Senator Barack Obama of Illinois, then a candidate for the Democratic Party's presidential nomination, gave a speech at the Constitution Center in Philadelphia, Pennsylvania on the enduring significance of race in American history. Though the event marked a critical juncture in Obama's quest to become the Democratic nominee, he saw its larger significance as well, casting his oration as a principled reflection on the continuing place of issues of race and faith in American public life.

Like his predecessors, Obama began with the words of the Constitution's Preamble, the hopes of those who had framed it, their failings in the process of framing it, and the ongoing struggle to repair those failings and bring American constitutional realities more in line with American constitutional aspirations:[8]

"We the people, in order to form a more perfect union."
    Two hundred and twenty one years ago, in a hall that still stands across the street, a group of men gathered and, with these simple words, launched America's improbable experiment in democracy. Farmers and scholars; statesmen and patriots who had traveled across an ocean to escape tyranny and persecution finally made real their declaration of independence at a Philadelphia convention that lasted through the spring of 1787.

The document they produced was eventually signed but ultimately unfinished. It was stained by this nation's original sin of slavery, a question that divided the colonies and brought the convention to a stalemate until the founders chose to allow the slave trade to continue for at least twenty more years, and to leave any final resolution to future generations.

Of course, the answer to the slavery question was already embedded within our Constitution—a Constitution that had at its very core the ideal of equal citizenship under the law; a Constitution that promised its people liberty, and justice, and a union that could and should be perfected over time.

And yet words on a parchment would not be enough to deliver slaves from bondage, or provide men and women of every color and creed their full rights and obligations as citizens of the United States. What would be needed were Americans in successive generations who were willing to do their part—through protests and struggle, on the streets and in the courts, through a civil war and civil disobedience and always at great risk—to narrow that gap between the promise of our ideals and the reality of their time.

Several months later, on the evening of November 4, 2008, Obama, now the Democratic presidential nominee, achieved a decisive victory in the 2008 general election. In his victory speech, the presumptive president, the first African American elected to the nation's highest office, acknowledged the history that he and his followers had made and related it back to the founding fathers:

> If there is anyone out there who still doubts that America is a place where all things are possible, who still wonders if the dream of our Founders is alive in our time, who still questions the power of our democracy, tonight is your answer....
>
> And to all those who have wondered if America's beacon still burns as bright: tonight we proved once more that the true strength of our nation comes not from the might of our arms or the scale of our wealth, but from the enduring power of our ideals—democracy, liberty, opportunity and unyielding hope.
>
> That's the true genius of America, that America can change. Our union can be perfected. And what we have already achieved gives us hope for what we can and must achieve tomorrow.[9]

In the days and weeks following Obama's speech, a host of commentators argued over whether his election indeed fulfilled the dreams of the founding fathers or whether any of them could even have conceived such a thing being possible. The verdict of these discussions came remarkably close to the line of argument sketched in this epilogue—that Obama was invoking not just the best aspirations of the founding fathers but the efforts of generations who came after them to narrow the gap between the ideals and the reality of the American experiment—to perfect the Union.[10]

The theme remains constant—and, indeed, it echoes the words of a great work of religion and law that was centuries old when the founding fathers began their labors, the Talmud. As the ancient Jewish sage Rabbi Tarfon counseled in *Ethics of the Fathers* (*Mishneh Pirke Avot* 2:21), "It is not thy duty to complete the work, but neither art thou free to desist from it."[11]

Appendix

The Founding Fathers: A Partial List

Nobody can agree on the complete list of the founding fathers, especially when we include the great number of Americans who did not hold political office in the new state governments, the Continental and Confederation Congresses, or the new government launched under the U.S. Constitution in 1789. This appendix provides a list divided into three groups: (1) the signers of the Declaration of Independence, (2) the framers of the Constitution, and (3) those who were neither signers nor framers but who played pivotal roles in the creation of the United States.

1. SIGNERS OF THE DECLARATION (BY STATE DELEGATION)

CONNECTICUT: Samuel Huntington, Roger Sherman, William Williams, Oliver Wolcott

DELAWARE: Thomas McKean, George Read, Caesar Rodney

GEORGIA: Button Gwinnett, Lyman Hall, George Walton

MARYLAND: Charles Carroll of Carrollton, Samuel Chase, William Paca, Thomas Stone

MASSACHUSETTS: John Adams, Samuel Adams, Elbridge Gerry, John Hancock, Robert Treat Paine

NEW HAMPSHIRE: Josiah Bartlett, Matthew Thornton, William Whipple

NEW JERSEY: Abraham Clark, John Hart, Francis Hopkinson, Richard Stockton, John Witherspoon

NEW YORK: William Floyd, Francis Lewis, Philip Livingston, Lewis Morris

NORTH CAROLINA: Joseph Hewes, William Hooper, John Penn

PENNSYLVANIA: George Clymer, Benjamin Franklin, Robert Morris, John Morton, George Ross, Benjamin Rush, James Smith, George Taylor, James Wilson

RHODE ISLAND: William Ellery, Stephen Hopkins

SOUTH CAROLINA: Thomas Heyward, Jr., Thomas Lynch, Jr., Arthur Middleton, Edward Rutledge

VIRGINIA: Carter Braxton, Benjamin Harrison, Thomas Jefferson, Francis Lightfoot Lee, Richard Henry Lee, Thomas Nelson, Jr., George Wythe

2. FRAMERS OF THE CONSTITUTION
   (BY STATE DELEGATIONS; ASTERISKS
   DENOTE SIGNERS)

CONNECTICUT: Oliver Ellsworth, William Samuel Johnson,* Roger Sherman*

DELAWARE: Richard Bassett,* Gunning Bedford Jr.,* Jacob Broome,* John Dickinson,* George Read*

GEORGIA: Abraham Baldwin,* William Few,* William Houstoun, William L. Pierce

MARYLAND: Daniel Carroll,* Daniel of St. Thomas Jenifer,* Luther Martin, James McHenry,* John Francis Mercer

MASSACHUSETTS: Elbridge Gerry, Nathaniel Gorham,* Rufus King,* Caleb Strong

NEW HAMPSHIRE: Nicholas Gilman,* John Langdon*

NEW JERSEY: David Brearly,* Jonathan Dayton,* William Churchill Houston, William Livingston,* William Paterson*

NEW YORK: Alexander Hamilton,* John Lansing, Jr., Robert Yates

NORTH CAROLINA: William Blount,* William Richardson Davie, Alexander Martin, Richard Dobbs Spaight,* Hugh Williamson*

PENNSYLVANIA: George Clymer,* Thomas Fitzsimons,* Benjamin Franklin,* Jared Ingersoll,* Thomas Mifflin,* Gouverneur Morris,* Robert Morris,* James Wilson*

SOUTH CAROLINA: Pierce Butler,* Charles Pinckney,* Charles Cotesworth Pinckney,* John Rutledge*

VIRGINIA: John Blair,* James Madison, Jr.,* George Mason, James McClurg, Edmund J. Randolph, George Washington,* George Wythe

3. OTHER FOUNDING FATHERS (AND MOTHERS)

Abigail Adams, wife of John Adams

John Quincy Adams, diplomat, U.S. senator from Massachusetts, secretary of state, president of the United States, U.S. representative from Massachusetts

Ethan Allen, war leader, founder of Vermont

Aaron Burr, war leader, U.S. senator from New York, New York attorney-general, vice president of the United States

George Clinton, war leader, governor of New York, vice president of the United States

Patrick Henry, lawyer, Virginia legislator, governor of Virginia

James Iredell, attorney, North Carolina legislator, associate justice of U.S. Supreme Court

John Jay, delegate to Continental Congress, president of Congress, diplomat, Confederation's Secretary for Foreign Affairs, first chief justice of the United States, governor of New York

Henry Knox, war leader, secretary of war

Henry Laurens, South Carolina legislator, delegate to Continental Congress, diplomat

William Maclay, Pennsylvania legislator, U.S. senator

John Marshall, diplomat, Virginia legislator, U.S. representative and secretary of state, fourth chief justice of the United States

James Monroe, war leader, Virginia legislator, U.S. senator, diplomat, governor of Virginia, secretary of war, secretary of state, president of the United States

Thomas Paine, pamphleteer

Mercy Otis Warren, author, pamphleteer, historian

Acknowledgments

THIS BOOK, THOUGH THE SHORTEST I HAVE written, was among the hardest to write. For this reason, I am even more grateful to those who have helped me along the way. I absolve them from any mistakes, errors of judgment, and wackosity remaining in these pages.

My first debts are to my mother, Marilyn Bernstein, and my brother, Steven J. Bernstein, and to the memories of my father, Fred Bernstein (1922–2001), and my sister, Linda A. Bernstein (1958–2004). Close behind those debts are those to my mentors, Henry Steele Commager (1902–1998) and Richard B. Morris (1904–1989). This book's title draws inspiration from Professor Morris's *The American Revolution Reconsidered* (New York: Harper & Row, 1967)—itself a response to J. Franklin Jameson's classic *The American Revolution Considered as a Social Movement* (Princeton, NJ: Princeton University Press, 1922).

Nancy E. Toff, my peerless editor at Oxford University Press, showed superhuman patience with me and provided the right mix of faith, encouragement, and gentle goading to get the book done. Its genesis came from an idle suggestion that I made to her, her swift recognition that there was more to the idea than I had realized, and her determination to see me—and make me, as needed—live up to the idea's possibilities. Many thanks also to her colleagues at Oxford—her assistant, Leora Bersohn; production editor Joellyn Ausanka; copy editor Arline Keithe; Rachel Perkins, who designed the book; and Jack Donner, who designed the section of photographs.

As this book's dedication testifies, I am also indebted to the New York University Legal History Colloquium, a group founded by Professor William E. Nelson of New York University School of Law in 1981 and presided over by him ever since. In 2005, Professor Daniel J. Hulsebosch became the Colloquium's co-presider. Bill and Dan have raised a standard to which the wise and honest of the fields of legal and constitutional history have always been able to repair. The Colloquium fosters rigorous inquiry, collegiality, and good humor— qualities that make the writing of history far less lonely and perilous. As the Colloquium's analogue to Benjamin Franklin, Professor John Phillip Reid has provided his own unique form of inspiration, both in his scholarship and in his sardonic deflating of pretension.* I have been a member of the Colloquium since 1983 and often have benefited from its vigorous, yet good-humored critiques. Other members of the Colloquium whose supportive and cogent comments aided me include J. H. Baker, Felice Batlan, Harold Forsythe (and his wife, Debra Jackson), Carla Spivack, Bernard Freamon, Deborah Malamud, James Oldham, Risa Goluboff, and Maribel Morey. In 2007–2008, Christopher Beauchamp, Sophia Z. Lee, and Gautham Rao, that year's Samuel I. Golieb Fellows at NYU Law School, were energetic and indispensable participants in the Colloquium. I found them especially insightful, constructively critical, and always encouraging. I greet them at the beginning of great careers.

Professor Joanne B. Freeman of Yale University and I have been talking and writing about the "founding guys" for more

---

*In addition, Professor Reid has put me in his debt by sharing his discovery of a previously unpublished manuscript by Franklin Pierce seeking to explain why New Hampshirites among the founding fathers deserve more respect and veneration than they receive.

than two decades, and I remain deeply grateful to her for enriching my understanding, as any careful student of this book's notes will find. (And thanks to Boo, the world's greatest birdie-buddy.) Joanne's mentor, Professor Peter S. Onuf, the Thomas Jefferson Foundation Professor of History at the University of Virginia, continues to be "mentor from heaven" (Joanne's phrase) to us all. In 2008, Peter organized the 2008 University of Virginia Jefferson Symposium in which he, Joanne, Professor David Thomas Konig of Washington University–St. Louis, and I addressed the topic "Thomas Jefferson: Friends and Foes." That creative, tumultuous symposium helped to teach me a great deal about the interactions both among the founding fathers and between them and posterity. I thank not just my fellow faculty members but also those who enrolled in the symposium and always kept us on our toes.

As Professor Charles L. Zelden of Nova Southeastern University, my scholarly brother, finished his landmark study of *Bush v. Gore* and the hidden crisis of American democracy, he managed to find time to read over my shoulder and to tell me where I was going right and where I was going wrong. Though he disclaims any expertise in early American history, he is an ideal reader, colleague, and friend. Charles also arranged for me to give a lecture at Nova titled "The Constitution as an Exploding Cigar," pieces of which found their way into chapters 3 and 4 of this book. So, too, another faithful friend and colleague, Professor Carla Spivack of Oklahoma City University Law School, arranged for me to give a faculty workshop presentation on that theme and a more formal lecture on the role of John Adams as a founding father. Assistant Dean Carol Buckler and Victoria Eastus of New York Law School arranged for me to give New York Law School's 2008 Constitution Day lecture and invited me to take part in the 2008 Faculty Presentation Day, where I presented and discussed some of the material appearing in chapters 1 and 4 of this book.

Margaret Klein, a good friend and widow of another good friend, the eminent historian Milton M. Klein of the University of Tennessee at Knoxville, proposed that I give the 2008 Milton

M. Klein Lecture at the University of Tennessee on the theme "How John Adams Became a Founding Father," portions of which helped to flesh out this book. I am indebted to her and to the University's History Department, especially Professor Robert Morrissey, for their kindness and collegiality.

Special thanks to Professor Annette Gordon-Reed of New York Law School and Rutgers University–Newark, treasured friend and colleague, whose work on Thomas Jefferson, Sally Hemings, the Hemings family, and their meaning in American history has done so much to transform our understandings of the American past and of the thorny and complex relationship between past and present. So also to Professor Felice J. Batlan of Chicago-Kent Law School, who has always had more faith in my work than I've had and whose own work on legal thought and social reform in the late nineteenth and early twentieth centuries sets a standard that I try to meet in mine; to Marian Angeles Ahumada Ruiz, deputy director of the Center for Political and Constitutional Studies in Madrid and professor of constitutional law at the Universidad Autónoma de Madrid Law Faculty, who always reminds me of the global context of the history I work on; and to George Athan Billias, professor emeritus of history at Clark University, and his wife, Margaret, for their unstinting support, encouragement, and friendship.

Peter Gibbon of Boston University's School of Education invited me to take part in three different teacher institutes on American history, two NEH institutes focusing on Thomas Jefferson and a Teaching American History program dealing with the American Founding. My profound thanks to Peter and his wife, Carol, and to Joan Musbach and Peter Wright, who as master teachers made the Jefferson institutes work without a hitch. I also thank the teachers who took part in all three institutes; their work on the "front lines" helps those of us in academia understand what we should be doing as scholars and teachers and how we should be doing it.

Once again Gaspare J. Saladino, co-editor of the *Documentary History of the Ratification of the Constitution and the Bill of Rights*, was a sounding board and a wise counselor, as were his colleagues John P. Kaminski and Richard Leffler, and the equally redoubtable team guiding the *Documentary History of the First Federal Congress*: Charlene Bangs Bickford, Kenneth Russell Bowling, Helen E. Veit, and Charles DiGiacomantonio. Many thanks also to the officers of the American Society for Legal History and the board of directors of H-LAW, the legal-history list-serv, with whom I've had the honor and pleasure to work for so long.

I owe a different but equally great debt to the fine actor Paul Giamatti, who in 2007–2008 regularly discussed with me his work in preparing to portray John Adams in the HBO miniseries of that name. His keen and perceptive questions about Adams and his intellectual and political world helped me to see those subjects afresh, and our discussions have contributed significantly not only to this book but to those that will follow.

Since 1991, I have been a member of the adjunct faculty of New York Law School. Under the leadership of Deans James Simon, Harry Wellington, and Richard A. Matasar, New York Law School continues to be a wonderful home for a historian masquerading as a law professor. I also thank valued faculty colleagues, chief among them William P. LaPiana, who first proposed me to the school and has always been my intellectual and academic rabbi; Edward A. Purcell, Jr., for his scholarly example and his incarnation of collegiality; Annette Gordon-Reed; Ruti Teitel; and many others. I also am grateful to the New York Law School's Mendik Library, its former director, Joyce Saltalamacchia, and her successor, Camille Broussard, and the many fine people there who make historical and legal scholarship possible, including William Mills, Michael McCarthy, Joseph Molinari, Paul Mastrangelo, and Grace Lee. And I am grateful to all the students who have taken a chance on one or another of my courses and have made sure that I not only teach but learn every time I walk into a classroom.

My friends, the "usual suspects" in my life, have never stinted in their insight, encouragement, and patience: Marilee B. Huntoon; Phillip A. Haultcoeur; Maralyn Lowenheim; Maureen K. Phillips and Joseph Newpol; Kathleen E. Spencer and Andrew McLean and their son, Aidan; Nathan D. Spencer and Jennifer McLean and their sons, Evan and Morgan; the documentarians *extraordinaire* Ron Blumer and Muffie Meyer and their daughter, Emma; April Holder and Michelle Waites; Kevin Griffin and Elissa Wynn; Michael A. Bellesiles; Shalom Doron, Esq.; Edward D. Young III, his wife, Gina Tillman-Young, and their children, Christa, Adam, Noah, Luke, Mary Maya, Peter, and Moses; Molly Myers and Hasan Rizvi and their son, Zane; and Internet friends Karen Spisak, Natalie D. Brown, Patrick Fiegenbaum, Marion Pavan, Robert K. Folkner, Philip Whitford, Tony Palumbo, Cynthia E. Nowak, and Kevin J. Hutchison.

Two friends did not live to see this book—the late Ron Carter, whose fine historical novels spanning the era from the American Revolution through the War of 1812 I read in manuscript, and the late Emil J. Lugo, one of the best teachers New York City's Stuyvesant High School ever had. Their memories always will be blessings to all who knew them.

The Sgantzos family—Victor, Helen, Mark, and Harry—run Clark's Restaurant in Brooklyn Heights, with the aid of Cesar Rendon, Miguel Bravo, Juan Perez, and Tommy Laoutas. The warm, friendly atmosphere of Clark's, a Brooklyn landmark, helped to bring this book into being in ways beyond listing.

As always, new books cannot be written without a steady supply of old books. Thanks therefore to John Carlberg, Mark Toneff, Theresa Buchheister, Hannah Messler, and Edward Sutton, and their former colleagues Brian Kleppin and Damien Cote, of the Strand Bookstore, a New York landmark for more than eighty years.

Finally, yet again I am grateful to Heights Books, Inc., and the wonderful people who work there, for all their support and generosity as I struggled to finish this book: Ned Futterman, Stanley Fogel, James Leopard, Robert E. Bullock, Darcy Sharon, Evan Walker-Wells, and above all Tracy M. Walsch, boss lady, trusted friend, and the best Shakespearean co-teacher any Law and Literature professor could have. (And thanks, George.)

Notes

1. Words, Images, Meanings

1. "Pomp and Circumstance," in Sandra Beasley, compiler, "Works in Progress," *American Scholar* 75:3 (Summer 2006): 12–16 (quote at 16).

2. "Harding Nominates Taft," *New York Times*, 23 June 1912, page 2 (viewed online May 25, 2008). I have not been able to locate an earlier use of this phrase or its early variant, whether by Harding or by anyone else.

3. William Safire, *Safire's Political Dictionary*, updated and expanded edition (New York: Oxford University Press, 2008), 260. Safire identifies the television writer as Richard Hanser. He also suggests that the phrase's first appearance was in a book by the New York attorney and popular historian Kenneth M. Umbreit, *Founding Fathers: Men Who Shaped Our Tradition* (New York: Harper & Brothers, 1941); however, Safire was misled by an erroneous citation in the *Oxford English Dictionary* giving the publication date of Umbreit's still valuable book as 1914 rather than 1941. Safire correctly notes that Harding, who tended to favor alliteration in his speeches, may have found this phrase irresistible, though the record now suggests that Harding coined it rather than merely popularizing it. Safire's landmark work is the source of the quotations for Harding's 1918 and 1921 speeches. For his 1920 acceptance speech, I used the version posted online by the *Wall Street Journal*: http://online.wsj. com/article_print/SB118971877847426817.html (viewed online 28 March 2008). In that speech, Harding assured his audience, "It was the intent of the founding fathers to give to this Republic a dependable and enduring popular government, representative in form, and it was designed to make political parties, not only the preserving sponsors, but the effective agencies

through which hopes and aspirations and convictions and conscience may be translated into public performance." He then mused, "I like to think there is something more than the patriotism and practical wisdom of the founding fathers. It is good to believe that maybe destiny held this New World Republic to be the supreme example of representative democracy and orderly liberty by which humanity is inspired to higher achievement." Oddly enough in 1921, the historian and documentary editor Max Farrand, famed for his authoritative *Records of the Federal Convention of 1787*, 3 vols. (New Haven, CT: Yale University Press, 1911; reissue, with a new fourth volume, 1937; reissue, with revised *Supplement* edited by James H. Hutson, 1987), and his *Framing of the Constitution of the United States* (New Haven, CT: Yale University Press, 1913), published a volume in the popular *Chronicles of America* series that Allen Johnson edited for Yale University Press that came close to but did not quite dock with Harding's coinage: Max Farrand, *The Fathers of the Constitution* (New Haven, CT: Yale University Press, 1921).

4. A sampling of the most important recent works includes: Gordon S. Wood, *Revolutionary Characters: What Made the Founding Fathers Different* (New York: Penguin Press, 2006); Joseph J. Ellis, *Founding Brothers: The Revolutionary Generation* (New York: Alfred A. Knopf, 2000); Joseph J. Ellis, *American Creation: Triumphs and Tragedies of the Founding of the Republic* (New York: Alfred A. Knopf, 2007); Bernard Bailyn, *Faces of Revolution: Personalities and Themes in the Struggle for Independence* (New York: Alfred A. Knopf, 1990); and Bernard Bailyn, *To Begin the World Anew: The Genius and the Ambiguities of the American Founders* (New York: Alfred A. Knopf, 2003). See also John P. Kaminski, ed., *The Founders on the Founders: Word Portraits from the American Revolutionary Era* (Charlottesville: University of Virginia Press, 2008).

5. Richard B. Morris, *Seven Who Shaped Our Destiny: The Founding Fathers as Revolutionaries* (New York: Harper & Row, 1973), passim.

6. Gary B. Nash, *The Unknown Revolution: The Unruly Birth of Democracy and the Struggle to Create America* (New York: Viking Press, 2005); Ray Raphael, *The First American Revolution: Before Lexington and Concord* (New York: New Press, 2002); Ray Raphael, *A People's History of the American Revolution: How Common People Shaped the Fight for Independence* (New York: New Press, 2001); Ray Raphael, *Founding Myths: Stories That Hide Our Patriotic Past* (New York: New Press, 2004); Woody Holton, *Unruly Americans and the Origins of the Constitution* (New York: Hill and Wang, 2007).

7. Cokie Roberts, *Founding Mothers: The Women Who Raised Our Nation* (New York: William Morrow, 2004); Cokie Roberts, *Ladies of Liberty: The Women Who Shaped Our Nation* (New York: William Morrow, 2008); Gail Collins, *America's Women: Four Hundred Years of Dolls, Drudges, Helpmates, and Heroines* (New York: William Morrow, 2003); Paul M. Zall, *Founding Mothers: Profiles of Ten Wives of America's Founding Fathers* (Westminster, MD: Heritage Books, 1981). For more scholarly studies, see Linda K. Kerber, *Women of the Republic:*

Intellect and Ideology in Revolutionary America (Chapel Hill: University of North Carolina Press for Institute of Early American History and Culture, 1980); Mary Beth Norton, *Liberty's Daughters: The Revolutionary Experience of American Women, 1750–1800* (Boston: Little, Brown and Company, 1980; reprint with new preface, Ithaca, NY: Cornell University Press, 1996); Carol Berkin, *First Generations: Women in Colonial America* (New York: Hill and Wang, 1996); Carol Berkin, *Revolutionary Mothers: Women in the Struggle for America's Independence* (New York: Alfred A. Knopf, 2005).

8. Francis J. Bremer, *John Winthrop: America's Forgotten Founding Father* (New York: Oxford University Press, 2003); Karl Campbell, *Senator Sam Ervin, Last of the Founding Fathers* (Chapel Hill: University of North Carolina Press, 2007); Stephen Frantzwich, *Founding Father: How C-SPAN's Brian Lamb Changed Politics in America* (Lanham, MD: Rowman & Littlefield, 2008).

9. Jeff Broadwater, *George Mason: Forgotten Founder* (Charlottesville: University Press of Virginia, 2006); Marty D. Mathews, *Forgotten Founder: The Life of Charles Pinckney* (Columbia: University of South Carolina Press, 2004); Jeffry H. Morrison, *John Witherspoon and the Founding of the American Republic* (Notre Dame, IN: Notre Dame University Press, 2005); Joseph A. Murray, *Alexander Hamilton: America's Forgotten Founder* (New York: Algora Publishing, 2007); and Nancy Isenberg, *Fallen Founder: The Life of Aaron Burr* (New York: Viking Press, 2007). For a book addressed to a popular audience, see Kenneth C. Davis, *America's Hidden History: Untold Tales of the First Pilgrims, Fighting Women, and Forgotten Founders Who Shaped a Nation* (New York: Collins, 2008).

10. On Native Americans, one study that has become the focus of scholarly and political controversy is Donald A. Grinde, Jr., and Bruce E. Johansen, *Exemplar of Liberty: Native America and the Evolution of Democracy* (Los Angeles: Native American Studies Center, University of California, Los Angeles, 1991). See also Bruce E. Johansen, *Forgotten Founders: How the American Indian Helped Shape Democracy* (Cambridge, MA: Harvard Common Press, 1987), and Jack C. Weatherford, *Indian Givers: How the Indians of America Transformed the World* (New York: Crown Publishers, 1988). For a valuable scholarly forum, see "Forum on the Iroquois Influence Thesis," *William and Mary Quarterly*, 3rd series, 33 (July 1996): 587–636. For other valuable perspectives, see Colin G. Calloway, *The American Revolution in Indian Country: Crisis and Diversity in Native American Communities* (Cambridge and New York: Cambridge University Press, 1995); Barbara Graymont, *The Iroquois in the American Revolution* (Syracuse, NY: Syracuse University Press, 1972); and Alan R. Taylor, *The Divided Ground: Indians, Settlers, and the Northern Borderland of the American Revolution* (New York: Alfred A. Knopf, 2006). On African Americans, see Richard S. Newman, *Freedom's Prophet: Bishop Richard Allen, the AME Church, and the Black Founding Fathers* (New York: New York University Press, 2008); Sylvia R. Frey, *Water from the Rock: Black Resistance in a Revolutionary Age* (Princeton, NJ: Princeton University Press,

1991); and Gary B. Nash, *The Forgotten Fifth: African Americans in the Struggle for Revolution* (Cambridge, MA: Harvard University Press, 2006). For an interesting comparative study, see Woody Holton, *Forced Founders: Indians, Debtors, Slaves, and the Making of the American Revolution in Colonial Virginia* (Chapel Hill: University of North Carolina Press for the Omohundro Institute of Early American History and Culture, 1999).

11. See T. C. W. Blanning, *The Culture of Power and the Power of Culture: Old Regime Eirope, 1660–1789* (Oxford: Clarendon Press, 2002); Tim Blanning, *The Pursuit of Glory: Europe 1648–1815* (New York: Viking, 2007); and R. R. Palmer, *The Age of the Democratic Revolution: A Political History of Europe and America*, 2 vols. (Princeton, NJ: Princeton University Press, 1959, 1964).

12. Robert A. McGuire, *To Form a More Perfect Union: A New Economic Interpretation of the United States Constitution* (New York: Oxford University Press, 2003); Holton, *Unruly Americans and the Origins of the Constitution*; Terry Bouton, *Taming Democracy: "The People," the Founders, and the Troubled Ending of the American Revolution* (New York: Oxford University Press, 2007); and see also the books cited in note 6.

13. John Adams to James Lloyd, 29 March 1815, in Charles Francis Adams, ed., *The Works of John Adams*...(Boston: Little, Brown and Company, 1850–1856), 10: 146–49 (quote at 149).

14. Seymour Martin Lipset, *The First New Nation: The United States in Historical and Comparative Perspective* (New York: Basic Books, 1963; new edition, New Brunswick, NJ: Transaction Publishers, 2003), passim. On civil religion, see generally Russell E. Richey and Donald G. Jones, eds., *American Civil Religion* (New York: Harper & Row, 1974). For another study taking seriously the creation of American national identity as a core component of the American founding, see Richard B. Bernstein with Kym S. Rice, *Are We to Be a Nation? The Making of the Constitution* (Cambridge, MA: Harvard University Press, 1987).

15. Here the work of Michael Kammen is of exceptional value: Michael Kammen, *A Machine That Would Go of Itself: The Constitution in American Culture* (New York: Alfred A. Knopf, 1986; new edition, with new introduction, New Brunswick, NJ: Transaction Publishers, 2006); Michael Kammen, *Mystic Chords of Memory: The Transformation of Tradition in American Culture* (New York: Alfred A. Knopf, 1991); Michael Kammen, *A Season of Youth: The American Revolution and the Historical Imagination* (New York: Alfred A. Knopf, 1978).

16. The literary historian and critic Van Wyck Brooks coined the phrase in an important article in 1918: Van Wyck Brooks, "On Creating a Usable Past," *The Dial* 64 (April 11, 1918): 337–41. For a valuable and eloquent series of meditations on this theme, see Henry Steele Commager, *The Search for a Usable Past and Other Essays in Historiography* (New York: Alfred A. Knopf, 1966). Recent work by David Lowenthal is also of

value on this subject: David Lowenthal, *The Past Is a Foreign Country* (Cambridge and New York: Cambridge University Press, 1986); David Lowenthal, *Possessed by the Past: The Heritage Crusade and the Spoils of History* (New York: Free Press, 1996; paperback edition under the title *The Heritage Crusade and the Spoils of History,* Cambridge and New York: Cambridge University Press, 1998).

17. John Dos Passos, *The Ground We Stand On: Some Examples from the History of a Political Creed* (New York: Harcourt, Brace, and Company, 1941), 3.

18. For a vigorous analysis of this point, see Nicholas Guyatt, "Father Knows Best" [review of Gordon S. Wood, *Revolutionary Characters*], *The Nation,* 9 October 2006, at 29–33.

19. Richard B. Morris, *The Emerging Nations and the American Revolution* (New York: Harper & Row, 1970); Timothy Garton Ash, *We the People: The Revolutions of '89 as Witnessed in Warsaw, Budapest, Berlin and Prague* (Cambridge, England: Granta Books, 1990). Ironically, the American edition of this book deleted the British edition's American references and changed its title accordingly: Timothy Garton Ash, *The Magic Lantern* (New York: Random House, 1990).

2. Contexts

1. A superb examination of how the delegates to the Second Continental Congress strove to keep pace with but not to get too far in front of the people's developing sentiment for independence is Pauline Maier, *American Scripture: Making the Declaration of Independence* (New York: Alfred A. Knopf, 1997; Vintage paperback, 1998).

2. On Franklin, the leading modern biographies are Edmund S. Morgan, *Benjamin Franklin* (New Haven, CT: Yale University Press, 2002); Gordon S. Wood, *The Americanization of Benjamin Franklin* (New York: Penguin Press, 2004); Walter Isaacson, *Benjamin Franklin: An American Life* (New York: Simon and Schuster, 2005); H. W. Brands, *The First American: The Life and Times of Benjamin Franklin* (New York: Doubleday, 2000); and James Campbell, *Rediscovering Benjamin Franklin* (La Salle, IL: Open Court, 1998). The best older biographies are Carl Van Doren, *Benjamin Franklin* (New York: Viking Press, 1938) and Esmond Wright, *Franklin of Philadelphia* (Cambridge, MA: Belknap Press of Harvard University Press, 1986). See also J. A. Leo LeMay, ed., *Benjamin Franklin: Writings* (New York: Library of America, 1987).

3. See the accounts in Van Doren, *Benjamin Franklin,* 336–55 (giving extensive extracts from the testimony); Brands, *The First American,* 373–76; and Wood, *Americanization,* 117–20. For a British perspective, see P. D. G. Thomas, *British Politics and the Stamp Act Crisis: The First Phase of the American Revolution 1763–1767* (Oxford: Clarendon Press, 1975).

4. See, e.g., Marcus Cunliffe, *George Washington: Man and Monument* (Boston: Little, Brown, 1958, and many later reprintings); John Rhodehamel, *The Great Experiment: George Washington and the American Republic* (New Haven, CT, and San Marino, CA: Yale University Press/Huntington Library, 1998); Robert F. Jones, *George Washington: Ordinary Man, Extraordinary Leader* (New York: Fordham University Press, 2002); John Rhodehamel, ed., *George Washington: Writings* (New York: Library of America, 1997); Glenn A. Phelps, *George Washington and American Constitutionalism* (Lawrence: University Press of Kansas, 1993); Garry Wills, *Cincinnatus: George Washington and the Enlightenment* (New York: Doubleday, 1984); John E. Ferling, *The First of Men: A Life of George Washington* (Knoxville: University of Tennessee Press, 1991); and Joseph J. Ellis, *His Excellency: George Washington* (New York: Alfred A. Knopf, 2004).

5. James Grant, *John Adams, Party of One* (New York: Farrar, Straus, & Giroux, 2005); Peter Shaw, *The Character of John* Adams (Chapel Hill: University of North Carolina Press for Institute of Early American History and Culture, 1975); Page Smith, *John Adams*, 2 vols. (Garden City, NY: Doubleday, 1961); Joseph J. Ellis, *Passionate Sage: The Character and Legacy of John Adams* (New York: W. W. Norton, 1992); Gilbert Chinard, *Honest John Adams* (Boston: Little, Brown, 1935; reprint ed., Gloucester, MA: Peter Smith, 1965); and David McCullough, *John Adams* (New York: Simon and Schuster, 2001).

6. Dumas Malone, *Jefferson and His Time,* 6 vols. (Boston: Little, Brown, 1948–1981); Merrill D. Peterson, *Thomas Jefferson and the New Nation* (New York: Oxford University Press, 1971); and R. B. Bernstein, *Thomas Jefferson* (New York: Oxford University Press, 2003).

7. Walter Stahr, *John Jay: Founding Father* (New York: Hambledon and London, 2005); Richard B. Morris, *John Jay, the Nation, and the Court* (Boston: Boston University Press, 1956); and Frank Monaghan, *John Jay*...(Indianapolis, IN: Bobbs-Merrill, 1937).

8. Jack N. Rakove, *James Madison and the Creation of the American Republic*, 3rd ed. (New York: Pearson Putnam, 2007); Irving N. Brant, *James Madison*, 6 vols. (Indianapolis, IN, and New York: Bobbs-Merrill, 1941–1961); Ralph Ketcham, *James Madison* (New York: Macmillan, 1971; reprint, Charlottesville: University Press of Virginia, 1998); Drew R. McCoy, *The Last of the Fathers: James Madison and the Republican Legacy* (Cambridge and New York: Cambridge University Press, 1989); and Trevor Colbourn, ed., *Fame and the Founding Fathers: Essays of Douglas Adair* (New York: W. W. Norton for the Institute of Early American History and Culture, 1974; reprint ed., Indianapolis, IN: Liberty Fund, 1998). See also Jack N. Rakove, ed., *James Madison: Writings* (New York: Library of America, 1999).

9. Broadus Mitchell, *Alexander Hamilton*, 2 vols. (New York: Macmillan, 1957, 1962); John C. Miller, *Alexander Hamilton: Portrait in Paradox* (New York:

Harper, 1958); Joanne B. Freeman, ed., *Alexander Hamilton: Writings* (New York: Library of America, 2001); and Ron Chernow, *Alexander Hamilton* (New York: Penguin Press, 2004).

10. The best study is Wood, *Americanization*.

11. The phrase is from Thomas Jefferson's first inaugural address, delivered on March 4, 1801.

12. See J. H. Elliott, *Empires of the Atlantic World: Britain and Spain in America, 1492–1830* (New Haven, CT: Yale University Press, 2006).

13. Colin Bonwick, *The American Revolution* (Charlottesville: University Press of Virginia, 1991), 31–55; E. J. Perkins, *The Economy of Colonial America* (New York: Columbia University Press, 1980); Jacob E. Cooke, *Tench Coxe and the Early Republic* (Chapel Hill: University of North Carolina Press for the Institute of Early American History and Culture, 1978).

14. Patricia U. Bonomi, *Under the Cope of Heaven: Religion, Society, and Politics in Colonial America*, updated edition (New York: Oxford University Press, 2003).

15. See Alexander Keyssar, *The Right to Vote: The Contested History of Democracy in the United States* (New York: Basic Books, 2000).

16. Thomas J. Curry, *The First Freedoms: Church and State in America to the Passage of the First Amendment* (New York: Oxford University Press, 1986); Forrest Church, *So Help Me God: The Founding Fathers and the First Great Battle over Church and State* (New York: Harcourt, 2007); and Stephen Waldman, *Founding Faith: Providence, Politics, and the Birth of Religious Freedom in America* (New York: Random House, 2008). See generally, for examination of conditions of religious belief, Bonomi, *Under the Cope of Heaven*.

17. Henry Adams, *History of the United States During the Administrations of Thomas Jefferson* (New York: Library of America, 1984), 5.

18. Linda K. Kerber, *Women of the Republic: Intellect and Ideology in Revolutionary America* (Chapel Hill: University of North Carolina Press for Institute of Early American History and Culture, 1980); Mary Beth Norton, *Liberty's Daughters: The Revolutionary Experience of American Women, 1750–1800* (Boston: Little, Brown, 1980; reprint with new preface, Ithaca, NY: Cornell University Press, 1996). For more popular studies, see Cokie Roberts, *Founding Mothers: The Women Who Raised Our Nation* (New York: William Morrow, 2004); Cokie Roberts, *Ladies of Liberty: The Women Who Shaped Our Nation* (New York: William Morrow, 2008); Gail Collins, *America's Women: Four Hundred Years of Dolls, Drudges, Helpmates, and Heroines* (New York: William Morrow, 2003); Paul M. Zall, *Founding Mothers: Profiles of Ten Wives of America's Founding Fathers* (Westminster, MD: Heritage Books, 1981).

19. Edith B. Gelles, *Portia: The World of Abigail Adams* (Bloomington: Indiana University Press, 1991); Edith B. Gelles, *First Thoughts: Life and Letters of Abigail Adams* (New York: Twayne Publishers, 1998); Edith B. Gelles, *Abigail and John: Portrait of a Marriage* (New York: William Morrow, forthcoming 2009).

20. Melvin Patrick Ely, *Israel on the Appomattox: A Southern Experiment in Black Freedom from the 1790s through the Civil War* (New York: Alfred A. Knopf, 2004) (Richard Randolph); Andrew Levy, *The First Emancipator: The Forgotten Story of Robert Carter, the Founding Father Who Freed His Slaves* (New York: Random House, 2005) (Robert Carter). See also Henry Wiencek, *An Imperfect God: George Washington, His Slaves, and the Creation of America* (New York: Farrar Straus Giroux, 2003); Franz Hirschfeld, *George Washington and Slavery: A Documentary Portrayal* (Columbia: University of Missouri Press, 1997); and François Furstenberg, *In the Name of the Father: Washington's Legacy, Slavery, and the Making of a Nation* (New York: Penguin Press, 2006). See also Annette Gordon-Reed, *The Hemingses of Monticello* (New York: W. W. Norton, 2008); Annette Gordon-Reed, *Thomas Jefferson and Sally Hemings: An American Controversy* (Charlottesville: University Press of Virginia, 1997).

21. Henry Louis Gates, Jr., *The Trials of Phillis Wheatley* (New York: Basic Civitas Books, 2003).

22. Thomas Jefferson (William Peden, ed.), *Notes on the State of Virginia* (Chapel Hill: University of North Carolina Press for the Institute of Early American History and Culture, 1955), esp. Query XVIII, "Manners," and compare Query XIV, "Laws." See the valuable discussion in Winthrop D. Jordan, *White Over Black: American Attitudes Toward the Negro, 1550–1812* (Chapel Hill: University of North Carolina Press for the Institute of Early American History and Culture, 1968), chapter 12. See also Charles A. Miller, *Jefferson and Nature: An Interpretation* (Baltimore: Johns Hopkins University Press, 1993), 56–87. For context, see Emmanuel Chukwudi Eze, ed., *Race and the Enlightenment: A Reader* (Cambridge, MA, and Oxford: Blackwell Publishers, 1997). For a terse summary, see R. B. Bernstein, *Thomas Jefferson* (New York: Oxford University Press, 2003), 61–62.

23. George Washington to Bryan Fairfax, 24 August 1774, in John C. Fitzpatrick, ed., *The Writings of George Washington* (Washington, DC: U.S. Government Printing Office, 1931–1944) [40 vols.], 3: 242. I found this quotation in a passionate and suggestive article, F. Nwabueze Okoye, "Chattel Slavery as the Nightmare of the American Revolutionaries," *William and Mary Quarterly,* 3rd series, 37:1 (January 1980): 4–28 (quote at 12 and note 45).

24. Samuel Johnson, *Taxation No Tyranny...*(1775), reprinted in Samuel Johnson (Arthur Murphy, ed.), *The Works of Samuel Johnson, LL.D., with an Essay on His Life and Genius* ("First Complete American Edition"), 2 vols. (New York: Alexander V. Blake, 1843), 2: 429–38 (quote at 437, col. 2).

25. Colin G. Calloway, *The American Revolution in Indian Country: Crisis and Diversity in Native American Communities* (Cambridge and New York: Cambridge University Press, 1995), Chapter 1, "The Peace That Brought No Peace"; Richard B. Morris, *The American Revolution Reconsidered* (New York: Harper & Row, 1967), Chapter 3; and Frederick S. Marks III, *Independence on Trial: Foreign Affairs and the Making of the Constitution* (Baton Rouge: Louisiana State University Press, 1973), passim.

26. Calloway, *American Revolution in Indian Country*.

27. Richard B. Morris, *The Forging of the Union, 1781–1789* (New York: Harper & Row, 1987), 162, and also see 162–93.

28. On this war, see Fred Anderson, *Crucible of War; The Seven Years' War and the Fate of Empire in British North America* (New York: Alfred A. Knopf, 2000). Anderson has also published an abridged version: Fred Anderson, *The War That Made America: A Short History of the French and Indian War* (New York: Viking, 2005).

29. Austin Woolrych, *Britain in Revolution, 1625–1660* (Oxford: Oxford University Press, 2002); Tim Harris, *Restoration: Charles II and His Kingdoms, 1660–1685* (London: Allen Lane, 2005); Tim Harris, *Revolution: The Great Crisis of the British Monarchy, 1685–1720* (London: Allen Lane, 2006); and J. H. Plumb, *The Growth of Political Stability in England, 1675–1725* (London: Macmillan, 1967).

30. One classic treatment is J. G. A. Pocock, *The Ancient Constitution and the Feudal Law: English Historical Thought in the Seventeenth Century* (Cambridge: Cambridge University Press, 1957; reprint with new introduction, 1987). For a different perspective, emphasizing the legal context, see the works of John Phillip Reid, in particular, John Phillip Reid, *Constitutional History of the American Revolution*, 4 vols. (Madison: University of Wisconsin Press, 1986–1993; abridged ed., 1995); and John Phillip Reid, *The Concept of Liberty in the Age of the American Revolution* (Chicago: University of Chicago Press, 1988). See also Ellis Sandoz, ed., *The Roots of Liberty: Magna Carta, Ancient Constitution, and the Anglo-American Tradition of Rule of Law* (Indianapolis, IN: Liberty Fund, 2008), passim.

31. Voltaire (Nicholas Cronk, ed.), *Letters Concerning the English Nation* (original ed., 1733; Oxford and New York: Oxford University Press, 1994); Charles Louis Secondat, Baron de Montesquieu (J. Robert Loy, ed./trans.), *The Persian Letters* (New York: Meridian Books, 1961); Charles Louis Secondat, Baron de Montesquieu (Anne M. Cohler, Basia Carolyn Miller, and Harold S. Stone, eds./trans.), *The Spirit of the Laws* (Cambridge: Cambridge University Press, 1989); and Jean Louis de Lolme (David Lieberman, ed./introduction), *The Constitution of England* (original ed., 1771; Indianapolis, IN: Liberty Fund, Inc., 2007).

32. So reports the National Public Radio online guide to the opera: www.npr.org/templates/story/story.php?storyId=9146854 (viewed online December 15, 2008).

33. Edmund S. Morgan and Helen M. Morgan, *The Stamp Act Crisis: Prologue to Revolution* (Chapel Hill: University of North Carolina Press for Institute of Early American History and Culture, 1953, 3rd ed., 1995); Edmund S. Morgan, ed., *Prologue to Revolution: Sources and Documents on the Stamp Act Crisis* (Chapel Hill: University of North Carolina Press for Institute of Early American History and Culture, 1959).

34. John Phillip Reid, *The Concept of Representation in the Age of the American Revolution* (Chicago: University of Chicago Press, 1989); for a still-valuable

older study, see J. R. Pole, *Political Representation in England and the Origins of the American Republic* (Berkeley and Los Angeles: University of California Press, 1966). See also Gordon S. Wood, *Representation in the American Revolution* (Charlottesville: University of Virginia Press, 2008). On the unrepresentative British parliament, see John Cannon, *Parliamentary Reform, 1640–1832* (Cambridge and New York: Cambridge University Press, 1973); and the old classic by Edward Porritt, assisted by Annie G. Porritt, *The Unreformed House of Commons: Parliamentary Representation Before 1832*, 2 vols. (Cambridge: Cambridge University Press, 1903).

35. Reid, *Constitutional History, passim;* John Phillip Reid, *In Defiance of the Law: The Standing-Army Controversy, the Two Constitutions, and the Coming of the American Revolution* (Chapel Hill: University of North Carolina Press, 1981); John Phillip Reid, "Book Review: The Ordeal by Law of Thomas Hutchinson," *New York University Law Review* 49 (October 1974): 593–613, reprinted in Hendrik Hartog, ed., *Law in the American Revolution and the Revolution in the Law* (New York: New York University Press, 1981), 20–45; John Phillip Reid, "The Irrelevance of the Declaration," in Hartog, ed., *Law in the American Revolution*, 46–89.

36. Benjamin Woods Larrabee, *The Boston Tea Party* (New York: Oxford University Press, 1964); Alfred H. Young, *The Shoemaker and the Tea Party: Memory and the American Revolution* (Boston: Beacon Press, 1999).

37. See generally Reid, *Constitutional History: Abridged Edition,* epilogue.

38. Quoted from John Adams to John Jay, 2 June 1785, in Charles Francis Adams, ed., *The Works of John Adams,* 10 vols. (Boston: Little, Brown and Company, 1850–1856), 8: 255–59. This letter reports Adams's account of his presenting credentials to George III as the first American minister to Great Britain; the quotation in the text is from the brief speech he made to the king on that occasion.

39. I. Bernard Cohen, *Benjamin Franklin's Science* (Cambridge, MA: Belknap Press of Harvard University Press, 1990); Joyce Chaplin, *The First Scientific American* (New York: Basic Books, 2007).

40. Michael Brian Schiffer, *Draw the Lightning Down: Benjamin Franklin and Electrical Technology in the Age of Enlightenment* (Berkeley and Los Angeles: University of California Press, 2003); James Delbourgo, *A Most Amazing Scene of Wonders; Electricity and Enlightenment in Early America* (Cambridge, MA: Harvard University Press, 2006); and I. Bernard Cohen, *Benjamin Franklin's Science* (Cambridge, MA: Belknap Press of Harvard University Press, 1990).

41. John Adams, *A Dissertation on the Canon and Feudal Law* (1765), reprinted in C. Bradley Thompson, ed., *The Revolutionary Writings of John Adams* (Indianapolis, IN: Liberty Fund, 2000), 21–35 (quote at 32–33).

42. M. N. S. Sellers, *American Republicanism: Roman Ideology in the United States Constitution* (New York: New York University Press, 1994); Carl J. Richard, *The Founders and the Classics: Greece, Rome, and the American Enlightenment*

(Cambridge; MA: Harvard University Press, 1994); and David J. Bederman, *The Classical Foundations of the American Constitution: Prevailing Wisdom* (Cambridge and New York: Cambridge University Press, 2008). *Contra* Paul A. Rahe, *Republics Ancient and Modern: Classical Republicanism and the American Revolution* (Chapel Hill: University of North Carolina Press, 1992; paperback ed. in 3 volumes with added bibliographies, 1994).

43. In addition to the many works of John Phillip Reid already cited, see James R. Stoner, Jr., *Common Law and Liberal Theory: Coke, Hobbes, and the Origins of American Constitutionalism* (Lawrence: University Press of Kansas, 1992); James R. Stoner, Jr., *Common-Law Liberty: Rethinking American Constitutionalism* (Lawrence: University Press of Kansas, 2003).

44. Donald S. Lutz, *Popular Consent and Popular Control: Whig Political Theory in the Early State Constitutions* (Baton Rouge: Louisiana State University Press, 1980); Donald S. Lutz, *The Origins of American Constitutionalism* (Baton Rouge: Louisiana State University Press, 1988); Donald S. Lutz, *A Preface to American Political Theory* (Lawrence: University Press of Kansas, 1991); and Donald S. Lutz, ed., *Colonial Origins of the American Constitution: A Documentary History* (Indianapolis, IN: Liberty Fund, 1998).

45. J. G. A. Pocock, *The Machiavellian Moment: Florentine Political Thought and the Atlantic Republican Tradition* (Princeton, NJ: Princeton University Press, 1975; 2nd ed., 2003).

46. Forrest McDonald, *Novus Ordo Seclorum: The Intellectual Origins of the Constitution* (Lawrence: University Press of Kansas, 1985); Carl L. Becker, *The Declaration of Independence: A Study in the History of Political Ideas* (New York: Harcourt, Brace, 1922; reprint, with new introduction, New York: Alfred A. Knopf, 1942, and Vintage paperback). On Montesquieu's influence in particular, see Anne M. Cohler, *Montesquieu's Comparative Politics and the Spirit of American Constitutionalism* (Lawrence: University Press of Kansas, 1988), and Paul M. Spurlin, *Montesquieu in America, 1760–1801* (Baton Rouge: Louisiana State University Press, 1940).

47. See, generally, the works cited in note 48 and Richard B. Bernstein with Kym S. Rice, *Are We to Be a Nation? The Making of the Constitution* (Cambridge, MA: Harvard University Press, 1987), Chapter 5.

48. See, generally, Peter Gay, *The Enlightenment: An Interpretation,* 2 vols. (New York: Alfred A. Knopf, 1965, 1970); Roy Porter, *The Creation of the Modern World: The Untold Story of the British Enlightenment* (New York: W. W. Norton, 2000); Jonathan I. Israel, *Radical Enlightenment: Philosophy and the Making of Modernity, 1650–1750* (Oxford: Oxford University Press, 2001), and Jonathan I. Israel, *Enlightenment Contested: Philosophy, Modernity, and the Emancipation of Man* (Oxford: Oxford University Press, 2006) (the first two of a projected three-volume history of the radical Enlightenment in Europe); Henry F. May, *The Enlightenment in America* (New York: Oxford University Press, 1976); Robert Ferguson, *The American Enlightenment, 1750–1820* (Cambridge,

MA: Harvard University Press, 1997); and Darren F. Staloff, *Hamilton, Adams, Jefferson: The Politics of Enlightenment and the American Founding* (New York: Hill & Wang, 2005). My work has been influenced above all by Henry Steele Commager, *Jefferson, Nationalism, and the Enlightenment* (New York: George Braziller, 1975), and Henry Steele Commager, *The Empire of Reason: How Europe Imagined and America Realized the Enlightenment* (New York: Anchor Press/Doubleday, 1977).

49. Porter, *Creation of the Modern World*, passim; Jenny Uglow, *The Lunar Men: Five Friends Whose Curiosity Changed the World* (New York: Farrar, Straus & Giroux, 2002), passim.

50. On Newton, see Richard N. Westfall, *Never at Rest: The Life of Isaac Newton* (Cambridge and New York: Cambridge University Press, 1980); Peter Ackroyd, *Newton* (New York: Nan A. Talese/Doubleday, 2008); Robert Iliffe, *Newton: A Very Short Introduction* (Oxford and New York: Oxford University Press, 2007); Patricia Fara, *Newton: The Making of Genius* (New York: Columbia University Press, 2002); and Mordechai Feingold, *The Newtonian Moment: Isaac Newton and the Making of Modern Culture* (New York: Oxford University Press, 2004).

51. Alexander Pope, "Epitaph. Intended for Sir Isaac Newton, in Westminster Abbey" (written and published 1730) in Alexander Pope (John Butt, ed.), *The Poems of Alexander Pope: A Reduced Version of the Twickenham Text* (New Haven, CT: Yale University Press, 1963), 808.

52. Philipp Blom, *Encyclopedie: The Triumph of Reason in an Unreasonable Age* (London: Fourth Estate, 2004); Robert Darnton, *The Business of Enlightenment: A Publishing History of the Encyclopedie, 1775–1800* (Cambridge, MA: Belknap Press of Harvard University Press, 1979).

53. See the appendix to Commager, *Empire of Reason,* on the definition of the term *philosophe.*

54. For an interesting exploration of this theme, see Staloff, *Hamilton, Adams, Jefferson.*

55. For a symposium pursuing this line of inquiry, see Roy Porter and Mikulas Teich, eds., *The Enlightenment in National Context* (Cambridge and New York: Cambridge University Press, 1981). For applications of this inquiry to specific nations, see, e.g., Porter, *Creation of the Modern World*, and Daniel Roche (Arthur Goldhammer, trans.), *France in the Enlightenment* (Cambridge, MA: Harvard University Press, 1998).

56. See generally the valuable books by Robert A. Ferguson, *Law and Letters in American Culture* (Cambridge, MA: Harvard University Press, 1984); Ferguson, *American Enlightenment*; and Robert A. Ferguson, *Reading the Early Republic* (Cambridge, MA: Harvard University Press, 2004).

57. Noah Webster first used the phrase in his 1787 pamphlet *An Examination into the Leading Principles of the Federal Constitution* (Philadelphia, 1787).

3. Achievements and Challenges

1. James Madison, *The Federalist No. 14*, in Alexander Hamilton, James Madison, and John Jay (Jacob E. Cooke, ed.), *The Federalist* (Middletown, CT: Wesleyan University Press, 1961), 83–89 (quote at 88). Cited hereafter as *The Federalist*, with page numbers.

2. Alexander Hamilton, *The Federalist No. 1*, in *The Federalist*, 1.

3. See the valuable monograph by David J. Siemers, *Ratifying the Republic: Federalists and Antifederalists in Constitutional Time* (Stanford, CA: Stanford University Press, 2004); see also Joanne B. Freeman, *Affairs of Honor: National Politics in the New Republic* (New Haven, CT: Yale University Press, 2001), ch. 1.

4. See generally Pauline Maier, *From Resistance to Revolution: Colonial Radicals and the Development of American Opposition to Britain, 1765–1776* (New York: Alfred A. Knopf, 1973).

5. The best studies are David Hackett Fischer, *Washington's Crossing* (New York: Oxford University Press, 2004); John E. Ferling, *Almost a Miracle: The American Victory in the War for Independence* (New York: Oxford University Press, 2007). See also Charles Royster, *A Revolutionary People at War: The Continental Army and American Character, 1775–1783* (Chapel Hill: University of North Carolina Press for the Institute of Early American History and Culture, 1979).

6. See generally Barry Schwartz, *George Washington: The Making of an American Symbol* (New York: Free Press/Macmillan, 1987).

7. The best treatment of this theme is Garry Wills, *Cincinnatus: George Washington and the Enlightenment* (New York: Doubleday, 1984).

8. The leading study, which needs updating, is Louise Burnham Dunbar, *A Study of "Monarchical" Tendencies in the United States from 1776 to 1801* (Urbana: University of Illinois, 1922; reprint ed., Chicago: Johnson Reprint Corporation, 1970). Dunbar, 82, quotes this report, giving her sources as *Pennsylvania Journal*, August 22, 1787, quoted in Max Farrand, ed., *The Records of the Federal Convention of 1787* (New Haven, CT: Yale University Press, 1911), 3: 73–74. The same item appeared in the *Pennsylvania Packet*, August 3, 1787, quoted in Farrand, *Records*, 3: 3.

9. On Lee, see J. Kent McGaughy, *Richard Henry Lee: A Portrait of an American Revolutionary* (Lanham, MD: Rowman & Littlefield, 2004).

10. The three best studies are Pauline Maier, *American Scripture: Making the Declaration of Independence* (New York: Alfred A. Knopf, 1997; Vintage paperback, 1998); Jay Fliegelman, *Declaring Independence: Jefferson, Natural Language, and the Culture of Performance* (Stanford, CA: Stanford University Press, 1993); and David Armitage, *The Declaration of Independence: A Global History* (Cambridge, MA: Harvard University Press, 2007). Older enlightening studies include Carl L. Becker, *The Declaration of Independence: A Study in the History of Political Ideas* (New York: Harcourt, Brace, 1922; reprint with new introduction, New York: Alfred A. Knopf, 1942); and

Garry Wills, *Inventing America: Jefferson's Declaration of Independence* (New York: Doubleday, 1978).

11. On this aspect of the Declaration, see the essay by John Phillip Reid, "The Irrelevance of the Declaration," in Hendrik Hartog, ed., *Law in the American Revolution and the Revolution of the Law* (New York: New York University Press, 1981), 46–89.

12. For a useful compilation, see James H. Hutson, ed., *A Decent Respect to the Opinions of Mankind: Congressional State Papers, 1774–1776* (Washington, DC: Library of Congress, 1975).

13. Armitage, *The Declaration of Independence: A Global History*, presents a thoughtful and innovative examination of the Declaration and its intended audiences. See also Fliegelman, *Declaring Independence*.

14. See, generally, Richard B. Morris, *The Peacemakers: The Great Powers and American Independence* (New York: Harper & Row, 1965); Ronald Hoffman and Peter J. Albert, eds., *Diplomacy and Revolution: The Franco-American Alliance of 1778* (Charlottesville: University Press of Virginia for the U.S. Capitol Historical Society, 1981); and Ronald Hoffman and Peter J. Albert, eds., *Peace and the Peacemakers: The Treaty of 1783* (Charlottesville: University Press of Virginia for the U.S. Capitol Historical Society, 1986).

15. One valuable perspective on this theme appears in Robert Middlekauff, *Benjamin Franklin and His Enemies* (Berkeley and Los Angeles: University of California Press, 1998).

16. Walter Stahr, *John Jay: Founding Father* (New York: Hambledon and London, 2005), 145–174.

17. See generally George C. Herring, *From Colony to Superpower: U.S. Foreign Relations Since 1776* (New York: Oxford University Press, 2008), 11–55; Frederick S. Marks III, *Independence On Trial: Foreign Affairs and the Making of the Constitution* (Baton Rouge: Louisiana State University Press, 1973); Richard B. Morris, *The American Revolution Reconsidered* (New York: Harper & Row, 1977), chapter III.

18. Herring, *From Colony to Superpower*, 56–92; Bradford Perkins, *Cambridge History of American Foreign Relations, I: The Creation of a Republican Empire* (Cambridge and New York: Cambridge University Press, 1993), 54–110. See also Peter S. Onuf and Nicholas Onuf, *Federal Union, Modern World: The Law of Nations in an Age of Revolutions, 1776–1814* (Madison, WI: Madison House, 1993); R. R. Palmer's still magisterial *The Age of the Democratic Revolution: A Political History of Europe and America, 1760–1800*, 2 vols. (Princeton, NJ: Princeton University Press, 1959–1964); and Louis Martin Sears, *George Washington and the French Revolution* (Detroit: Wayne State University Press, 1960).

19. Samuel Eliot Morison, "Dissent in the War of 1812," in Samuel Eliot Morison, Frederick Merk, and Frank Freidel, *Dissent in Three American Wars* (Cambridge, MA: Harvard University Press, 1970), chapter 1. On the war

itself, see Reginald Horsman, *The Causes of the War of 1812* (Philadelphia: University of Pennsylvania Press, 1962); Reginald Horsman, *The War of 1812* (New York: Alfred A. Knopf, 1969); Steven Watts, *The Republic Reborn: War and the Making of Liberal America, 1790–1820* (Baltimore: Johns Hopkins University Press, 1987); Roger H. Brown, *The Republic in Peril: 1812* (New York: Columbia University Press, 1964); Donald R. Hickey, *The War of 1812: A Forgotten Conflict* (Urbana: University of Illinois Press, 1989); and Herring, *From Colony to Superpower*, 93–133. See also James M. Banner, Jr., *To the Hartford Convention: The Federalists and the Origins of Party Politics in Massachusetts, 1789–1815* (New York: Alfred A. Knopf, 1970).

20. Thomas Jefferson to Roger C. Weightman, June 24, 1826, Library of Congress.

21. Benjamin Franklin, speech to the Convention, 17 September 1787, in Max Farrand, ed., *The Records of the Federal Convention of 1787,* 3 vols. with 1987 supplement (New Haven, CT: Yale University Press, 1966, 1987), 2: 641–43.

22. Thomas Jefferson to John Adams, February 28, 1796, in Lester J. Cappon, ed., *The Adams-Jefferson Letters,* 2 vols. (Chapel Hill: University of North Carolina Press for Institute of Early American History and Culture, 1959), 1: 260.

23. An excellent short treatment is Bernard Bailyn, *The Origins of American Politics* (New York: Alfred A. Knopf, 1968). For a dramatic case study, see Patricia U. Bonomi, *The Lord Cornbury Scandal: The Politics of Reputation in British America* (Chapel Hill: University of North Carolina Press for the Omohundro Institute of Early American History and Culture, 2000).

24. John Adams to James Warren, 11 April 1776, in Robert J. Taylor et al., eds., *The Papers of John Adams,* 3rd series, 10 vols. (Cambridge, MA: Belknap Press of Harvard University Press, 1977–), 4: 132. The authoritative modern text of *Thoughts on Government* appears in 86–93.

25. On Paine, see Eric Foner, *Tom Paine and Revolutionary America* (New York: Oxford University Press, 1976; updated edition, 2005); John Keane, *Tom Paine: A Political Life* (Boston: Little, Brown, 1995); Jack Fruchtman, *Thomas Paine: Apostle of Freedom* (New York: Four Walls Eight Windows, 1994); Gregory Claeys, *Thomas Paine: Social and Political Thought* (Boston: Unwin Hyman, 1989); and Mark Philp, *Paine* (Oxford and New York: Oxford University Press, 1989). For an overview of the literature on Paine, see R. B. Bernstein, "Review Essay: Rediscovering Thomas Paine," *New York Law School Law Review* 39 (1994): 873–929.

26. See, generally, the work of Donald S. Lutz and Willi Paul Adams. Donald S. Lutz, *Popular Consent and Popular Control: Whig Political Theory in the Early State Constitutions* (Baton Rouge: Louisiana State University Press, 1980); Donald S. Lutz, *The Origins of American Constitutionalism* (Baton Rouge: Louisiana State University Press, 1988); Willi Paul Adams (Rita and Robert Kimber, trans.), *The First American Constitutions: Republican Ideology and the Making of the State Constitutions in the Revolutionary Era* (Chapel Hill: University

of North Carolina Press for the Institute of Early American History and Culture, 1980; expanded edition, Lanham, MD: Madison House, 2001).

27. See the useful short treatment by Bernard Schwartz, *The Great Rights of Mankind* (New York: Oxford University Press, 1977). The most recent life of Mason is Jeff Broadwater, *George Mason: Forgotten Founder* (Chapel Hill: University of North Carolina Press, 2006).

28. John Phillip Reid, *Constitutional History of the American Revolution: Abridged Edition* (Madison: University of Wisconsin Press, 1995), "Epilogue."

29. William A. Polf, *1777: The Political Revolution and New York's First Constitution* (Albany: New York State Bicentennial Commission, 1977).

30. See, generally, Robert J. Taylor, ed., *Massachusetts, Colony to Commonwealth: Documents on the Foundation of Its Constitution, 1775–1780* (Chapel Hill: University of North Carolina Press for the Institute of Early American History and Culture, 1961); Oscar Handlin and Mary Handlin, eds., *The Popular Sources of Political Authority: Documents on the Massachusetts Constitution of 1780* (Cambridge, MA: Harvard University Press, 1966); Ronald M. Peters, Jr., *The Massachusetts Constitution of 1780: A Social Compact* (Amherst: University of Massachusetts Press, 1978); Samuel Eliot Morison, "The Struggle over the Adoption of the Constitution of Massachusetts, 1780," *Massachusetts Historical Society Proceedings* 50 (1916–1917): 353–412; and "Symposium: The Massachusetts Constitution of 1780," *Suffolk University Law Review* 14 (1980): 841–1010.

31. Judith N. Shklar, *Montesquieu* (Oxford and New York: Oxford University Press, 1989); Anne M. Cohler, *Montesquieu's Comparative Politics and the Spirit of American Constitutionalism* (Lawrence: University Press of Kansas, 1988); Paul M. Spurlin, *Montesquieu in America, 1760–1801* (Baton Rouge: Louisiana State University Press, 1940).

32. The leading study of the framing of the Articles remains Merrill M. Jensen, *The Articles of Confederation …* (Madison: University of Wisconsin Press, 1940; rev. ed., 1971), supplemented and sometimes challenged by Jack N. Rakove, *The Beginnings of National Politics: An Interpretive History of the Continental Congress* (New York: Alfred A. Knopf, 1979).

33. See, e.g., Richard B. Morris, *The American Revolution Reconsidered* (New York: Harper & Row, 1967), chapter 3; Frederick A. Marks III, *Independence on Trial: Foreign Affairs and the Making of the Constitution* (Baton Rouge: Louisiana State University Press, 1973).

34. For two authoritative yet contrasting histories of the Confederation, see Merrill M. Jensen, *The New Nation* (New York: Alfred A. Knopf, 1950), and Richard B. Morris, *The Forging of the Union, 1781–1789* (New York: Harper & Row, 1987).

35. See Richard B. Bernstein with Kym S. Rice, *Are We to Be a Nation? The Making of the Constitution* (Cambridge, MA: Harvard University Press, 1987), 170, for a discussion of the delegates' abandonment of the word "nation" on June 20, 1787.

36. Bernstein with Rice, *Are We to Be a Nation?*, chapter 6; Clinton L. Rossiter, *1787: The Grand Convention* (New York: Macmillan, 1966); Charles Warren, *The Making of the Constitution* (Boston: Little, Brown, 1926, 1937); Carol Berkin, *A Brilliant Solution: Inventing the American Constitution* (New York: Harcourt, 2003); and Max Farrand, *The Framing of the Constitution of the United States* (New Haven, CT: Yale University Press, 1913); all these are reliable accounts of the Convention and its work.

37. On ratification, see Patrick Conley and John P. Kaminski, eds., *The Constitution and the States* (Madison, WI: Madison House, 1989); Robert A. Rutland, *The Ordeal of the Constitution* (Norman: University of Oklahoma Press, 1966); and Bernstein with Rice, *Are We to Be a Nation?*, chapter 7. The great documentary resource is Merrill M. Jensen, John P. Kaminski, Gaspare J. Saladino, Richard Leffler, and Charles E. Schoenleber, eds., *Documentary History of the Ratification of the Constitution and the Bill of Rights, 1787–1791* (Madison: State Historical Society of Wisconsin, 1976–), now nearing completion. See also Bernard Bailyn, ed., *The Debate on the Constitution*, 2 vols. (New York: Library of America, 1993); Herbert J. Storing, with the assistance of Murray Dry, eds., *The Complete Anti-Federalist*, 7 vols. (Chicago: University of Chicago Press, 1981), esp. volume 1, published separately in paperback as *What the Anti-Federalists Were For*. Pauline Maier's forthcoming history of ratification is eagerly awaited by all students of the topic.

38. This is a central argument of Richard B. Bernstein, *Amending America: If We Love the Constitution So Much, Why Do We Keep Trying to Change It?* (New York: Times Books/Random House, 1993; paperback, Lawrence: University Press of Kansas, 1995). See also David E. Kyvig, *Explicit and Authentic Acts: Amending the U.S. Constitution, 1776–1995* (Lawrence: University Press of Kansas, 1996).

39. Helen E. Veit, Kenneth Russell, Bowling, and Charlene Bangs Bickford, eds., *Creating the Bill of Rights: The Documentary Record from the First Federal Congress* (Baltimore: Johns Hopkins University Press, 1991), is an excellent documentary history. See also Patrick T. Conley and John P. Kaminski, eds., *The Bill of Rights and the States* (Madison, WI: Madison House, 1992); Stephen L. Schechter and Richard B. Bernstein, eds., *Contexts of the Bill of Rights* (Albany: New York State Commission on the Bicentennial of the Constitution, 1990).

40. See the valuable series *Commentaries on the Constitution: Public and Private*, volumes 13–18 of Jensen, Kaminski, Saladino, Leffler, and Schoenleber, *Documentary History of the Ratification of the Constitution and the Bill of Rights, 1787–1791*. See also Bailyn, *The Debate on the Constitution*.

41. See, generally, Bernstein, *Amending America*, and Kyvig, *Explicit and Authentic Acts*.

42. This section is deeply indebted to the excellent new book by Edward A. Purcell, Jr., *Originalism, Federalism, and the American Constitutional Experiment:*

A Historical Inquiry (New Haven, CT: Yale University Press, 2007). See also Peter S. Onuf, *Origins of the Federal Republic: Jurisdictional Controversies in the United States, 1776–1787* (Philadelphia: University of Pennsylvania Press, 1973), David C. Hendrickson, *Peace Pact: The Lost World of the American Founding* (Lawrence: University Press of Kansas, 2005); Forrest McDonald, *States' Rights and the Union: Imperium in Imperio, 1776–1876* (Lawrence: University Press of Kansas, 2000); and Rogan E. Kersh, *Dreams of a More Perfect Union* (Ithaca, NY: Cornell University Press, 2001).

43. See McDonald, *States' Rights and the Union*, passim.

44. Harry M. Ward, *The United Colonies of New England, 1643–90* (New York: Vantage Press, 1961).

45. Harry M. Ward, *"Unite or Die": Intercolony Relations, 1690–1763* (Port Washington, NY: Kennikat Press, 1971); David S. Lovejoy, *The Glorious Revolution in America* (New York: Harper & Row, 1972; new edition, Middletown, CT: Wesleyan University Press, 1987).

46. Timothy J. Shannon, *Indians and Colonists at the Crossroads of Empire; The Albany Congress of 1754* (Ithaca, NY: Cornell University Press, 2000); Robert C. Newbold, *The Albany Congress and Plan of Union of 1754* (New York: Vantage Press, 1955).

47. Jerrilyn Green Marston, *King and Congress: The Transfer of Political Legitimacy, 1774–1776* (Princeton, NJ: Princeton University Press, 1987).

48. On the origins of the Articles, see Merrill M. Jensen, *The Articles of Confederation…*(Madison: University Press of Wisconsin, 1940, 1970). On the Confederation, the best case for the Articles appears in Merrill M. Jensen, *The New Nation: A History of the United States during the Confederation, 1781–1789* (New York: Alfred A. Knopf, 1950); a measured critique appears in Jack N. Rakove, *The Beginnings of National Politics: An Interpretive History of the Confederation Congress* (New York: Alfred A. Knopf, 1979). The leading account is now Richard B. Morris, *The Forging of the Union, 1781–1789* (New York: Harper & Row, 1987).

49. See H. James Henderson, *Party Politics in the Continental Congress* (New York: McGraw-Hill, 1974); Rakove, *Beginnings of National Politics*; and Jensen, *The New Nation.*

50. See the writings contained in Volume 1 of James Wilson (Kermit L. Hall and Mark David Hall, eds.), *The Collected Works of James Wilson*, 2 vols. (Indianapolis, IN: Liberty Fund, 2007).

51. See, generally, Clinton Rossiter, *Alexander Hamilton and the Constitution* (New York: Harcourt, Brace & Co., 1964); Gerald Stourzh, *Alexander Hamilton and the Idea of Republican Government* (Stanford, CA: Stanford University Press, 1970); and John Lamberton Harper, *American Machiavelli: Alexander Hamilton and the Origins of U.S. Foreign Policy* (Cambridge and New York: Cambridge University Press, 2004).

52. Thomas Jefferson to James Madison, December 20, 1787, Jefferson Papers, LC.

53. My reading of Jefferson is based on Peter S. Onuf, *Jefferson's Empire: The Language of American Nationhood* (Charlottesville: University Press of Virginia, 2000), and Peter S. Onuf, *The Mind of Thomas Jefferson* (Charlottesville: University of Virginia Press, 2007); it also draws on my earlier research and argument in R. B. Bernstein, *Thomas Jefferson* (New York: Oxford University Press, 2003; paperback ed. with emendations, 2005).

54. Glenn A. Phelps, *George Washington and American Constitutionalism* (Lawrence: University Press of Kansas, 1993); Richard B. Morris, *John Jay, the Nation, and the Court* (Boston: Boston University Press, 1967).

55. This point is based on discussions with Richard Samuelson and on a careful review of the leading studies of John Adams's political thought: Correa Moylan Walsh, *The Political Science of John Adams* (New York: G. P. Putnam's Sons, 1915); Zoltan Haraszti, *John Adams and the Prophets of Progress* (Cambridge, MA: Harvard University Press, 1952); Edward Handler, *America and Europe in the Political Thought of John Adams* (Cambridge, MA: Harvard University Press, 1964); John R. Howe, Jr., *The Changing Political Thought of John Adams* (Princeton, NJ: Princeton University Press, 1966); John Patrick Diggins, *John Adams* (New York: Henry Holt, 2004); and above all C. Bradley Thompson, *John Adams and the Spirit of Liberty* (Lawrence: University Press of Kansas, 1998).

56. The leading study is Drew R. McCoy, *The Last of the Fathers: James Madison and the Republican Legacy* (Cambridge and New York: Cambridge University Press, 1989). See also Ralph Ketcham, *James Madison* (New York: Macmillan, 1971; reprint ed., Charlottesville: University Press of Virginia, 1998); Jack N. Rakove, *James Madison and the Creation of the American Republic*, 3rd ed. (New York: Pearson Putnam, 2007); and Lance Banning, *The Sacred Fire of Liberty: James Madison and the American Founding* (Ithaca, NY: Cornell University Press, 1995).

57. See, generally, Michael A. Foley, *The Silence of Constitutions: Gaps, "Abeyances" and Political Temperament in the Maintenance of Government* (London and New York: Routledge, 1989).

58. James M. McPherson, *Crossroads of Freedom: Antietam* (New York: Oxford University Press, 2004).

59. This section is deeply indebted to the arguments of Joanne B. Freeman, *Affairs of Honor: National Politics in the New Republic* (New Haven, CT: Yale University Press, 2001).

60. This sense of Madison's learning process is a central theme of Banning, *Sacred Fire of Liberty*.

61. For a discussion of ratification in general and *The Federalist* in particular, see Bernstein with Rice, *Are We to Be a Nation?*, chapter 7 and sources cited.

62. On politics in Virginia, see the still valuable classic treatment by Charles S. Sydnor, *Gentlemen Freeholders: Political Practices in Washington's Virginia* (Chapel Hill: University of North Carolina Press for the Institute of Early American History and Culture, 1952), often reprinted in paperback under the title *American Revolutionaries in the Making*.

63. The sketch presented in the following pages draws on my work on Jefferson, my biography of him, and recent monographs, including Jeremy D. Bailey, *Thomas Jefferson and Executive Power* (Cambridge and New York: Cambridge University Press, 2007). In addition, I am profoundly indebted to many conversations on this subject with Prof. Joanne B. Freeman of Yale University.

64. John Adams to Timothy Pickering, 6 August 1822, in Charles Frances Adams, ed., *The Works of John Adams*..., 10 vols. (Boston: Little, Brown, 1850–1856), 2: 154.

65. Danbury, Connecticut, Baptist Association to Thomas Jefferson, October 7, 1801, and Thomas Jefferson to Danbury, Connecticut, Baptist Association, January 1, 1802, Library of Congress. On this subject, see Daniel L. Dreisbach, *Thomas Jefferson and the Wall of Separation Between Church and State* (New York: New York University Press, 2002).

66. Abraham Lincoln to Henry L. Pierce and others, April 6, 1859, in Roy P. Basler, ed., *Collected Works of Abraham Lincoln*, 9 vols. (New Brunswick, NJ: Rutgers University Press, 1953–1955), 3: 374–76 (quote at 375).

67. John Adams to Benjamin Rush, November 11, 1807, in John A. Schutz and Douglass G. Adair, eds., *The Spur of Fame: Dialogues of John Adams and Benjamin Rush, 1805–1813* (San Marino, CA: Huntington Library Press, 1966), 97–98.

68. John Adams quoted and discussed in Freeman, *Affairs of Honor*, 48.

69. Freeman, *Affairs of Honor*, Chapter 2, passim. Freeman coined the phrase "grammar of political combat." This entire discussion is deeply indebted to Freeman's reading of Jefferson as politician.

70. John Marshall, *The Life of George Washington*..., 5 vols. (Philadelphia: Printed and Published by G. P. Wayne, 1804–1807); John Marshall, *The Life of George Washington: Special Edition for Schools* (1838; reprint edited by Robert Faulkner and Paul Carrese, Indianapolis, IN: Liberty Fund, 2000).

71. R. B. Bernstein, Review of J. Jefferson Looney, ed., *The Papers of Thomas Jefferson: Retirement Series*, Volume 1, 4 March to 15 November 1809, *Journal of the Early Republic* 26:4 (Winter 2006): 682–98.

72. Thomas J. Curry, *The First Freedom: Church and State in America to the Passage of the First Amendment* (New York: Oxford University Press, 1986); Edwin S. Gaustad, *Faith of the Founders: Religion and the New Nation, 1776–1826* (Waco, TX: Baylor University Press, 2004).

73. Letter from John Adams to Abigail Adams, September 16, 1774 [electronic edition]. *Adams Family Papers: An Electronic Archive*. Massachusetts Historical Society. www.masshist.org/digitaladams/.

74. William G. McLoughlin, *New England Dissent, 1630–1833: The Baptists and the Separation of Church and State*, 2 vols. (Cambridge, MA: Harvard University Press, 1971); William G. McLoughlin, *Soul Liberty: The Baptists' Struggle in New England, 1630–1833* (Hanover, NH: University Press of New England for Brown University Press, 1991).

75. See Merrill D. Peterson and Robert C. Vaughan, eds., *The Virginia Statute for Religious Freedom: Its Evolution and Consequences in American History* (Cambridge and New York: Cambridge University Press, 1988); Thomas E. Buckley, S.J., *Church and State in Revolutionary Virginia, 1776–1787* (Charlottesville: University Press of Virginia, 1977).

76. J. R. Pole, *The Pursuit of Equality in American History*, rev. ed. (Berkeley and Los Angeles: University of California Press, 1993).

77. Donald L. Robinson, *Slavery in the Structure of American Politics, 1765–1820* (New York: Harcourt, Brace Jovanovich, 1971); Duncan J. MacLeod, *Slavery, Race, and the American Revolution* (Cambridge and New York: Cambridge University Press, 1974); David Brion Davis, *The Problem of Slavery in the Age of Revolution, 1770–1823* (Ithaca, NY: Cornell University Press, 1973); David Brion Davis, *Inhuman Bondage: The Rise and Fall of Slavery in the New World* (New York: Oxford University Press, 2006); Betty Wood, *The Origins of American Slavery: Freedom and Bondage in the English Colonies* (New York: Hill and Wang, 1998); Ira Berlin, *Many Thousands Gone: The First Two Centuries of Slavery in North America* (Cambridge, MA: Belknap Press of Harvard University Press, 2000); Ira Berlin, *Generations of Captivity: A History of African-American Slaves* (Cambridge, MA: Belknap Press of Harvard University Press, 2004); Gary B. Nash, *Race and Revolution* (Madison, WI: Madison House, 1990); Gary B. Nash, *The Forgotten Fifth: African Americans in the Age of Revolution* (Cambridge, MA: Harvard University Press, 2006); and Matthew Mason, *Slavery and Politics in the Early American Republic* (Chapel Hill: University of North Carolina Press, 2006). A brilliant close-focus examination of the relations between an enslaving family and an enslaved family, both linked by ties of blood, is Annette Gordon-Reed, *The Hemingses of Monticello: An American Family* (New York: W. W. Norton, 2008), which follows up on and expands discussion of these issues in Annette Gordon-Reed. *Thomas Jefferson and Sally Hemings: An American Controversy* (Charlottesville: University Press of Virginia, 1997; paperback ed., 1999).

78. See the summary discussion in Bernstein with Rice, *Are We to Be a Nation?*, 175–78.

79. Max Farrand, ed., *The Records of the Debates of the Federal Convention of 1787*, 3 vols. with 1987 supplement edited by James H. Hutson (New Haven, CT: Yale University Press, 1911, 1937, 1966, 1987), 2: 372 (notes of James Madison).

80. William M. Wiecek, *The Sources of Antislavery Constitutionalism in America, 1760–1848* (Ithaca, NY: Cornell University Press, 1977); Ronald G. Walters, *The Antislavery Appeal: Abolitionism After 1830* (Baltimore: Johns Hopkins University Press, 1976); James Brewer Stewart, *Holy Warriors: The Abolitionists and American Slavery* (New York: Hill and Wang, 1996).

81. On the voting-rights amendments, see Bernstein, *Amending America*, 112–116, 128–134, 136–139; Charles L. Zelden, *Voting Rights on Trial: A Handbook*

with *Cases, Laws, and Documents* (Santa Barbara, CA: ABC-CLIO, 2002); and Alexander Keyssar, *The Right to Vote: The Contested History of Democracy in the United States* (New York: Basic Books, 2000).

82. Bradford Perkins, *The Cambridge History of American Foreign Relations, Volume I: The Creation of a Republican Empire, 1776–1865* (Cambridge and New York: Cambridge University Press, 1993); George C. Herring, *From Colony to Superpower: U.S. Foreign Relations Since 1776* (New York: Oxford University Press, 2008).

83. Edward S. Corwin, *The President: Office and Powers, 1787–1957: History and Analysis of Practice and Opinion*, 4th rev. ed. (New York: New York University Press, 1957), 171: "The Constitution is an invitation to struggle for the privilege of directing American foreign policy. The power to determine the substantive content of American foreign policy is a divided power, with the lion's share falling usually, though by no means always, to the President." See also Harold Hongju Koh, "Why the President (Almost) Always Wins in Foreign Relations: The Lessons of the Iran-Contra Affair," *Yale Law Journal* 97:7 (June 1988): 1255–1342; Harold Hongju Koh, *The National Security Constitution: Sharing Power after the Iran-Contra Affair* (New Haven, CT: Yale University Press, 1990); and Louis Fisher, *Constitutional Conflicts Between Congress and the President*, 5th rev. ed. (Lawrence: University Press of Kansas, 2007).

84. Ralph Adams Brown, *The Presidency of John Adams* (Lawrence: University Press of Kansas, 1975).

85. Jeremy D. Bailey, *Thomas Jefferson and Executive Power* (Cambridge and New York: Cambridge University Press, 2007); Dumas Malone, *Jefferson the President: First Term, 1801–1805* (Boston: Little, Brown, 1970).

86. Dumas Malone, *Jefferson the President: Second Term, 1805–1809* (Boston: Little, Brown, 1974), mounts a defense more notable for its enthusiasm than its persuasiveness.

87. J. C. A. Stagg, *Mr. Madison's War: Politics, Diplomacy, and Warfare in the Early American Republic, 1783–1830* (Princeton, NJ: Princeton University Press, 1983).

88. Thomas Jefferson to Samuel Kercheval, July 13, 1816, Library of Congress.

89. John Adams to Samuel Adams, May 1, 1784, Samuel Adams Papers, Bancroft Collection, Rare Books and Manuscripts Division, The New York Public Library, Astor, Lenox, and Tilden Foundations.

90. See the discussions in Leonard D. White, *The Federalists* (New York: Macmillan, 1948); James D. Hart, *The American Presidency in Action: 1789* (New York: Macmillan, 1948); and Charles A. Miller, *The Supreme Court and the Uses of History* (Cambridge, MA: Harvard University Press, 1969). See also *Myers v. United States*, 272 U.S. 52 (1926) and *Humphrey's Executor v. United States*, 295 U.S 602 (1935).

91. Senator Maclay's diary is best used in the splendid modern edition that is Volume 9 of the *Documentary History of the First Federal Congress*. See Kenneth Russell Bowling, Helen E. Veit, and Charlene Bangs Bickford, eds., *The Diary of William Maclay and Other Notes of Senate Debates*...(Baltimore: Johns Hopkins University Press, 1989).

92. See, generally, Clinton Rossiter, *Alexander Hamilton and the Constitution* (New York: Harcourt, Brace, and World, 1964). Joanne B. Freeman, ed., *Alexander Hamilton: Writings* (New York: Library of America, 2001), conveniently collects authoritative texts of these reports.

93. George C. Edwards, *Why the Electoral College Is Bad for America* (New Haven, CT: Yale University Press, 2001), 86 and note 34.

94. On the election of 1800, see Bernstein, *Thomas Jefferson*, 124–128, and sources cited. Edwards, *Why the Electoral College Is Bad for America*, is the best indictment of the institution. For the best defense of the electoral college, see Judith A. Best, *The Case Against Direct Election of the President: A Defense of the Electoral College* (Ithaca, NY: Cornell University Press, 1975); Judith A. Best, *The Choice of the People? Debating the Electoral College* (Lanham, MD: Rowman and Littlefield, 1986).

95. See Michael Stokes Paulsen, "Someone Should Have Told Spiro Agnew," in William N. Eskridge, Jr., and Sanford Levinson, eds., *Constitutional Stupidities, Constitutional Tragedies* (New York: New York University Press, 1998), 75–76.

96. Robert K. Merton, "The Unanticipated Consequences of Purposive Social Action," *American Sociological Review* 1:6 (December 1936): 894–904. Though it was coined by Merton, many writers attribute this phrase to the late Senator Daniel Patrick Moynihan (D-NY) and other political and social thinkers sometimes labeled neoconservatives. Much of Moynihan's best and most influential work in the social sciences does parallel the arguments first offered by Merton. See, for example, the discussion of Moynihan in E. J. Dionne, *Why Americans Hate Politics: The Death of the Democratic Process* (New York: Simon and Schuster, 1991; new edition, 2004), 60–61.

4. Legacies

1. John Adams to Abigail Adams, 26 April 1777 (electronic edition). *Adams Family Papers: An Electronic Archive*. Massachusetts Historical Society. www.masshist.org/digitaladams/.

2. John Higham, *History: Professional Scholarship in America*, updated edition (Baltimore: Johns Hopkins University Press, 1989); Peter Novick, *That Noble Dream: The "Objectivity Question" and the American Historical Profession* (Cambridge and New York: Cambridge University Press, 1988); Richard Hofstadter, *The Progressive Historians: Turner, Beard, Parrington* (New York:

Alfred A. Knopf, 1968); and, for an account that sets American historical scholarship in a global context, J. W. Burrow, *A History of Histories: Epics, Chronicles, Romances and Inquiries from Herodotus and Thucydides to the Twentieth Century* (New York: Alfred A. Knopf, 2008), 423–519.

3. John Jay, *The Federalist No. 2*, in *The Federalist*, 8–13 (quote at 10–11).

4. The best account is still Clinton L. Rossiter III, *1787: The Grand Convention* (New York: Macmillan, 1966), passim. For an account valuable only as an incarnation of what the historian Wesley Frank Craven called "the legend of the Founding Fathers," see Catherine Drinker Bowen, *Miracle at Philadelphia* (Boston: Atlantic-Little, Brown, 1967). On that legend, see Wesley Frank Craven, *The Legend of the Founding Fathers* (New York: New York University Press, 1956; reprint, Ithaca, NY: Cornell University Press, 1965).

5. James Madison, *The Federalist No. 37*, in Alexander Hamilton, James Madison, and John Jay (Jacob E. Cooke, ed.), *The Federalist* (Middletown, CT: Wesleyan University Press, 1961), 231–39.

6. Luther Martin, *The Genuine Information …*, in Max Farrand, ed., *The Records of the Federal Convention of 1787*, revised edition in 4 volumes including 1987 supplement edited by James H. Hutson (New Haven, CT: Yale University Press, 1987), 3: 178.

7. See John K. Alexander, *The Selling of the Constitutional Convention: A History of News Coverage* (Madison, WI: Madison House, 1987); see also the review by Richard B. Bernstein and Stephen L. Schechter, *William and Mary Quarterly*, third series, 50:1 (January 1993): 224–26.

8. Merrill D. Peterson, *Adams and Jefferson: A Revolutionary Dialogue* (Athens: University of Georgia Press, 1976); Stuart Leibiger, *Founding Friendship: George Washington, James Madison, and the Creation of the American Republic* (Charlottesville: University Press of Virginia, 1999). A study of the history of the friendship between James Madison and Alexander Hamilton is badly needed.

9. See, e.g., Joanne B. Freeman, *Affairs of Honor: National Politics in the New Republic* (New Haven, CT: Yale University Press, 2001), chapter 5; James Horn, Jan Ellen Lewis, and Peter S. Onuf, eds., *The Revolution of 1800: Democracy, Race, and the New Republic* (Charlottesville: University of Virginia Press, 2002); and R. B. Bernstein, *Thomas Jefferson* (New York: Oxford University Press, 2003), 128–34.

10. For the correspondence, see Charles Francis Adams, ed., *Correspondence Between John Adams and Mercy Warren, Relating to the "History of the American Revolution,"* Massachusetts Historical Society, *Collections*, fifth series, IV (Boston, 1878). For a scholarly modern edition of her *History*, see Mercy Otis Warren (Lester H. Cohen, ed.), *History of the Rise, Progress and Termination of the American Revolution. Interspersed with Biographical, Political and Moral Observations* (Indianapolis, IN: Liberty Fund, 1989).

11. John A. Schutz and Douglass Adair, eds., *The Spur of Fame: Dialogues of John Adams and Benjamin Rush, 1805–1812* (San Marino, CA: Huntington Library,

1966; reprint, Indianapolis, IN: Liberty Fund, 2001). On Adams's campaign for vindication in the eyes of posterity, see Joseph J. Ellis, *Passionate Sage: The Character and Legacy of John Adams* (New York: W. W. Norton, 1993; reprint, with new introduction, 2001).

12. The most useful discussion is Merrill D. Peterson, *Adams and Jefferson: A Revolutionary Dialogue* (Athens: University of Georgia Press, 1976). For the correspondence, see Lester J. Cappon, ed., *The Adams-Jefferson Letters . . .* , 2 vols. (Chapel Hill: University of North Carolina Press for the Institute of Early American History and Culture, 1959).

13. See, for example, the letters collected in Adrienne Koch and William Peden, eds., *The Life and Selected Writings of Thomas Jefferson* (New York: Modern Library, 1943, reset edition, 1998), 159–72.

14. On Jefferson's reaction to Marshall's *Life of Washington*, see Freeman, *Affairs of Honor*, chapter 2; Herbert J. Sloan, "Presidents as Historians," in Richard Alan Ryerson, ed., *John Adams and the Founding of the Republic* (Boston: Massachusetts Historical Society, 2001), 266–83. On Adams's quest for historical vindication, see Ellis, *Passionate Sage*, and Zoltan Haraszti, *John Adams and the Prophets of Progress* (Cambridge, MA: Harvard University Press, 1952). On the Adams–Jefferson correspondence, see Peterson, *Adams and Jefferson*; for the correspondence itself, see Cappon, ed., *Adams-Jefferson Letters*. On Madison, see Drew McCoy, *The Last of the Fathers: James Madison and the Republican Legacy* (Cambridge and New York: Cambridge University Press, 1989).

15. Thomas Jefferson to John Trumbull, 8 January 1818, Library of Congress. See also Peter de Bolla, *The Fourth of July: And the Founding of America* (London: Profile, 2007). For the painting, see this book's title page.

16. Many of these letters are reprinted in Farrand, ed., *The Records of the Federal Convention of 1787*, Volume III, passim.

17. Thomas Jefferson (Thomas Jefferson Randolph, ed.), *Memoir, Correspondence, and Miscellanies: From the Papers of Thomas Jefferson*, 4 vols. (Charlottesville, VA: F. Carr, 1829).

18. John Marshall, *The Life of George Washington . . .* , 5 vols. (Philadelphia: Printed and Published by G. P. Wayne, 1804–1807); John Marshall, *The Life of George Washington: Special Edition for Schools* (1838; reprint edited by Robert Faulkner and Paul Carrese, Indianapolis, IN: Liberty Fund, 2000).

19. John Adams (Charles Francis Adams, ed.), *The Works of John Adams, Second President of the United States . . .* , 10 vols. (Boston: Little, Brown, and Company, 1850–1856); John Quincy Adams and Charles Francis Adams, *The Life of John Adams, Begun by John Quincy Adams and Completed by Charles Francis Adams* (Philadelphia: J. B. Lippincott, 1871).

20. William Cabell Rives, *History of the Life and Times of James Madison* (Boston: Little, Brown, and Company, 1866–1868). On Rives, see Drew R. McCoy, *The Last of the Fathers: James Madison and the Republican Legacy* (Cambridge and New York: Cambridge University Press, 1989), 323–69.

21. Hofstadter, *Progressive Historians*, part I.

22. On 1826, see Andrew J. Burstein, *America's Jubilee: How in 1826 a Generation Remembered Fifty Years of American Independence* (New York: Alfred A. Knopf, 2001).

23. Abraham Lincoln, "Address before the Young Men's Lyceum of Springfield, Illinois," January 27, 1838, in Roy P. Basler, ed., *The Collected Works of Abraham Lincoln* (New Brunswick, NJ: Rutgers University Press, 1953), 1: 108–15.

24. On the coining of this phrase by Van Wyck Brooks, see note 16 to chapter 1. See also Henry Steele Commager, *The Search for a Usable Past: And Other Essays in American History* (New York: Alfred A. Knopf, 1966).

25. On Confederate nationalism, see Drew Gilpin Faust, *The Creation of Confederate Nationalism: Ideology and Identity in the Civil War South* (Baton Rouge: Louisiana State University Press, 1988), and on the uses that Lincoln made of the founding fathers, see Garry Wills, *Lincoln at Gettysburg: The Words that Remade America* (New York: Simon and Schuster, 1992).

26. James Russell Lowell, "The Place of the Independent in Politics: An Address Delivered before the Reform Club of New York, at Steinway Hall, April 13, 1888," in James Russell Lowell, *Literary and Political Addresses* (Boston and New York: Houghton, Mifflin and Company, 1891), 190–221 (quote at 206). See also Michael Kammen, *A Machine That Would Go of Itself: The Constitution in American Culture* (New York: Alfred A. Knopf, 1986).

27. Karal Ann Marling, *George Washington Slept Here* (Cambridge, MA: Harvard University Press, 1988).

28. Rebecca Edwards, *New Spirits: Americans in the Gilded Age, 1865–1905* (New York: Oxford University Press, 2006), passim; Morton Keller, *Affairs of State: Public Life in Late Nineteenth-Century America* (Cambridge, MA: Belknap Press of Harvard University Press, 1977), passim.

29. On Beard, see Hofstadter, *Progressive Historians*, part III. For two powerful counterblasts to Beard's *Economic Interpretation of the Constitution*, see Robert E. Brown, *Charles Beard and the Constitution* (Princeton, NJ: Princeton University Press, 1955), and Forrest McDonald, *We the People: The Economics Origins of the Constitution* (Chicago: University of Chicago Press, 1958). For a modern attempt to present a neo-Beardian interpretation, see Robert McGuire, *To Form a More Perfect Union: A New Economic Interpretation of the United States Constitution* (New York: Oxford University Press, 2003).

30. See, e.g., Walton H. Hamilton and Douglass Adair, *The Power to Govern* (New York: W. W. Norton, 1937); Irving N. Brant, *Storm over the Constitution* (Indianapolis, IN: Bobbs-Merrill, 1937).

31. See Herbert Croly, *The Promise of American Life* (New York: Macmillan, 1909), 27–51.

32. Daniel J. Boorstin, *The Genius of American Politics* (Chicago: University of Chicago Press, 1952).

33. Richard Hofstadter, *The American Political Tradition: And the Men Who Made It* (New York: Alfred A. Knopf, 1948), chapter 1.

34. See the discussion in Richard Kluger's landmark history *Simple Justice* (New York: Alfred A. Knopf 1975; revised edition, 2004). A germinal work is Winthrop D. Jordan, *White over Black: American Attitudes Toward the Negro, 1550–1812* (Chapel Hill: University of North Carolina Press for the Institute of Early American History and Culture, 1968).

35. Two classic older works are Donald I. Robinson, *Slavery in the Structure of American Politics, 1765–1820* (New York: Harcourt, Brace Jovanovich, 1971), and Duncan MacLeod, *Slavery, Race, and the American Revolution* (Cambridge: Cambridge University Press, 1974). See also the powerful critique by Paul L. Finkelman, *Slavery and the Founders: Race and Liberty in the Age of Jefferson*, revised edition (Armonk, NY: M. E. Sharpe, 2001). A differing perspective appears in Don E. Fehrenbacher, *The Dred Scott Case* (New York: Oxford University Press, 1978), and Don E. Fehrenbacher (completed by Ward M. McAfee), *The Slaveholding Republic: An Account of the United States Government's Relations to Slavery* (New York: Oxford University Press, 2001).

36. On this point, see Gordon S. Wood, *Revolutionary Characters: What Made the Founding Fathers Different* (New York: Penguin Press, 2006), and Gordon S. Wood, *The Purpose of the Past: Reflections on the Use of History* (New York: Penguin Press, 2008). For similar comments, see the introduction to Joseph J. Ellis, *American Creation: Triumphs and Tragedies at the Founding of the Republic* (New York: Alfred A. Knopf, 2007), 12: "The currently hegemonic narrative within the groves of academe—race, class, and gender are the privileged categories of analysis—customarily labels (and libels) the founders as racists, classists, and sexists, a kind of rogues' gallery rather than a gallery of greats." For a more nuanced argument on these lines in the context of an examination of the historical and current roles of heroes in American life and culture, see Peter H. Gibbon, *A Call to Heroism: Renewing America's Vision of Greatness* (New York: Atlantic Monthly Press, 2002).

37. Lester J. Cappon, "A Rationale for Historical Editing Past and Present," *William and Mary Quarterly*, 3rd series, 23:1 (January 1966): 56–75.

38. These projects include editions of the papers of George Washington, the Adams family, Thomas Jefferson, James Madison, Alexander Hamilton, Benjamin Franklin, John Marshall, and John Jay. Other projects have collected the surviving papers of George Mason, Henry Laurens, Nathanael Greene, and others.

39. William W. Freehling, *The Reintegration of American History* (New York: Oxford University Press, 1994), chapter 1. See also the discussion in Richard B. Bernstein, "Review Essay: Charting the Bicentennial," *Columbia Law Review* 87 (December 1987): 1565–1624. Among the projects noted in text are Merrill M. Jensen, John P. Kaminski, Gaspare J. Saladino, Richard Leffler,

and Charles E. Schoenleber, eds., *The Documentary History of the Ratification of the Constitution and the Bill of Rights, 1787–1791* (Madison: State Historical Society of Wisconsin, 1976–); Merrill M. Jensen, Robert A. Becker, and Gordon denBoer, eds., *The Documentary History of the First Federal Elections, 1788–1790* (Madison: University of Wisconsin Press, 1976–1990); Linda Grant DePauw, Charlene Bangs Bickford, Kenneth R. Bowling, Helen E. Veit, and Charles D. Giacomantonio, eds., *The Documentary History of the First Federal Congress* (Baltimore: Johns Hopkins University Press, 1972–); and Maeva Marcus et al., eds., *The Documentary History of the Supreme Court of the United States, 1789–1800* (New York: Columbia University Press, 1985–2006).

40. On Adams, see, e.g., James Grant: *John Adams, Party of One* (New York: Farrar, Straus & Giroux, 2005); Peter Shaw, *The Character of John Adams* (Chapel Hill: University of North Carolina Press for the Institute of Early American History and Culture, 1975); and Richard Alan Ryerson, ed., *John Adams and the Founding of the Republic* (Boston: Massachusetts Historical Society/Distributed by Northeastern University Press, 2000).

41. The best one-volume overview of such scholarship is Peter S. Onuf, ed., *Jeffersonian Legacies* (Charlottesville: University Press of Virginia, 1993). See also Peter S. Onuf, *Jefferson's Empire: The Language of American Nationhood* (Charlottesville: University Press of Virginia, 2000); Peter S. Onuf, *The Mind of Thomas Jefferson* (Charlottesville: University of Virginia Press, 2007). R. B. Bernstein, *Thomas Jefferson* (New York: Oxford University Press, 2003), is another example of scholarship benefiting from the documentary-editing revolution, as is Kevin Hayes, *The Road to Monticello: The Life and Mind of Thomas Jefferson* (New York: Oxford University Press, 2008).

42. Sherman Edwards and Peter Stone, *1776: A Musical Play* (New York: Viking Press, 1970). This *1776* should not be confused with David McCullough, *1776* (New York: Simon and Schuster, 2005).

43. Daniel Lessard Levin, *Representing Popular Sovereignty: The Constitution in American Political Culture* (Albany: State University of New York Press, 1999). For one history of a bicentennial celebration that noted the problems discussed in text, see Richard B. Bernstein et al., *Where the Experiment Began: New York City and the Two Hundredth Anniversary of George Washington's Inauguration: Final Report of the New York City Commission on the Bicentennial of the Constitution* (New York: New York City Commission on the Bicentennial of the Constitution, 1989).

44. The best-known exemplars are Joseph J. Ellis, *Founding Brothers: The Revolutionary Generation* (New York: Alfred A. Knopf, 2000), which won the 2001 Pulitzer Prize for History, and David McCullough, *John Adams* (New York: Simon and Schuster, 2001), which won the 2002 Pulitzer Prize for Biography. The critical literature is enormous. See, for example, Sean Wilentz, "America Made Easy: John Adams Is Not the Hero We Need, and David McCullough Is Not the Historian We Need," *The New Republic*

(July 2, 2001), 40ff; and H. W. Brands, "Founders Chic," *The Atlantic Monthly*, September 2003, available on the Internet at www.theatlantic.com/ doc/200309/brands (viewed online December 14, 2008), with an accompanying "Web-only" interview titled "Ordinary People," www.theatlantic. com/doc/200308u/int2003–08–07 (viewed online December 14, 2008). The phrase's point of origin is Evan Thomas, "Founders Chic: Live from Philadelphia," *Newsweek*, July 9, 2001, 48–49. The article's tag line read: "They cut political deals and stabbed each other in the back on the way to inventing freedom: Why Jefferson, Adams and their brethren are suddenly hot again." The article is available on the Internet at www.newsweek.com/ id/78672 (viewed December 13, 2008).

45. See, for example, Bruce Ackerman, *The Failure of the Founding Fathers: Jefferson, Marshall, and the Rise of Presidential Democracy* (Cambridge, MA: Belknap Press of Harvard University Press, 2005).

46. Warren G. Harding, "Address on the Dedication of the Lincoln Memorial," *New York Times*, May 31, 1922, pp. 1, 3 (quote on page 3). I first came across this quotation from Harding's 1922 speech in Andrew Ferguson, *Land of Lincoln: Adventures in Abe's America* (New York: Grove Press, 2007), 265.

47. A wonderful website—www.io.com/'janis/quiz/quiz1.html—allows you to answer a series of questions and that tells you, based on your answers, whether you're most like George Washington, John Adams, Thomas Jefferson, Alexander Hamilton, or Thomas Paine. A similar website—www.selectsmart.com/FREE/select.php?client=founders—uses Washington, Adams, Jefferson, Hamilton, Paine, James Madison, Benjamin Franklin, and Aaron Burr as its comparison spectrum.

48. Merrill D. Peterson, *The Jefferson Image in the American Mind* (New York: Oxford University Press, 1960; new edition, Charlottesville: University Press of Virginia, 1998); Francis D. Cogliano, *Thomas Jefferson: Reputation and Legacy* (Edinburgh and Charlottesville: Edinburgh University Press/ University of Virginia Press, 2006). For a summary treatment, see the epilogue to Bernstein, *Thomas Jefferson*.

49. Stephen Knott, *Alexander Hamilton and the Persistence of Myth* (Lawrence: University Press of Kansas, 2002).

50. Douglass Adair (Trevor Colbourn, ed.), *Fame and the Founding Fathers: Essays of Douglass Adair* (New York: W. W. Norton for the Institute of Early American History and Culture, 1974; reprint ed., Indianapolis, IN: Liberty Fund, 1998); Irving N. Brant, *James Madison*, 6 vols. (Indianapolis, IN: Bobbs-Merrill, 1941–1961).

51. Walter Stahr, *John Jay: Founding Father* (New York: Hambledon and London, 2005); Richard B. Morris, *John Jay, the Nation, and the Court* (Boston, MA: Boston University Press, 1967); Richard B. Morris, *Seven Who Shaped Our Destiny: The Founding Fathers as Revolutionaries* (New York: Harper & Row, 1973).

52. Bernstein, "Charting the Bicentennial," 1622. See also Louis Fisher, *Constitutional Dialogues: Interpretation as Political Process* (Princeton, NJ: Princeton University Press, 1988).

53. Alexander Hamilton, *The Federalist No. 78*, the first of Hamilton's six essays defending the judicial branch of the general government created by the Constitution, focused on the goal of vindicating the existence of the federal judiciary against claims that it was either dangerous or unnecessary by focusing on its vital function of interpreting the Constitution to defend it against encroachment by Congress, the executive, or the states.

54. James H. Hutson, "The Creation of the Constitution: The Integrity of the Documentary Record," *Texas Law Review* 65 (1986): 1–40.

55. Merrill M. Jensen, John P. Kaminski, Gaspare J. Saladino, Richard Leffler, and Charles Schoenleber, eds., *The Documentary History of the Ratification of the Constitution and the Bill of Rights, 1787–1791* (21 volumes to date) (Madison: State Historical Society of Wisconsin, 1976–).

56. Jonathan Elliot, ed., *Debates in the Several State Conventions on the Adoption of the Federal Constitution, as Recommended by the General Convention at Philadelphia in 1787, second edition, with considerable additions*, 5 vols. (Philadelphia: J. B. Lippincott, and Washington, DC: Taylor & Maury, 1836–1859). The first edition appeared in 1827, and many editions and reprints appeared through the following decades and well into the twentieth century.

57. The first edition was Henry D. Gilpin, ed., *The Papers of James Madison: Purchased by Order of the Congress, Being His Correspondence and Reports of Debates during the Congress of the Confederation, and His Reports of Debates in the Federal Convention; Now Published from the Original Manuscripts, Deposited in the Department of State, by Direction of the Joint Library Committee of the Congress, under the Supervision of Henry D. Gilpin*, 3 vols. (Washington, DC: Langtree & O'Sullivan, 1840). J. & H. G. Langley and Allston Mygatt issued reprint editions in New York in 1840 and in Mobile, Alabama, in 1842, respectively.

58. (1) United States Department of State, Bureau of Rolls and Library, *Documentary History of the Constitution of the United States of America, 1786–1870: Derived from the Records, Manuscripts, and Rolls Deposited in the Bureau of Rolls and Library of the Department of State*, 3 vols. (Washington, DC: United States Department of State, 1894–1905); (2) Max Farrand, ed., *The Debates of the Federal Convention of 1787*, 3 vols. (New Haven, CT: Yale University Press, 1911; revised ed. in 4 volumes, 1937; revised ed., 1966; revised ed. with new *Supplement* edited by James H. Hutson, 1987); (3) James Madison (James Brown Scott with Gaillard Hunt, eds.), *The Debates in the Federal Convention of 1787* (New York: Oxford University Press, 1920, and many later reprints); (4) Charles C. Tansill, ed., *Documents Illustrative of the Formation of the Union of the American States* (Washington, DC: U.S. Government Printing Office, 1927, and later reprints).

59. Jack N. Rakove, "Early Uses of *The Federalist*," in Charles R. Kesler, *Saving the Revolution: The Federalist Papers and the American Founding* (New York: Free Press/Macmillan, 1987), 234–49.

60. See the discussion in Joseph M. Lynch, *Negotiating the Constitution: The Earliest Debates over Original Intent* (Ithaca, NY: Cornell University Press, 1999), 63, 250 (notes 67 and 86), and 255 (note 84).

61. The clearest exposition of Hamilton's fiscal policies remains Forrest McDonald, *Alexander Hamilton* (New York: W. W. Norton, 1979).

62. Lance Banning, *The Jeffersonian Persuasion* (Ithaca, NY: Cornell University Press, 1978), passim; Drew R. McCoy, *The Elusive Republic: Political Economy in Jeffersonian America* (Chapel Hill: University of North Carolina Press for the Institute of Early American History and Culture, 1980); E. James Ferguson, *The Power of the Purse: A History of American Public Finance, 1776–1790* (Chapel Hill: University of North Carolina Press for the Institute of Early American History and Culture, 1960).

63. See, generally, Kenneth R. Bowling, *The Creation of Washington, D.C.: The Idea and the Location of the Nation's Capital* (Fairfax, VA: George Mason University Press, 1991).

64. A useful modern edition is Alexander Hamilton and James Madison (Morton J. Frisch, ed.), *The Pacificus-Helvidius Debates of 1793: Toward the Completion of the American Founding* (Indianapolis, IN: Liberty Fund, 2007).

65. A thorough recent study is Lynch, *Negotiating the Constitution.* See the excellent review of this book by Jack N. Rakove, "Review of Joseph M. Lynch, Negotiating the Constitution: The Earliest Debates over Original Intent," H-Law, H-Net Reviews, July, 1999. URL: www.h-net.org/reviews/showrev. cgi?path=26403931988556. See also Jack N. Rakove, *Original Meanings: Politics and Ideas in the Making of the Constitution* (New York: Alfred A. Knopf, 1996); Jack N. Rakove, ed., *Interpreting the Constitution: The Debate over Original Intent* (Boston, MA: Northeastern University Press, 1990); and Leonard W. Levy, *Original Intent and the Framers' Constitution* (New York: Macmillan, 1988).

66. Bernstein, *Jefferson*, 141–43; Jon R. Kukla, *A Wilderness So Immense: The Louisiana Purchase and the Future of America* (New York: Alfred A. Knopf, 2003), 301–9 and Appendix D, 359–61; Dumas Malone, *Jefferson the President: First Term, 1801–1805* (Boston: Little, Brown, 1971), 311–32; Perkins, *Creation of a Republican Empire*, 111–46; and Lawrence S. Kaplan, *Thomas Jefferson: Westward the Course of Empire* (Wilmington, DE: Scholarly Resources, 1999), 136–39.

67. William Wiecek, *The Origins of Antislavery Constitutionalism in America, 1760–1848* (Ithaca, NY: Cornell University Press, 1977).

68. Alvan Stewart, "Response to Governor Marcy's Message, 1836," in Luther Rawson Marsh, ed., *Writings and Speeches of Alvan Stewart on Slavery* (New York: A. B. Burdick, 1860), 59–85 (quote at 74 [emphasis in original]).

69. See H. Jefferson Powell, "The Principles of '98: An Essay in Historical Retrieval," *Virginia Law Review* 80 (1994): 689–743.

70. *Dred Scott v. Sandford*, 60 U.S. (19 Howard) 393 (1857). The authoritative study is Don E. Fehrenbacher, *The Dred Scott Case* (New York: Oxford University Press, 1978). For two recent challenging readings of *Dred Scott* that dispute Fehrenbacher's interpretation, see Austin Allen, *Origins of the Dred Scott Case: Jacksonian Jurisprudence and the Supreme Court, 1837–1857* (Athens: University of Georgia Press, 2006), and Mark Graber, *Dred Scott and the Problem of Constitutional Evil* (Cambridge and New York: Cambridge University Press, 2006).

71. Harold Holzer, *Lincoln at Cooper Union: The Speech That Made Lincoln President* (New York: Simon and Schuster, 2004).

72. See, e.g., for Confederate nationalism, Faust, *The Creation of Confederate Nationalism,* and for the uses that Lincoln made of the founding fathers, Wills, *Lincoln at Gettysburg.*

73. See, for example, Leo Pfeffer, *Church, State, and Freedom* (Boston: Beacon Press, 1967) (separationist) and Robert L. Cord, *Separation of Church and State; Historical Fact and Current Fiction* (New York: Lambeth Press, 1982) (accommodationist). The literature is vast, and the entire controversy deserves a history of its own.

74. See generally Rakove, *Original Meanings,* passim.

75. John Jay, Charge to the Grand Jury of the Circuit Court for the District of New York, 12 April 1790, reprinted in Maeva Marcus, ed., *The Documentary History of the Supreme Court of the United States, 1789–1800,* 8 vols. (New York: Columbia University Press, 1985–2006), *Volume Two: The Justices on Circuit, 1790–1794* (quote at 26).

76. Alexander M. Bickel, *The Least Dangerous Branch: The Supreme Court at the Bar of Politics* (Indianapolis, IN: Bobbs-Merrill, 1962; reprint ed., with new introduction by Harry H. Wellington, New Haven, CT: Yale University Press, 1986), 103.

Epilogue

1. For an account that denies that self-government is a constitutional value because the American people govern themselves under a constitution more than two centuries old, see Paul A. Kahn, *Legitimacy and History: Self-Government in American Constitutional Theory* (New Haven, CT: Yale University Press, 199x). For a vigorous critique, see Richard B. Bernstein, "Book Review," *Journal of American History* 81:2 (September 1994): 667–68.

2. We know almost nothing of the origins of this key phrase, or of the Preamble in general, save that it was the handiwork of Gouverneur Morris, a New Yorker serving as a Pennsylvania delegate, whom the Committee of Style and Arrangement named to prepare the Constitution's final draft. On Morris, see William Howard Adams, *Gouverneur Morris: An Independent Life*

(New Haven, CT: Yale University Press, 2003); 163–64 (brief discussion of Morris's drafting of Preamble but without reference to "more perfect Union"). On the centrality of Article V's amending process to the success of the Constitution in the ratification controversy of 1787–1788, see Richard B. Bernstein, *Amending America: If We Love the Constitution So Much, Why Do We Keep Trying to Change It?* (New York: Times Books/Random House, 1993), 22–30.

3. My discussion is informed throughout by the valuable recent study by Rogan Kersh, *Dreams of a More Perfect Union* (Ithaca, NY: Cornell University Press, 2001).

4. On Douglass, see William S. McFeely, *Frederick Douglass* (New York: W. W. Norton, 1991); Nathan Irvin Huggins, *Slave and Citizen: The Life of Frederick Douglass* (Boston: Little, Brown, 1980); and James Oakes, *The Radical and the Republican: Frederick Douglass and Abraham Lincoln* (New York: W. W. Norton, 2007). John Stauffer, *Giants: The Parallel Lives of Frederick Douglass and Abraham Lincoln* (New York: Twelve, 2008), appeared too late for use here. On this speech, see James L. Colaiaco, *Frederick Douglass and the Fourth of July* (New York: Palgrave Macmillan, 2006). For the text of Douglass's speech, I have used Ted Widmer, ed., *American Speeches: Political Oratory from the Revolution to the Civil War* (New York: Library of America, 2006), 526–52.

5. For the text of King's speech, I have used Ted Widmer, ed., *American Speeches: Political Oratory from Abraham Lincoln to Bill Clinton* (New York: Library of America, 2006), 556–73. Two leading discussions are Taylor Branch, *Parting the Waters: America in the King Years, 1954–1963* (New York: Simon and Schuster, 1987), 846–87 (esp. 881–83); and David J. Garrow, *Bearing the Cross: Martin Luther King, Jr., and the Southern Christian Leadership Conference* (New York: William Morrow, 1986), 283–88.

6. On Jordan, see Mary Beth Rogers, *Barbara Jordan: American Hero* (New York: Bantam, 1998). On this speech, see L. H. LaRue, *Political Discourse: A Case Study of the Watergate Affair* (Athens: University of Georgia Press, 1988). For the text of Jordan's speech, I have used Widmer, ed., *American Speeches: Lincoln to Clinton*, 695–99.

7. On Marshall, see Mark Tushnet, *Making Civil Rights Law: Thurgood Marshall and the Supreme Court, 1936–1961* (New York: Oxford University Press, 1994); Mark V. Tushnet, *Making Constitutional Law: Thurgood Marshall and the Supreme Court, 1961–1991* (New York: Oxford University Press, 1997); and Juan Williams, *Thurgood Marshall: American Revolutionary* (New York: Times Books, 1998). For the text of Marshall's address, originally delivered at the annual seminar of the San Francisco Patent and Trademark Law Association in Maui, Hawaii, on May 6, 1987, I have used that version published as Thurgood Marshall, "Commentary: Reflections on the Bicentennial of the United States Constitution," *Harvard Law Review*, 101:1 (November 1987): 1–5.

8. "Barack Obama's Speech on Race," *New York Times*, March 19, 2008, online at www.nytimes.com/2008/03/18/us/politics/18text-obama.html?_r=1& ref=politics&oref=slogin (viewed online October 5, 2008).

9. "Transcript: Obama's Victory Speech," *New York Times*, November 5, 2008, online at www.nytimes.com/2008/11/04/us/politics/04text-obama.html? pagewanted=1&sq=november%204%202008%20obama%20speech&st= cse&scp=1 (viewed online November 30, 2008). On election night, Obama became the presumptive president; not until December 15, 2008, when the members of the electoral college met to cast their votes, did he become president-elect. For an interesting novel exploring the unsettled constitutional questions raised by this interregnum, see Jeff Greenfield, *The People's Choice* (New York: G. P. Putnam's Sons, 1995).

10. See, for example, Brent Staples, "Savoring the Undertones and Lingering Subtleties of Obama's Victory Speech," *New York Times*, "The Board Blog, http:// theboard.blogs.nytimes.com/2008/11/07/savoring-the-undetones-and-lingering-subtleties-of-obamas-victory-speech/ (viewed online November 30, 2008); Brent Staples, "Obama's Victory Speech: A Response to Comments," *New York Times*, "The Board Blog," http://theboard.blogs.nytimes. com/2008/11/10/obamas-victory-speech-a-response-to-comments/ (viewed online November 30, 2008); and the comments appended to both blog entries. See also James Wood, "Talk of the Town—Close Reading: Victory Speech," *The New Yorker*, November 17, 2008, www.newyorker. com/talk/2008/11/17/081117ta_talk_wood (viewed online December 14, 2008). For a dissenting view on Obama's vision of the American founding advancing the claims of Samuel Adams, see Ira Stoll, "Is Barack Obama the Founding Fathers' Dream Come True? Not Quite," *New York Daily News*, November 7, 2008, www.nydailynews.com/opinions/2008/11/07/2008-11-07_is_barack_obama_the_founding_fathers_dre.html (viewed online November 30, 2008).

11. *Sayings of the Fathers: Pirke Aboth: The Hebrew Text, with English Translation and Commentary by Rabbi Joseph H. Hertz* (West Orange, NJ: Behrman House, 1986), at 45.

Further Reading

This book expands and refines arguments that I made in my first book—Richard B. Bernstein with Kym S. Rice, *Are We to Be a Nation? The Making of the Constitution* (Cambridge, MA: Harvard University Press, 1987). Interested readers will find further documentation, both via primary sources and historical scholarship, of many of the arguments in chapters 2 and 3.

Understanding the founding fathers begins with reading their own words. The Library of America has issued a series of wonderful volumes for many of the key figures and events examined here: J. A. Leo LeMay, ed., *Benjamin Franklin: Writings* (New York: Library of America, 1987); Joanne B. Freeman, ed., *Alexander Hamilton: Writings* (New York: Library of America, 2001); Merrill D. Peterson, ed., *Thomas Jefferson: Writings* (New York: Library of America, 1984); Jack N. Rakove, ed., *James Madison: Writings* (New York: Library of America, 1999); Eric Foner, ed., *Thomas Paine: Collected Writings* (New York: Library of America, 1995); John H. Rhodehamel, ed., *George Washington: Writings* (New York: Library of America, 1997); Bernard Bailyn, ed., *The Debate on the Constitution*, 2 vols. (New York: Library of America, 1993); and John H. Rhodehamel, ed., *The American Revolution: Writings from the War of Independence* (New

York: Library of America, 2001). The Library of America is also working to prepare a volume or volumes for John Adams.

In a class by itself is John P. Kaminski, ed., *The Founders on the Founders: Word Portraits from the American Revolutionary Era* (Charlottesville: University of Virginia Press, 2008).

The best one-volume history of the American Revolution is Robert Middlekauff, *The Glorious Cause: The American Revolution, 1763–1789* (New York: Oxford University Press, 1982; revised edition, 2005). Two books by John E. Ferling complement Middlekauff's account—*Almost a Miracle: The American Victory in the War for Independence* (New York: Oxford University Press, 2007) and *A Leap in the Dark: The Struggle to Create the American Republic* (New York: Oxford University Press, 2003). Richard B. Morris, *The Forging of the Union, 1781–1789* (New York; Harper & Row, 1987), is the premier history of the United States during the Confederation period and deserves to be restored to print; but readers will also find valuable Merrill M. Jensen, *The Articles of Confederation: An Interpretation of the Social-Constitutional History of the American Revolution* (Madison: University of Wisconsin Press, 1948; reprint, 1970); Jensen, *The New Nation: A History of the United States during the Confederation, 1781–1789* (New York: Alfred A. Knopf, 1950); Jensen, *The Founding of a Nation: A History of the American Revolution, 1763–1776* (New York: Oxford University Press, 1968; reprint, Indianapolis, IN: Hackett, 2004); and Jensen, *The American Revolution Within America* (New York: New York University Press, 1974). Three other books by Richard B. Morris are recommended: *The American Revolution Reconsidered* (New York: Harper & Row, 1967); *The Emerging Nations and the American Revolution* (New York: Harper & Row, 1970); and *Seven Who Shaped Our Destiny: The Founding Fathers as Revolutionaries* (New York: Harper & Row, 1973). Jack N. Rakove, *The Beginnings of National Politics: An Interpretive History of the Continental Congress* (New York: Alfred A. Knopf, 1999), and his *Original Meanings: Politics and Ideas in the Making of the Constitution* (New York: Alfred A. Knopf,

1996), are indispensable, as are three studies by Pauline Maier: *From Resistance to Revolution* (New York: Alfred A. Knopf, 1972; paperback reprint, New York: W. W. Norton, 1991); *The Old Revolutionaries: Political Lives in the Age of Samuel Adams* (New York: Alfred A. Knopf, 1980; paperback reprint, New York: W. W. Norton, 1991); and *American Scripture: Making the Declaration of Independence* (New York: Alfred A. Knopf, 1997).

On the American Enlightenment or the Enlightenment in America, see the following: Henry Steele Commager, *Empire of Reason: How Europe Imagined and America Realized the Enlightenment* (New York: Anchor Press/Doubleday, 1977); Commager, *Jefferson, Nationalism, and the Enlightenment* (New York: George Braziller, 1975); Douglass G. Adair (Trevor Colbourn, ed.), *Fame and the Founding Fathers: Essays of Douglass Adair* (New York; W. W. Norton for the Institute of Early American History and Culture, 1974; reprint, Indianapolis, IN: Liberty Fund, Inc., 1998); Henry F. May, *The Enlightenment in America* (New York: Oxford University Press, 1976); I. Bernard Cohen, *Science and the Founding Fathers; Science in the Political Thought of Jefferson, Adams, Franklin, and Madison* (New York: W. W. Norton, 1995; revised paperback ed., 1997); and Robert A. Ferguson, *The American Enlightenment, 1750–1820* (Cambridge, MA: Harvard University Press, 1997). Two other books by Ferguson are especially illuminating on the difficulty of ordering the world with words: *Law and Letters in American Culture* (Cambridge, MA: Harvard University Press, 1984) and *Reading the Early Republic* (Cambridge, MA: Harvard University Press, 2004).

On the framing of the Constitution see Clinton L. Rossiter, *1787: The Grand Convention* (New York: Macmillan, 1966); Carol Berkin, *A Brilliant Solution: Inventing the American Constitution* (New York: Harcourt, 2002); Max Farrand, *The Framing of the Constitution of the United States* (New Haven, CT: Yale University Press, 1913); and Charles Warren, *The Making of the Constitution* (Boston: Little, Brown, 1926, 1937). The peerless compilation of primary documents is Max Farrand, ed., *The Records of the Federal Convention of 1787*, 4 vols. (including 1987 supplement edited by James H. Hutson) (New Haven, CT:Yale University Press, 1911, 1937, 1966, 1987).

On the political history of the early republic see Joanne B. Freeman, *Affairs of Honor: National Politics in the New Republic* (New Haven, CT:Yale University Press, 2001); Francis D. Cogliano, *Revolutionary America, 1763–1815: A Political History* (London and New York: Routledge, 1999; second edition, 2009); and Paul E. Johnson, *The Early American Republic, 1789–1829* (New York: Oxford University Press, 2007).

On individual founding fathers see Edmund S. Morgan, *Benjamin Franklin* (New Haven, CT: Yale University Press, 2002); Esmond Wright, *Franklin of Philadelphia* (Cambridge, MA: Harvard University Press, 1986); Marcus Cunliffe, *George Washington: Man and Monument* (Boston: Little, Brown, 1958, and many reprints); Glenn A. Phelps, *George Washington and American Constitutionalism* (Lawrence: University Press of Kansas, 1993); Robert F. Jones, *George Washington: Ordinary Man, Extraordinary Leader* (New York: Fordham University Press, 2002); John Rhodehamel, *The Great Experiment: George Washington and the American Republic* (New Haven, CT:Yale University Press, 1999); James Grant, *John Adams: Party of One* (New York: Farrar, Straus Giroux, 2005); Zoltan Haraszti, *John Adams and the Prophets of Progress* (Cambridge, MA: Harvard University Press, 1952); C. Bradley Thompson, *John Adams and the Spirit of Liberty* (Lawrence: University Press of Kansas, 1998); Peter Shaw, *The Character of John Adams* (Chapel Hill: University of North Carolina Press for the Institute of Early American History and Culture, 1975); Joseph J. Ellis, *Passionate Sage: The Character and Legacy of John* Adams (New York: W. W. Norton, 1993); Edith B. Gelles, *Portia: The World of Abigail Adams* (Bloomington: Indiana University Press, 1992); Gelles, *First Thoughts: Life and Letters of Abigail Adams* (New York: Twayne, 1998), reprinted in paperback as *Abigail Adams: A Writing Life* (London and New York: Routledge,

2002); Gelles, *Abigail and John: Portrait of a Marriage* (New York: William Morrow, forthcoming); R. B. Bernstein, *Thomas Jefferson* (New York: Oxford University Press, 2003; paperback, 2005); Merrill D. Peterson, *Thomas Jefferson and the New Nation* (New York; Oxford University Press, 1971); Peter S. Onuf, ed., *Jeffersonian Legacies* (Charlottesville: University Press of Virginia, 1993); Onuf, *Jefferson's Empire:The Language of American Nationhood* (Charlottesville: University Press of Virginia, 2000); Onuf, *The Mind of Thomas Jefferson* (Charlottesville: University Press of Virginia, 2007); Kevin P. Hayes, *The Road to Monticello:The Life and Mind of Thomas Jefferson* (New York: Oxford University Press, 2008); Jeremy D. Bailey, *Thomas Jefferson and Executive Power* (Cambridge and New York: Cambridge University Press, 2007); Ralph Ketcham, *James Madison* (New York: Macmillan, 1971; reprint, Charlottesville: University Press of Virginia, 1998); Jack N. Rakove, *James Madison and the Creation of the American Republic*, 3rd ed. (New York: Pearson/ Longman, 2007); Forrest McDonald, *Alexander Hamilton* (New York: W. W. Norton, 1979); Ron Chernow, *Alexander Hamilton* (New York: Penguin Press, 2004); Gerald Stourzh, *Alexander Hamilton and the Idea of Republican Government* (Stanford, CA: Stanford University Press, 1970); Forrest McDonald, *Alexander Hamilton* (New York:W. W. Norton, 1979); Karl-Friedrich Walling, *Republican Empire: Alexander Hamilton on War and Free Government* (Lawrence: University Press of Kansas, 1999); John Lamberton Harper, *American Machiavelli: Alexander Hamilton and the Origins of U.S. Foreign Policy* (Cambridge and New York: Cambridge University Press, 2005); Richard B. Morris, *John Jay, the Nation, and the Court* (Boston: Boston University Press, 1967); Walter Stahr, *John Jay: Founding Father* (New York: Hambledon and London, 2005).

On what history has made of the founding fathers see Wesley Frank Craven, *The Legend of the Founding Fathers* (New York: New York University Press, 1957); Michael G. Kammen, *A Season of Youth: The American Revolution and the Historical Imagination* (New York: Knopf, 1978); Kammen, *A Machine That Would Go of Itself:The*

Constitution and American Culture (New York: Alfred A. Knopf, 1986, and reprint editions); Kammen, *Mystic Chords of Memory: The Transformation of Tradition in American Culture* (New York: Alfred A. Knopf, 1991); and Karal Ann Marling, *George Washington Slept Here: Colonial Revivals and American Culture, 1876–1986* (Cambridge, MA: Harvard University Press, 1988). Two more general books by David Lowenthal posit the distinction between "history" and "heritage" at the core of current debates: *The Past Is a Foreign Country* (Cambridge and New York: Cambridge University Press, 1986), and *Possessed by the Past: The Heritage Crusade and the Spoils of History* (New York: Free Press, 1996), reprinted in paperback as *The Heritage Crusade and the Spoils of History* (Cambridge and New York: Cambridge University Press, 1998).

On the reputations of individual founding fathers see Merrill D. Peterson, *The Jefferson Image in the American Mind* (New York: Oxford University Press, 1960; reprint, with new foreword, Charlottesville: University Press of Virginia, 1998); Francis D. Cogliano, *Thomas Jefferson: Reputation and Legacy* (Charlottesville: University of Virginia Press, 2006); Annette Gordon-Reed, *Thomas Jefferson and Sally Hemings: An American Controversy* (Charlottesville: University Press of Virginia, 1997; reprint with new introduction, 1999); Jan Ellen Lewis and Peter S. Onuf, eds., *Sally Hemings and Thomas Jefferson: History, Memory, and Civic Culture* (Charlottesville: University Press of Virginia, 1999); Annette Gordon-Reed, *The Hemingses of Monticello: An American Family* (New York: W. W. Norton, 2008); Peter S. Onuf, ed., *Jeffersonian Legacies* (Charlottesville: University Press of Virginia, 1993); Stephen Knott, *Alexander Hamilton and the Persistence of Myth* (Lawrence: University Press of Kansas, 2002); Nian-sheng Huang, *Benjamin Franklin in American Thought and Culture, 1790–1990* (Philadelphia: American Philosophical Society, 1994); Barry Schwartz, *George Washington: The Making of an American Symbol* (New York: Free Press/Macmillan, 1987).

On original intent see Leonard W. Levy, *Original Intent and the Framers' Constitution* (New York: Macmillan, 1987); Jack N. Rakove,

Original Meanings: Politics and Ideas in the Making of the Constitution (New York: Alfred A. Knopf, 1996); Rakove, ed., *Interpreting the Constitution: The Debate Over Original Intent* (Boston: Northeastern University Press, 1990); Joseph M. Lynch, *Negotiating the Constitution: The Earliest Debates Over Original Intent* (Ithaca. NY: Cornell University Press, 1999); Jonathan O'Neill, *Originalism in American Law and Politics: A Constitutional History* (Baltimore: Johns Hopkins University Press, 2005); Dennis J. Goldford, *The American Constitution and the Debate over Originalism* (Cambridge and New York: Cambridge University Press, 2005); Alan Gibson, *Interpreting the Founding: Guide to the Enduring Debates over the Origins and Foundations of the American Republic* (Lawrence: University Press of Kansas, 2006); Alan Gibson, *Understanding the Founding: The Crucial Questions* (Lawrence: University Press of Kansas, 2007). See also, for an innovative and challenging critique, Martin S. Flaherty, "History 'Lite' in Modern American Constitutionalism," *Columbia Law Review* 95 (1995): 523–90.

As this book was nearing completion, the McConnell Center at the University of Louisville sponsored a research project to identify forgotten founding fathers. In the fall of 2008, the Center published its report, Gary L. Gregg II and Mark David Hall, eds., *America's Forgotten Founders* (Louisville, KY: Butler Books, 2008), identifying the top ten forgotten founders as James Wilson, George Mason, Gouverneur Morris, John Jay, Roger Sherman, John Marshall, John Dickinson, Thomas Paine, Patrick Henry, and John Witherspoon. The book is an interesting blend of historical rediscovery and reflection on the cultural and political significance of the founding fathers.

Index